WATERLOO VOICES 1815

WATERLOO

VOICES

1815

THE BATTLE AT FIRST HAND

MARTYN
BEARDSLEY

AMBERLEY

First published 2015

Amberley Publishing
The Hill, Stroud
Gloucestershire, GL5 4EP

www.amberley-books.com

Copyright © Martyn Beardsley, 2015

The right of Martyn Beardsley to be identified
as the Author of this work has been asserted in
accordance with the Copyrights, Designs and
Patents Act 1988.

ISBN 978 1 4456 1982 8 (hardback)
ISBN 978 1 4456 1990 3 (ebook)

British Library Cataloguing in Publication Data.
A catalogue record for this book is available
from the British Library.

Typesetting and Origination by Amberley
Publishing.
Printed in the UK.

CONTENTS

INTRODUCTION

There have been countless books on the Battle of Waterloo, which is hardly surprising given its historical importance, the sheer awful drama of the day, and the fascination the battle holds for those interested in military tactics and generalship. Published accounts started to appear within months of the battle itself in the summer of 1815, and this book, marking as it does Waterloo's bicentenary, will no doubt be one of several other new contributions to the field. However, I'm no expert in battlefield tactics; I wanted to offer up something a little bit different. Having always had a particular fascination for personal historical accounts, particularly things like diaries and correspondence (the diaries of Pepys and Francis Kilvert, the Bronte letters, etc.), it struck me that a reasonably original approach, and one which I knew would interest me as a reader, would be to do the same with Waterloo – a book consisting almost solely of the words of those who were there at the time.

My two concerns were that there might not be enough material, and that what material there was would have been left to us almost exclusively by the educated officer class of soldier. I was pleasantly surprised to discover that I was wrong on both counts. Firstly, there were plenty of reminiscences to choose from. It's almost impossible to underestimate the impact the battle and its outcome had on the psyche of the British, who had been living in fear of a French invasion, led by the megalomaniacal but charismatic and much feared Napoleon, for many years. In an age before twenty-four-hour news and instant media coverage, there was an almost insatiable hunger for first-hand accounts, and they continued to appear almost until the last ageing eyewitnesses faded away. Over the decades, many a local newspaper featured a 'last survivor of Waterloo' story.

And by no means were all Waterloo memoirs written by officers. (Not that I have anything against officers! The image of stuffy, aloof, callous British colonels and generals has been image much overegged by Hollywood and meekly parroted by the British film and TV industry – eager students of what I call the 'Mel Gibson School of English History'.) As you will see in the pages that follow, there is no shortage of sensitive, moving and compelling personal stories by such men. It's also interesting that the image of the crusty old officer itself is not entirely accurate, either; note in the mini-biographies at the end of the book how many men of all ranks were in their thirties and even twenties. There are quite a few reminiscences from among the ordinary rank and file, and I must admit to having a soft spot for fellow Nottinghamian Private Charles Stanley's letter to his 'Dear Cusson', telling of his 'Verry ruf march'. If anything, the unconventional, phonetic spelling helps us to hear the voice of the man himself far better than any edited and corrected version would have.

During the course of my research into the backgrounds of the men mentioned in this book, I noted two things in particular. One was the number that had been wounded, sometimes quite seriously, fighting the French before Waterloo, yet who still took part in that battle. The other was how many of those who had been part of Wellington's highly successful Peninsular campaign were also present at Waterloo. However, these were mostly senior officers. In writings about the event there are often references to the absence of battle-tested units, still stationed across the Atlantic following the war of 1812 against America. It's been calculated that only around seven to eight thousand of Wellington's 25,000 British soldiers were Peninsular veterans, and you will see that more than one old soldier believed the Allies would have won a more decisive and perhaps less costly victory if only the old Peninsular army could have been deployed again at Waterloo.

Not all of the accounts in this book are by witnesses to the battle itself, but the viewpoints of such people as Charlotte Eaton and Magdalene De Lancey help to convey the building tensions before Waterloo, the horror and carnage afterwards, and, in Lady De Lancey's case, the sense of personal loss.

AUTHOR'S NOTE

Wherever possible, I have tried to leave the spelling and punctuation of these stories in their original form, but some minor changes have been made for clarity and consistency. I've also done my best to put these accounts into chronological order. In many cases the author himself has not been specific regarding what point in the day he is referring to, and in such cases I have endeavoured to find some clue from the names or events he mentions. Nevertheless, a certain amount of guesswork has invariably been involved, so I apologise in advance to any purists who might come across entries which are 'out of order'. The biographical notes in the appendix aren't, by any means, intended to represent a comprehensive 'Who's Who' of Waterloo. Most names appearing in this book, whether as actual eyewitnesses or merely mentioned within an account, do have entries; but in some cases I have been unable to track down enough, if any, information to warrant inclusion.

Charlotte Eaton's name will crop up frequently during the course of this book, and it's worth mentioning that this is her married name and that at the time of Waterloo she was actually Charlotte Waldie.

Part I

THE ROAD TO WAR

By 1815, Britain, along with an ever-changing coalition of other European nations, had been at war with France for over twenty years. Since the alarm caused by France's overthrow of her monarchy, later exacerbated by panic at Napoleon's rapid rise and belligerent territorial ambitions, much blood had been shed on the battlefield. But non-combatants suffered too. War had affected wheat imports to Britain, for example, and the country was afflicted by inflation, higher taxation, hardship and social unrest. This was also the era of Luddism, and there had for some time been a fear that revolutionary fever might spread across the channel. However, the seemingly invincible Napoleon was beginning to look human after all. His Russian campaign had culminated in the indescribably harrowing retreat from Moscow, his army of around 400,000 or more (some accounts say up to 600,000) being reduced to approximately – and almost unbelievably – 20,000, through death, injury, disease, imprisonment and desertion. His star was finally waning. Further costly military defeats dismayed a war-weary France, and Napoleon's eventual abdication and exile to Elba in 1814 seemed to at last herald an end to what some have called the true First World War – involving as it did all the major powers and featuring conflict across several continents. In France, a new king, Louis XVIII, was installed, and the banished Napoleon's attempted suicide failed only because the poisoned pill he swallowed was, to borrow a modern phrase, past its sell-by date. It seemed as if the old order in the world was being restored.

But not all those in France dismayed by the human and monetary cost of years of continual warfare were necessarily disenchanted with the Republican ideal itself, especially when Louis XVIII soon resumed the old ostentatiously profligate royal ways. A clandestine Bonapartist movement flourished on the mainland, and on Elba Napoleon took advantage of lax naval security to slip away and stage a triumphal return to Paris in March 1815.

What became known as the Hundred Days had begun.

I

NAPOLEON RETURNS

John Smart of Brixham, aged fourteen[29]
It must have been about the end of March, 1815 for the date is historical, that Brixham, in common with the rest of England, was startled from its repose by the great news. Bonaparte had escaped from Elba! Old Isaac Yeo, who traded with a fish-cart to Totnes, first told us of the rumours, for he heard that the telegraph to Plymouth had been working more than usual, and that the troops there had been mustered in marching order. In those days the semaphore telegraph could transmit simple messages in half an hour from London to Plymouth.

Sergeant John Douglas, 3rd Battalion, The Royal Scots[15]
Early in the month of April, being in town one evening, the mail coach passing through had a large placard fastened to the boot, on which was printed in large characters, that no mistake might occur, 'Bonaparte escape from Elba'. On reading this, off I started for the barracks. 'Come on my boys, you may be getting your knapsacks in order ... ' On May 1st, 1815, we marched with the old tune of 'The girl I left behind me.'

Sergeant William Lawrence, 40th Foot[8]
Thence we proceeded on our route to Portsmouth, and had a very pleasant voyage with fair weather prevailing; but when near England we fell in with an English frigate, which informed us that Napoleon Buonaparte had left the island of Elba with a small force and had landed in France to collect more troops. This was indeed a disappointment to me, for I felt sure that if he again intended disturbing Europe, we should have to be on the scene again. But in another way it caused no small amount of stir on board, for the young officers, who were looking ravenously forward to promotion, were so rejoiced at the news that they treated all the men to an extra glass of grog, to make everybody as lively as themselves.

Gunner John Edwards, Royal Horse Artillery[1]
My dear Brother, I reseved your Kind Letter and I am Happy to Hear from you and with Plesur I take up my pen to informe you That I am in Good Helth at present and I hope you and your wife and family Are the same. After Wee marched from Birmingham to Warley wee Remained theire But a short time, the route Came for us. We marched to Woolwich and we were fitted out for pursuing searvice and messing. Happy I was we were reddy in 14 Dayes then wee embarked at Ramsgate and after a plesunt passage of 24 oures at sea wee landed at hostend in Flanderes.

A quartermaster-sergeant, Royal Scots Dragoon Guards[43]
... many a man left behind him a wife and children unprotected and unprovided for. On going ashore [before departure] we had the opportunity of witnessing the most distressing scenes of women parting from their husbands, their faces covered with tears, and some of them with a child on their back and one in each hand, calling out from the shore to their husbands on board the transports, many of whom they would never meet again.

Lt John McDonald 1/23rd Royal Welch Fusiliers to his father[44]
We are all in high spirits. Quite delighted for we received our order for embarkation this morning ... Every person quite astonished at the progress Bonaparte has made ... We embark tomorrow morning at nine o'clock about seven hundred as fine men as ever fixed bayonets.

'CW, a sergeant of the Guards'[12]
My departure from England was very sudden ... After having been so long absent in Holland, Sicily, Spain and France, I thought Europe was weary of war, and that I was safe and comfortably situated with my family at home ... Yet, amidst all the sufferings of my mind, in parting from my friends, I felt it my duty to go in search of that enemy of peace, The Tyrant of the World; and if it were required, to die for the cause; for I was fully sensible we were defending truth and justice.

William Gavin, 1st Battalion, 71st Highland Light Infantry[13]
We were tossed about St. George's Channel for eight days, in the most unhappy way ever experienced, in the evening on the coast of Wales, and morning that of Ireland. We met a vessel at sea who informed us that Napoleon had advanced as far as Lyons ... We sailed for Deal, and sent our heavy baggage on shore, and embarked in fishing smacks for Ostend. The sea ran mountains high, so much so that the smack I was on board of was half under water ... We remained at Deal two days; got fresh provisions for the men and sailed for Ostend, which we made in twelve hours. It was about ten at night when we got to the harbour, and at a certain state of the tide it is dangerous to enter. They have signals, well known to the English smugglers and fishermen, when to enter or when to remain outside the bar. We happened to arrive at the wrong time, and were obliged to remain outside till morning, when we landed and were ordered immediately to Ghent. We embarked on board

boats in the evening and proceeded to Bruges, and stopped at the English Hotel, kept by Mr Carpenter, formerly of Limerick. Next day we proceeded to Ghent by the canal. We remained here a few days and then marched to Fresne (through Audenarde, etc.), where we remained two days. We were then ordered to Leuse, and were quartered with the 2nd Battalion of the Rifles.

Soldier of the 71st, or Glasgow Regiment, Highland Light Infantry[23]
I had now been seven years a soldier, and, therefore, hoped for my discharge ... Had I called myself seventeen, I should have now been free; but I scorned to lie ... I wanted but a few months to be free. I sought my discharge, but was refused. I was almost tempted to desert. I lamented my becoming a soldier, at his time ... To be so near home, and almost free, and yet to be sent across the Atlantic, was very galling ... I knew not what to do. I kept my honour and embarked ... When on our way [to America] a schooner fired a gun and brought us to, and gave us orders for Deal. My heart bounded with joy: 'Freedom, freedom!' ... my mind dwelt on nothing but home ... We landed all our heavy baggage at Deal, then sailed round to Gravesend and disembarked. We lay there only one afternoon, then were put on board the smacks, and were landed at Antwerp ...

2

BELGIUM: PREPARATIONS AND RUMOURS

Ensign Edmund Wheatley, King's German Legion[26]
2 April – While dressing to go out to a party [in Tournai] the girl came in pale and aghast telling me the Cannon was planted 'sur la grande place' with lighted matches, and that Boney was at Lille.

Sergeant Major Edward Cotton, 7th Hussars[3]
The regiment I belonged to disembarked at Ostend on the 21st of April, and we soon found there was work in hand. Swords were to be ground and well pointed, and the frequent inspections of arms, ammunition, camp equipage, etc., plainly announced that we were shortly about to take the field. The army, soon after our arrival, had, in consequence of a *secret memorandum* issued by the duke of Wellington to the chief officers in command, drawn closer together, in the probable expectation of an attack, and our great antagonist was not the sort of man to send us word of the when and the where. Louis XVIII, with his suite and a train of followers, being with us at Ghent, we were not destitute of information. Napoleon was as well informed of all that transpired in Belgium as if it had taken place at the Tuileries. Things continued in this state until June, when, from various rumours, we began to be more on the alert.

Private Charles Stanley, 1st King's Dragoon Guards[32]
Brusels Flemish Flanders May 15th 1815 Dear Cusson I take this
Oppetunety of Riting to you hoping this will find you all In gud
helth as it leves me at Pressent I Thank God for It I have ad a Verry
Ruf march Since i sow you at Booton we am onley 15 miles From
Mr Boney Part Harmey wish we Expect To have a Rap at him
Everry Day We have the Most Cavilrey of the English that Ever
was None at One time and in Gud Condishon and Gud sperrits we
have lost a few horses by hour Marshing I have the Plesure to say
my horse Is Better Everry Day Wish i think im to be the Best frend
i have at Pressant there is no dout Of us Beting the Confounded
Rascald it ma Cost Me my Life and a meaney more that will onley
Be the forting of War my Life i set ne store By at all ...

We have one gud thing Cheap that is Tobaco and Everrything
a-Cordnley Tobaco is 4d Per 1b Gin is 1s 8d Per Galland that is 2
1/2 Per Quart and Everrything In Perposion hour alounse Per Day
is One Pound of Beef a Pound and half of Bred half a Pint o Gin But
the worst of all we dont get it Regeler and If we dont get it the Day
it is due we Luse it wish It is ofton the Case i asure you My Dear
Lad I hop Wot Ever may Comacros your mind to trobel You wish
i hope nothing will I hope you never will think Of Being a Soldier
I Asure you it is a Verry Ruf Consarn ... I hope you will Excuse my
Bad Inditing and Spelling my Love to Aunt and Cussons ...

Lady Magdalene, wife of Colonel Sir William Howe De Lancey[4]
I arrived at Brussels on Thursday, 8th June 1815, and was much
surprised at the peaceful appearance of that town ... Now and then
a pang would cross my mind at the prospect of the approaching
campaign, but I chased away the thought, resolved not to lose the
present bliss by dwelling on the chance of future pain. Sir William
promised to let me know as soon as he knew himself, everything
concerning the movement of the army ... After some consideration,
he decided that upon the commencement of hostilities I should go

to Antwerp, and there remain till the end of the campaign, which might last months. He wished me not to think of going along with him, because the rear of a great army was always dangerous, and an unfit situation for a woman; and he wished not to draw me into any scenes, or near any danger ... He little thought I should be in the midst of horrors I would not pass again for any being now living. On Wednesday the 14th, I had a little alarm in the evening with some public papers, and Sir William went out with them, but returned in a short time; and it passed by so completely, that Thursday forenoon was the happiest day of my life; but I cannot recollect a day of my short married life that was not perfect. I shall never get on if I begin to talk of what my happiness was; but I dread to enter on the gloomy past, which I shudder to look back upon, and I often wonder I survived it. We little dreamt that Thursday was the last we were to pass together, and that the storm would burst so soon.

Charlotte Eaton, travel writer[22]
The country [on the road to Brussels] is thickly covered with neat cottages, scattered hamlets, and small farm-houses: the fields were waving with tall, luxuriant crops of corn, and far from wearing the appearance of the theatre of war, it seemed to be the abode of peace and plenty ... The ... cottage children, bare-footed and bare-headed, frequently pursued the carriage for miles, keeping pace with the horses, tumbling as they went along, singing Flemish patriotic songs, the burden of which was invariably, 'Success to the English, and destruction to the French'; and crying with unwearied perseverance, 'Vive les Anglaises!' 'Dat for Napoleon!' expressing at the same time, by an emphatic gesture, cutting off his head. They threw bouquets of flowers into the carriage, twisted their little sunburnt faces into the most extraordinary grimaces, and kept whirling round on their hands and feet, in imitation of the rotatory motion of a wheel.

Near Brussels we passed a body of Brunswick troops (called

Black Brunswickers). They were dressed in black, and mounted upon black horses, and their helmets were surmounted with tall nodding plumes of black horsehair, which gave them a most sombre and funereal appearance ... Some of these black, ominous looking men kept before us, and entered Brussels along with us. Everything wore a military aspect; and the number of troops of different nations, descriptions, and dresses, which filled the town, made it look very gay. Soldiers' faces, or at least their white belts and red coats, were to be seen at every window; and in our slow progress through the streets we were delighted to see the British soldiers, and particularly the Highlanders, laughing and joking, with much apparent glee, with the inhabitants.

Gunner John Edwards, Royal Horse Artillery[1]
Flanderes is a verrey fine cunterey and verrey fine Groves and Riveres and one of the finest Knells in the woorld. wee marched through Brussels and Gent and manney other fine townes.

Lt-Colonel William Tomkinson, 16th Light Dragoons[42]
The men cannot stand the good treatment they receive from the persons on whom they are billeted, and some instances of drunkenness has occurred. The old Peninsular men know their best chance of good treatment is being civil ... and the inhabitants finding them not inclined to give trouble, generally repay them by something to drink, which, being spirits, *sometimes* overcomes them in a morning.

Lt John Kincaid, 95th Rifle Brigade[18]
Brussels was, at that time, thronged with British temporary residents, who, no doubt, in the course of the two last days, must have heard, through their military acquaintance, of the immediate prospect of hostilities. But accustomed, on their own ground, to hear of those things as a piece of news in which they were not

personally concerned, and never dreaming of danger in streets crowded with the gay uniforms of their countrymen, it was not until their defenders were summoned to the field that they were fully sensible of their changed circumstances; and the suddenness of the danger multiplying its horrors, many of them were now seen running about in the wildest state of distraction.

Sergeant Thomas Morris, 73rd Foot[20]

On the 15th of June, some of the officers and men were playing at ball against the gable-end of a house in the village, when an orderly dragoon brought despatches from General Halkett, who commanded our brigade, ordering us to fall in immediately, and proceed to the town of Soignes. The men were scattered about, variously engaged; but they soon understood, from the roll of the drum and the tones of the bugle, that their attendance was immediately necessary, in marching order. About four o'clock the order came, and by six we had fallen in, and were off. On our arrival at Soignes we found the town filling fast with troops. There was evidently something extraordinary in this sudden movement, but no one knew the cause. About nine o'clock that night we had one day's provision served out, and as the meat was raw, we thought it advisable to cook it, not knowing how we might be situated next day. At twelve o'clock at night we fell in; and in another hour had left the town behind us, and soon entered what is very appropriately called the 'dark wood of Soignes'.

Napoleon

I will depart this night to place myself at the head of my armies; the movements of the different hostile corps render my presence there indispensable.

3

A PLACE CALLED WATERLOO

Charlotte Eaton, travel writer[22]

Major Wylie ... was with us in a minute. Breathless with haste, he could scarcely articulate that hostilities had commenced! Our amazement may be conceived: at first we could scarcely believe him to be in earnest. 'Upon my honour,' exclaimed Major Wylie ... 'it is quite true; and the troops are ordered to be in readiness to march at a moment's notice; and we shall probably leave Brussels to-morrow morning.' In answer to our eager inquiries, he then told us that this unexpected intelligence had only just arrived; that he had that moment left the Duke of Wellington's table, where he had been dining with a party of officers; and that, just as the dessert had been set upon the table, a courier had arrived, bringing dispatches from Marshal Blucher, announcing that he had been attacked by the French: but although the fighting was hot, it seemed to be Blucher's opinion that it would most probably be nothing more than a mere skirmish. While the Duke was reading the dispatches, the Prince of Orange, General Mufflin, and some other foreign officers had come in. After a short debate, the Duke, expecting that the blow would be followed up, and believing that it was the enemy's plan to crush the English army, and take

Brussels, immediately ordered the troops to be in readiness to take the field at a moment's notice ...

'However, after all, this may end in nothing,' said Major Wylie ... 'We may have to march to-morrow morning, or we may not march these three weeks: but the Duke expects another dispatch from Blucher, and that will settle the business.' And so saying, Major Wylie went away to dress for a ball. Yes, a ball! For the Duke of Wellington, and his aides-de-camp, and half of the British officers, though they expected to go to a battle to-morrow, were going to a ball to-night, at the Duchess of Richmond's; and to the ball they did accordingly go.

Gunner John Edwards, Royal Horse Artillery[1]
It was at Brussels where Louis the 18th was. I seed him there 2 or 3 times. wee Remained there 12 Dayes. the Rout came at 11 o'Clock on the Evning of the 15 June. wee marched all that night and it rained verrey hard all that night the action of the 16th begun before wee could get up.

Charlotte Eaton, travel writer[22]
But we were not destined long to enjoy the sweets of repose. Scarcely had I laid my weary head on the pillow, when the bugle's loud and commanding call sounded from the Place Royale. 'Is that the call to arms?' I exclaimed, starting up in the bed ... At half-past two we were roused by a loud knocking at our room door, and my brother's voice calling to us to get up instantly, not to lose a moment, that the troops were under arms were marching out against the French and that Major Llewellyn was waiting to see us before he left Brussels. Inexpressibly relieved to find that this nocturnal alarm was occasioned by the departure of Major Llewellyn, not by the arrival of the French ... we got up with the greatest alacrity, and hastily throwing some clothes about us, flew to see Llewellyn, who was waiting on the stairs ...

By the light of a candle in my brother's room, we sat down for a few minutes on some boxes, scarcely able to believe our senses, that all this was real, and almost inclined to doubt whether it was not a dream: but the din of war which resounded in our ears too painfully convinced us that it was no illusion of phantasy: we could scarcely even 'snatch a fearful joy,' for not for a single moment could we banish from our minds the impression, that in a few moments we must part, perhaps for ever, and that this hurried interview might prove our last. We could only gaze intently upon each other, as if to retain a lasting remembrance of the well-known countenance, should we indeed be destined to meet no more: we could only utter incoherent words or disjointed speeches. While he still lingered, we heard his charger, which his servant held in the court-yard below, neighing and pawing the ground, as if impatient of his master's delay, and eager to bear him to the field. Our greetings and adieus were equally hurried. We bade him farewell, and saw him go to battle.

Captain Archibald Leach, 95th Rifles[24]
Soon after dark on the evening of the 15th the drums beat to arms, and the bugles sounded to assemble the division ... We then advanced [from Brussels] by the road through the forest of Soignie, and halted near the village of Waterloo ... No one who has campaigned need be told, that a multiplicity of rumours, reports, speculations, and calculations, most of them vague, contradictory, and unfounded, are the forerunners of the advance of an army.

Charlotte Eaton, travel writer[22]
As the dawn broke, the soldiers were seen assembling from all parts of the town, in marching order, with their knapsacks on their backs, loaded with three days' provision. Unconcerned in the midst of the din of war, many a soldier laid himself down on

a truss of straw, and soundly slept, with his hands still grasping his firelock; others were sitting contentedly on the pavement, waiting the arrival of their comrades. Numbers were taking leave of their wives and children, perhaps for the last time, and many a veteran's rough cheek was wet with the tears of sorrow. One poor fellow, immediately under our windows, turned back again and again, to bid his wife farewell, and take his baby once more in his arms; and I saw him hastily brush away a tear with the sleeve of his coat, as he gave her back the child for the last time, wrung her hand, and ran off to join his company, which was drawn up on the other side of the Place Royale. Many of the soldiers' wives marched out with their husbands to the field, and I saw one young English lady mounted on horseback, slowly riding out of town along with an officer, who, no doubt, was her husband.

Charlotte Eaton, travel writer[22]

Soon afterwards the 42nd and 92nd Highland regiments marched through the Place Royale and the Park with their bagpipes playing before them, while the bright beams of the rising sun shone full on their polished muskets, and on the dark waving plumes of their tartan bonnets ... Alas! we little thought that even before the fall of night these brave men, whom we now gazed at with so much interest and admiration, would be laid low! During the whole night, or rather morning, we stood at the open window, unable to leave these sights and sounds of war, or to desist for a moment from contemplating a scene so new, so affecting, and so deeply interesting to us. Regiment after regiment formed and marched out of Brussels; we heard the last word of command March! the heavy measured uniform tread of the soldiers' feet upon the pavement, and the last expiring note of the bugles, as they sounded from afar.

Charlotte Eaton, travel writer[22]
Sir Philip Belson and Major Llewellyn ... felt quite at their ease; 'being certain,' they said, 'of overtaking the regiment at a place called Waterloo where the men were to stop to cook.'

Colonel Augustus Frazer, Royal Horse Artillery[5]
I have just learned that the Duke moves in half an hour. Wood thinks to Waterloo, which we cannot find on the map: this is the old story over again. I have sent Bell to Delancey's office, where we shall learn the real name, &c. The whole place is in a bustle. Such jostling of baggage, of guns, and of waggons. It is very useful to acquire a quietness and composure about all these matters; one does not mend things by being in a hurry. Adieu! I almost wonder I can write so quietly. But nothing can be done to-day. My horse is ready when the signal for mounting shall be given.

'Portrait of Wellington by a German'[11]
Wellington is forty-seven years of age. Any one who should see him among a thousand officers, would immediately discover him to be the general. A well-proportioned figure, about the middle size, no tendency to corpulence, yet no want of flesh, all muscle and activity; the soldier in his dress, that is, plain and becoming, without any thing fantastical or vain; an aquiline nose, a small mouth, a free open forehead, every feature of the serious countenance defined and regular; a dark, ardent, and expressive eye; the vigour of health manifest over the whole person: – this is Wellington's exterior. He is quiet and unassuming in his manners; his temperance is an example to all who value a clear head, and this he preserves even amid the fatigues of war. He sleeps little; but, when in cantonments, likes to sleep regularly, during the hours before and after midnight. He is no friend to exterior pomp nor glitter, and is

as far from avarice as from prodigality; not a single instance can be adduced, from the history of any one of his campaigns, of his having practised extortion, or required any thing for himself. In his whole air, there is a great, exalted, and dignified gravity, which, however, is not repulsive ... Wellington, as it regards professional intimacies, appears cold and reserved; a demeanour without which a general can never pretend to lasting greatness. He is strict with his soldiers, maintains the most exact subordination, and is yet adored by the whole army, which readily follows with boundless confidence wherever he leads it. What has especially gained him the love of his men is, that he is in the highest degree just; that he exercises the most assiduous care for the supply of the army, and that he personally examines whether the soldier has any grounds for complaints which admit of remedy ...

Major General Sir William Ponsonby[37]
There seems to be in England a decided feeling of war & perfect confidence as to the successful results.

Wellington[45]
I have got an infamous army, very weak and ill-equipped, and a very inexperienced staff.

Colonel Augustus Frazer, Royal Horse Artillery[5]
Now for Bonaparte, the disturber of all the great, as well as of all the little folks of this lower world.

Lord William Pitt Lennox[31]
The map was found and spread out before them. The Duke scrutinised it closely. 'I have made arrangements to meet him at Quatre Bras,' he observed, 'and if I find myself not strong enough to stop him there, I shall fall back towards Blucher, and

fight him *here*.' The Duke pointed to the open country, where he made a mark with his thumb-nail ... The field has since enjoyed a world-wide fame. Its name, as is well-known, was taken from a village of insignificant houses existing there.

Part II

QUATRE BRAS

There were actually two battles on 16 June, two days before Waterloo itself. Napoleon attacked Blucher's Prussians at Ligny, roughly south-east of Waterloo and Quatre Bras, and beat them after a very fierce battle causing Blucher to withdraw northwards towards Wavre, about twelve miles to the east of Wellington. Blucher himself had been lucky to survive, having been trapped beneath his stricken horse while leading one of several ultimately futile charges. Napoleon's overall strategy was to keep Wellington and Blucher apart and defeat them separately, and control of the crossroad at Quatre Bras was key to this. The French left wing under Marshal Ney moved to take the critical junction. Ney initially had about 42,000 men and Wellington only about 6,000, but Ney was later to be criticised for waiting until the afternoon before launching his attack, meaning that Lt-General Picton was able to come up with reinforcements, with others arriving as the day wore on.

4

THE FORCES GATHER

'*Extract of a letter from a private of the 42d Regiment*'[11]
On the 15th, about twelve o'clock at night, we turned out, and at two in the morning marched from the city of Brussels, to meet the Enemy, who were advancing in great force on that city.

Corporal Dickson, Scots Greys[33]
I remember how the trumpets roused us at four o'clock on the morning of Friday the 16th June 1815, and how quickly we assembled and fell in!

Sergeant Edward Costello, 95th Rifles[19]
All things arranged, we passed the gates of Brussels, and descended the wood of Soignies, that leads to the little village of Waterloo. It was the 16th – a beautiful summer morning – the sun slowly rising above the horizon and peeping through the trees, while our men were as merry as crickets, laughing and joking with each other, and at times pondered in their minds what all this fuss, as they called it, could be about; for even the old soldiers could not believe the enemy were so near. We halted at the verge of the wood, on the left of the road, behind the village of Waterloo, where we remained for

some hours; the recruits lay down to sleep, while the old soldiers commenced cooking. I could not help noticing while we remained here, the birds in full chorus, straining their little throats as if to arouse the spirits of the men to fresh vigour for the bloody conflict they were about to engage in. Alas! how many of our brave companions, ere that sun set, were no more! About nine o'clock, the Duke of Wellington with his staff, came riding from Brussels and passed us to the front; shortly afterwards, orders were given to the Rifles to fall in and form the advanced-guard of our division, and follow. We moved on through the village of Waterloo, and had not proceeded far, when, for the first time, we heard distant cannon; it was, I believe, the Prussians engaged on our extreme left.

Corporal Dickson, Scots Greys[33]
Three days' biscuits were served out to us; and after long marches for we did fifty miles that one day before we reached Quatre Bras we joined the rest of our brigade under Sir William Ponsonby.

Private George Farmer, 11th Light Dragoons[25]
We had mustered for field exercise, ourselves in undress, and the saddles strapped – as the expression is when we ride them without cloaks or valises – when an orderly dragoon was observed approaching at speed, and making straight for the officer in command. He was the bearer of intelligence that the French, on the previous day, had attacked and defeated the Prussians at Ligne; and that Napoleon, with the bulk of his army, was in full march to attack the positions of the English. In an instant we received the word to gallop horses, pack up, and accoutre; and in an incredibly short space of time the whole regiment mustered beside its alarm-post, in every respect prepared for action. Let me not forget to mention that, like an old soldier as I was, I took care not to move without a stock of provisions for myself, as well as for my charger. All the men carried their nose-bags filled with corn, and a supply of hay behind them, sufficient for four-and-twenty

hours; but the young hands forgot that men, as well as horses, are little fit for work when they are starving. I had a lump of bacon and a loaf of bread in my haversack, of which not many hours elapsed ere I experienced the great benefit. ... we could distinguish the smoke as it curled over the woods of Quatre Bras and were no longer at a loss to tell that artillery was firing sharply ... We gave the jaded horses the spur, and kept them on the trot till full five-and-twenty miles were encompassed ... The cannonade became louder, and mixed with it was the short sharp rattle of musketry ... Finally, groups of persons were seen approaching, whom, on our nearing one another, we recognised to be the wounded, some of whom appeared to be suffering much, though they all bore themselves nobly under their pain. Poor fellows, they drew to one side that we might pass, and cheered lustily. 'Push on, push on,' was their cry, 'you are very much wanted; for there is no cavalry up.'

Charlotte Eaton, travel writer[22]
Our consternation may be imagined when we were told that a dreadful cannonade had been heard from the Pare, in the very direction which our army had taken, and that it was supposed they must have been attacked by the French within a few miles of Brussels. At first I was utterly incredulous; I could not, would not believe it; but, hurrying to the Pare, we were too soon, too incontestably convinced of the dreadful truth, by ourselves hearing the awful and almost incessant thunder of the guns apparently very near to us. For many hours this tremendous cannonade continued, while, unable to gain any intelligence of what was passing, ignorant of everything, except of the fact, proclaimed by the loud and repeated voice of war, that there was a battle, we listened in a state of terrible uncertainty and suspense, and thought with horror, in the roar of every cannon, that our brave countrymen were every moment falling in agony and death.

An officer in the army of the Duke of Brunswick[11]
About 10 o'clock, we arrived at Quatre Bras, where we found part of the Nassau troops engaged, and heard that the French advanced very fast, and were exceedingly strong. We then went on a hill to observe their approach; but hardly had they perceived the number of officers, but the rascals fired at us with grenades: so we were obliged to leave the spot, and I narrowly escaped being killed.

'Extract of a letter from an officer in the Guards'[11]
We marched up towards the Enemy, at each step hearing more clearly the fire of musquetry; and as we approached the field of action, we met constantly waggons full of men, of all the various nations under the Duke's command, wounded in the most dreadful manner. The sides of the road had a heap of dying and dead, very many of whom were British: such a scene did, indeed, demand every better feeling of the mind to cope with its horrors; and too much cannot be said in praise of the Division of Guards, the very largest part of whom were young soldiers, and volunteers from the Militia, who had never been exposed to the fire of an enemy, or witnessed its effects.

Lt John Kincaid, 95th Rifle Brigade[18]
On ascending the rising ground, where stands the village of Quatre Bras, we saw a considerable plain in our front, flanked on each side by a wood; and on another acclivity beyond, we could perceive the enemy descending towards us, in most imposing numbers. Quatre Bras, at that time, consisted of only three or four houses; and, as its name betokens, I believe, stood at the junction of four roads, on one of which we were moving; a second, inclined to the right; a third, in the same degree to the left; and the fourth, I conclude, must have gone backwards; but, as I had not an eye in that direction, I did not see it.

'*Extract of a letter from an officer in the Guards*'[11]

Assured of my safety, you will doubtless be anxious for an account of the three eventful days I have witnessed; and therefore I lose no time in gratifying your curiosity, particularly as I am aware of your desire to be informed of every thing relating to your friends the Guards. ... as we approached the town, we heard distinctly a constant roar of cannon; and we had scarcely rested ourselves, and commenced dressing the rations, which had been served out at Enghien, when an Aide-de-camp from the Duke of Wellington arrived, and ordered us instantly under arms, and to advance with all speed to Les Quatre Bras, where the action was going on with the greatest fury, and where the French were making rapid strides towards the object they had in view, which was to gain a wood, called 'Bois de Bossu;' a circumstance calculated to possess them of the road to 'Nivelles,' and to enable them to turn the flank of the British and Brunswickers, and to cut off the communication between them and the other forces which were coming up. The order was, of course, instantly obeyed; the meat which was cooking, was thrown away; the kettles, &c. packed up, and we proceeded, as fast as our tired legs would carry us, towards a scene of slaughter, which was a prelude well calculated to usher in the bloody tragedy of the 18th.

Picton's men, whom Wellington had ordered to take cover, were first bombarded by Ney's artillery. Ney then attacked in four powerful columns. French columns were accustomed to breaking opponents employing line formation, or even caused them to flee before being engaged. The British philosophy, however, was that a line would always bring more firepower to bear than a column, as long as men kept their nerve. Picton's line maintained its discipline in the face of the oncoming enemy, even receiving French fire and taking casualties without reply until the range was adjudged right. Finally, the order to fire was barked out along the line; Picton's men let off a devastating close-range volley and followed it up with a rapid rate of firing which caused carnage among the French.

5

NEY ATTACKS

An officer in the army of the Duke of Brunswick[11]
About 12 o'clock we returned; and the Duke strongly expressed
his wish of having an opportunity of meeting the French in equal
force with his troops. To his great satisfaction, the Royal Scotch,
the Hanoverians, and his own corps, arrived betwixt one and two
o'clock. Tired and hungry as they were, they sang as they passed
the Duke, abusing and swearing against Buonaparte, wishing that
they might soon meet him, and have an opportunity of setting the
soldiers of the Grande Nation to rights. Hardly had we marched
half an hour, when we saw the French expecting us on a hill. The
Duke of Wellington then ordered to collect the troops as quick as
possible, and to prepare for battle. At 2 o'clock all was ready, and
the attack began. The battle was very bloody, but we compelled
the Enemy to retreat.

Unknown soldier of the 3rd Battalion of the Royals[11]
I have great pleasure in detailing the conduct of the gallant 3rd
Battalion of the Royal Scots; and though I have been present with
the regiment at the battles of Busaco, Salamanca, Vittoria, Fuenres
d'Honor, both stormings of San Sebastian, the passage of the

Bidassoa, &c. (all of which they bore a most conspicuous part, and suffered most severely), I can assure you they never evinced more steadiness and determined bravery than at the late battle. About half-past one o'clock on the 16th, the battalion was taken from its place in the centre of the 5th division, by a movement to its own left, by order of Sir Thomas Picton, and instantly by command of that lamented officer brought into action by a charge upon a column of the Enemy: it succeeded beyond our most sanguine expectations in routing this column, who afterwards formed under the protection of their cavalry, and then commenced a most galling fire upon us, which we returned with the utmost steadiness and precision.

The battalion was brought into action under the most trying circumstances imaginable, and continued so for a long time; but they never for one moment lost sight of that character which upon former trials they had so well earned and maintained. The ground through which they moved was planted with corn that took the tallest men up to the shoulders; and the Enemy by this, and the advantage of the rising ground, threw in volley after volley of grape [i.e. grapeshot, consisting of many small balls packed into a canvas bag and which scatter after being fired from a cannon] and musketry, which did astonishing execution. After being engaged for some time in a line, the battalion was formed into a square to resist the Enemy's cavalry, who were then advancing in great force; and I have the pride of stating, that though charged six or seven times by an infinite superiority of numbers, the French cavalry never for an instant made the slightest impression upon the square of the Royal Scots.

'Extract of a letter from an officer in the Guards'[11]
We arrived at the very moment the French skirmishers were appearing. We dashed in and cut them up properly, though our loss was severe. Out of 84, I had only 43 left in my company. At

night the remains of the battalion bivouacked at the head of the road, and during the night we received a strong reinforcement. They call this the action of Quatre Bras (where two high roads cross).

'Extract of a letter from a private of the 42d Regiment'[11]

About three o'clock in the afternoon of the 16th, we came up with them. Our whole force did not exceed 12,000 men, who were fatigued with a long march of upwards of twenty miles, encumbered with knapsacks and other luggage. The day was uncommonly warm and no water to be had on the road; however, we were brought up in order of battle. The French being strongly posted in a thick wood, to the number of 40,000 men, including cavalry and lancers, gave us very little time to look round us ere the fight commenced on both sides, in an awful and destructive manner, they having every advantage of us, both as to position and numbers, particularly in cavalry, and the British dragoons had not yet come up. The French cavalry charged the British line of infantry three different times, and did much execution, until we were obliged to form squares of battalions, in order to turn them, owing either to their own superior quickness, or to the want of ardour in the Belgians, the latter were left behind; and in a field of high standing corn, a column of French Lancers advanced upon them. Col. Macara ordered the regiment to form a square, in doing which two companies were left out, or were rather in the act of falling in, when they were pierced by the Lancers, and in one moment overwhelmed, and literally annihilated. The Lancers then attacked the square, and repeated the charge several times. One half of them were also mowed down, together with the brave Colonel; upon which Lieut-Col. Dick took the command, though wounded by a musket-ball; he succeeded in rallying and forming them into a diminished square, and thus presented an undaunted resistance to the Enemy. The

Lieutenant Colonel was at length, from the loss of blood, carried from the field; but the gallant remnant of the men succeeded in putting the Lancers to flight.

Captain Alexander Cavalie Mercer, Royal Horse Artillery[35]
It might have been, as nearly as I can collect [*sic*], about three p.m., when Sir Augustus Frazer galloped up, crying out, 'Left limber up, and as fast as you can.' The words were scarcely uttered when my gallant troop stood as desired in a column of sub-divisions, left in front, pointing towards the main ridge. 'At a gallop, march!' and away we flew, as steadily and compactly as if at a review. I rode with Frazer, whose face was as black as a chimney sweep's from the smoke, and the jacket-sleeve of his right arm torn open by a musket-ball or case-shot, which had merely grazed his flesh ... we were ascending the reverse slope of the main position. We breathed a new atmosphere – the air was suffocatingly hot, resembling that from an oven. We were enveloped in thick smoke ... and *malgré* [despite] the incessant roar of cannon and musketry, could distinctly hear around us a mysterious humming noise, like that which one hears of a summer's evening proceeding from myriads of black beetles; cannon-shot, too, ploughed the ground in all directions, and so thick was the hail of balls and bullets that it seemed dangerous to extend one's arm lest it should be torn off. In spite of the serious situation in which we were, I could not help being somewhat amused at the astonishment expressed by our kind-hearted surgeon (Hitchins), who heard for the first time this sort of informal *carillon* about his ears, began staring round in the wildest and most comic manner ... exclaiming, 'My God, Mercer, what is that? What *is* all that noise? How curious – how very curious!' And then when a cannon-shot rushed hissing past, '*There! There!* What *is* it all?'

'*Extract of a letter from an officer in the Guards*'[11]
The moment we caught a glimpse of them, we halted, formed, and having loaded, and fixed bayonets, advanced; the French immediately retiring; and the very last man who attempted to re-enter the wood, was killed by our Grenadiers. At this instant, our men gave three glorious cheers, and, though we had marched fifteen hours without any thing to eat and drink, save the water we procured on the march, we rushed to attack the Enemy.

Captain Alexander Cavalie Mercer, Royal Horse Artillery[35]
The Brunswickers were falling fast – the shot every moment making great gaps in their squares, which officers and sergeants were actively employed in filling up by pushing their men together, and sometimes thumping them ere they could make them move. These were the very boys whom I had but yesterday seen throwing away their arms, and fleeing panickstricken [sic] from the very sound of our horse's feet.

Charlotte Eaton, travel writer[22]
No authentic intelligence could be gained; and every minute we were assailed with the most absurd and contradictory stories. One moment we heard that the allied army had obtained a complete victory; that the French had been completely repulsed, and had left twenty thousand dead upon the field of battle. Gladly would I have believed the first part of this story, but the twenty thousand dead I could not swallow. Then again we were told that the French, 180,000 strong, had attacked the British, that the Belgians had abandoned their arms and fled, that our troops were literally cut to pieces, and that the French were advancing to Brussels. Then an English gentleman stopped his carriage to tell us, that he had been out farther than anybody, and that he had actually seen the engagement, which was between the French and the Prussians, and that old Blucher had given the rascals a complete beating.

We had not gone ten paces farther, before another man, in a great hurry, advised us to set off instantly if we wished to make our escape; that he was on the point of going, for that certain intelligence had been received 'that the French had won the battle, and that our army was retreating in the utmost confusion.' I never remember to have felt so angry in my life; and I indignantly exclaimed, that such a report deserved only to be treated with contempt, and that it must be false, for that the English would never retreat in confusion. The man seemed a little ashamed of himself, and Mr H. advised him 'by all means to take care of himself, and set off directly.' We hastened on. Presently we met another of Mr H.'s wise friends, who assured us, with a face of the greatest solemnity, 'that the day was going against us; that the battle was as good as lost; that our troops had been driven back from one position after another; and that the artillery and baggage had commenced the retreat; that all the horses would be seized for the service of the army; and that in two hours it would be impossible to get away.'

Sergeant Critchley of the 1st or Royal Dragoons[11]
Dear Tom, I came off pretty safe, my horse shot through the leg, and myself slightly wounded with a bayonet, but nothing to signify of any consequence; in short, there were but few escaped wounds or scars. The French had the better of the day about 12 o'clock at noon, when the Belgians turned their backs to them, and left the British infantry to the mercy of the world; and the French advanced upon that part of the line, and would have had possession of it in a few minutes, had it not been for our brigade making a rapid charge, which took such effect, and repulsed them, and drove them to confusion, which lightened the hearts of our infantry, and encouraged them to rally together, which was of great service at that point.

Unknown officer[11]

We found that we had come at the critical moment, when the Enemy were actually in possession of a large wood, commanding all four roads, and cutting off our communication with Marshal Blucher. The 3d division had been driven from the wood, and the Guards were ordered to re-take it. The Enemy's tirailleurs retired as we advanced, till at length we passed the wood, and found ourselves in the presence of an immense body of French cavalry ready to charge. From the difficulties of the ground, we could not manoeuvre, and retired into the wood; the cavalry charged in after us, did us no harm, and were all cut to pieces; but their light troops advanced in such numbers, as to oblige us to evacuate the wood at ten o'clock, after four hours hard fighting, till night closed the business. We lost here in the first brigade, Lord Hay, Barrington, Brown, and Cross, killed; Askew, Adair, Miller, Streatfield, Townsend [Townshend], Stuart, Croft, Fludyer, and Luthel, wounded. I received a contusion in my right instep from a musket shot, and a bayonet scratch over the eye; but neither of any consequence.

'Extract of a letter from an officer in the Guards'[11]

As we entered the wood, a few noble fellows, who sunk down overpowered with fatigue, lent their voice to cheer their comrades. The trees were so thick, that it was beyond any thing difficult to effect a passage. As we approached, we saw the Enemy behind them, taking aim at us: they contested every bush, and at a small rivulet running through the wood, they attempted a stand, but could not resist us, and we at last succeeded in forcing them out of their possessions. The moment we endeavoured to go out of this wood, (which had naturally broken us,) the French cavalry charged us; but we at last found the third battalion, who had rather skirted the wood, and formed in front of it, where they afterwards were in hollow square, and repulsed all the attempts of the French cavalry to break them. Our loss was most tremendous, and nothing could exceed the desperate work of the evening; the French infantry and cavalry fought most desperately; and after a conflict of nearly three hours, (the obstinacy of which could find no parallel, save in the slaughter it occasioned,) we had the happiness to find ourselves complete masters of the road and wood, and that we had at length defeated all the efforts of the French to outflank us, and turn our right, than which nothing could be of greater moment to both parties.

Charlotte Eaton, travel writer[22]

All this time we could hear nothing of what was really passing; or these idle tales and unfounded rumours were unworthy of a moment's attention, and did not give us a moment's alarm; but the poor Belgians, not knowing what to make of all this, and nearly frightened out of their senses, firmly expected the French in Brussels before the morning; for their terror of them was so great and so deeply rooted, that they believed nothing on earth could stop their advance. Our consternation may be imagined when we were told that a dreadful cannonade had been heard from the Pare, in the very direction which our army had taken, and that it was supposed they must have been attacked by the French within a few miles of Brussels. At first I was utterly incredulous; I could not, would not believe it; but, hurrying to the Pare, we were too soon, too incontestably convinced of the dreadful truth, by ourselves hearing the awful and almost incessant thunder of the guns apparently very near to us. For many hours this tremendous cannonade continued, while, unable to gain any intelligence of what was passing, ignorant of everything, except of the fact, proclaimed by the loud and repeated voice of war, that there was a battle, we listened in a state of terrible uncertainty and suspense, and thought with horror, in the roar of every cannon, that our brave countrymen were every moment falling in agony and death.

Sergeant Thomas Morris, 73rd Foot[20]
Among the occurrences of the day I may mention the following:
– On our entrance into the battle, we met a young man, a private
of the 92nd regiment, whose arm had been taken off close to the
shoulder by a cannon-ball. On passing us he exclaimed, 'Go on,
73rd, give them pepper! I've got my Chelsea commission!' Poor
fellow! I should think, from the nature of his wound, he must have
bled to death in half an hour, unless he obtained the most prompt
and efficient surgical attendance, which he was not likely to do, as
there were so many wounded waiting their turn to be attended to.
I never was struck by a ball; but I have often noticed that those
who are, do not always feel it at the time.

Captain Alexander Cavalie Mercer, Royal Horse Artillery[35]
Our first gun had scarcely gained the interval between their
[Brunswicker] squares, when I saw through the smoke the leading
squadrons of the advancing column coming at a brisk trot, and
not more than one hundred yards distant ... I immediately ordered
the line to be formed for action – *case-shot!* [or cannister shot – a
collection of small balls, as with grapeshot, but encased within a
metal canister rather than canvas. Only effective at short range.]
And the leading gun was unlimbered and commenced firing almost
as soon as the word was given ... The very first round, I saw,
brought down several men and horses. They continued, however,
to advance. I glanced at the Brunswickers, and that glance told me
it would not do ... both squares appeared too unsteady ... Still they
persevered in approaching us (the first round had brought them
to a walk), though slowly, and it seemed they would ride over us
... at the instant I thought it was all over with us, they turned to
either flank and filed away rapidly to the rear. Retreat of the mass,
however, was not so easy. Many facing about and trying to force
their way through the body of the column, that part next to us
became a mob, into which we kept a steady fire ...

An officer in the army of the Duke of Brunswick[11]
About half past four the French advanced again, and appeared double the number of the Allied Army; but no fear was shown. The cannonade began most horribly, which in some respects put the train and baggage in confusion: however, the troops stood, and fought like lions; so the French were again obliged to retreat, and were driven back to their position. Here they had a great advantage, being covered by a little wood, where they had placed all their artillery and riflemen. The Duke of Wellington most likely knew this, and ordered a fresh attack, to get the French out of the wood. The troops advanced, the Brunswick division on the left wing. When they came near the wood, the French commenced a horrible fire with artillery and case-shot, which occasioned a great loss to our corps, in this attack, which was about 7 o'clock in the evening, the Duke was unfortunately killed on the spot by a case-shot. At this moment I was not far from his highness, and ordered our small carriage, thinking that he was only wounded – when, alas! to my inexpressible sorrow, I found he was dead. My feelings I cannot describe, but you will be able to form to yourself an idea.

Marshal Michel Ney[9]
On the 16th, I received orders to attack the English in their position at Quatre Bras. We advanced towards the enemy with an enthusiasm difficult to be described. Nothing resisted our impetuosity. The battle became general, and victory was no longer doubtful, when, at the moment that I intended to order up the first corps of infantry, which had been left by me in reserve at Frasnes, I learned that the Emperor had disposed of it without adverting me of the circumstance, as well as of the division of Girard of the second corps, on purpose to direct them upon St. Amand, and to strengthen his left wing, which was vigorously engaged with the Prussians. The shock which this intelligence gave me, confounded

me. Having no longer under me more than three divisions, instead of the eight upon which I calculated, I was obliged to renounce the hopes of victory; and, in spite of all my efforts, in spite of the intrepidity and devotion of my troops, my utmost efforts after that could only maintain me in my position till the close of the day. About nine o'clock, the first corps was sent me by the Emperor, to whom it had been of no service. Thus twenty-five or thirty thousand men were, I may say, paralized, and were idly paraded during the whole of the battle from the right to the left, and the left to the right, without firing a shot. It is impossible for me, Sir, not to arrest your attention for a moment upon these details, in order to bring before your view all the consequences of this false movement, and, in general, of the bad arrangements during the whole of the day.

'Extract of a letter from John Marshall, private, 10th Dragoons'[11]
On the 16th of June, our troops were in motion. At day-break in the morning, the British were advancing with all possible speed towards the Enemy, who was waiting our approach, and had already made an attack upon some Hanoverian troops, and on that account we had a forced march. The brigade to which I belong, marched a distance of about fifty miles, taking their posts the same evening about seven o'clock; and being the first cavalry that arrived, we remained under arms all night, during which time several brigades of cavalry, and most of our infantry, arrived. But the enemy was so strongly posted, that it was thought prudent not to attack them in their works, but to fall back ... The enemy, seeing us retreat, were quite delighted, and followed us with all speed, cheering and hallooing at us, thinking to alarm and frighten; but in this they were disappointed, for we did not lose a man, although they attempted to charge us several times; but our skirmishers kept them back, in spite of all their boasted bravery.

Captain George Jones[11] [Not named in source account, but identified as author in *Waterloo Roll Call*.]

At the Battle on the 16th of June, a brave Major of the 42d Highlanders [Captain, Acting Major Archibald Menzies], preferring to fight on foot in front of his men, had given his horse to hold to a little drummer-boy of the regiment. After some severe fighting with the French Horse Cuirassiers and Lancers, and after receiving several severe wounds, he fell from loss of blood near a brave private, Donald Mackintosh, of his corps, who was mortally wounded at the same instant. The little drummer-lad had left the horse, to assist poor Donald: a lancer seeing the horse, thought him a fair prize, and made a dash at him. This did not escape the watchful and keen eye of the dying Highlander, who, with all the provident spirit of his country 'ruling strong, even in death,' groaned out, 'Hoot man, ye manna tak that beast, 't belangs to oor Captain here.' The lancer, understanding little of his brogue, and respecting less his writhing gestures, seized on the horse. Donald loaded his musket once more, shot him dead, – and the next moment fell back, and expired content. An officer of the Cuirassiers, at this time, observing our poor Major still bestirring himself, rode up, and stooping from his charger, aimed to dispatch him with his sword; our resolute Major seized his leg, and still grappled with him so stoutly, that he pulled him off his horse upon him. Another lancer, observing this struggle, galloped up, and, to relieve his officer, attempted to spear the Major, who, by a sudden jerk and desperate exertion, placed the Frenchman, in the nick of the necessity, in his arms before him, who received the mortal thrust below his cuirass, and in this condition continued lying upon him, with his sword in his hand, for near ten minutes.

The Major, unconscious that he had received a death-wound, expected all this time to receive his own at his hand. At last the French Officer raised himself, ran or staggered a few yards, and then fell to struggle or to rise no more. Another private of his regiment now came up, and asked his Major what he could do to assist him? 'Nothing, my good friend, but load your piece and finish me.' 'But your eye still looks lively (said the poor fellow); if I could move you to the 92d, fighting hard by, I think you would yet do well.' With the aid of a fellow soldier, he was moved as the man proposed, and soon seen by an intimate friend, Colonel Cameron, commanding the 92d, who instantly ordered him every succour possible. A blanket and four men carried him a little in the rear. While they were raising him, Colonel Cameron exclaimed, 'God bless you; I must be off – the devils (meaning the lancers) are at us again – I must stand up to them.' He did so, and in a few minutes, stretched dead on the bed of honour, finished his mortal career of glory in the bold defence of his country. It is a pleasure to add, that the brave Major is still alive, wearing the honourable decoration and marks of sixteen severe wounds received in this unequal and arduous conflict, and lame too from a severe wound received before, at the storming of Badajoz.

Anonymous account[11]
As on these occasions the first object of attack being the commanding officers, Col. Muttlebury was closely pursued by two lancers, towards two Hanoverian guns, the only artillery then present, the Colonel, by a sudden jerk of his horse, let the lancers pass him, at that moment some grape shot from the Hanoverian guns laid his pursuers on the ground; and the gallant officer escaped unhurt.

The French mounted attack after attack, and the outnumbered Allies were in genuine danger of being over-run despite their brave defence of Quatre Bras. But the French were taking heavy casualties, and the arrival of more British units finally altered the balance. By early evening Wellington was able to order a counter-attack which pushed Ney right back. There was no clear winner of the battle itself – but Wellington remained in control of the crossroads.

6

'LET ME SEE THE COLOURS'

'Extract of a letter from a private of the 42d Regiment'[11]
Still they sent up fresh forces, and as often we beat them back. The battle lasted until it was quite dark, when the Enemy began to give way, our poor fellows who were left alive following them as long as they could see, when night put an end to the fatigues of a well-fought day. Thousands on both sides lay killed and wounded on the field of battle; and, as the greater part of the action lay in corn fields along a vast track of country, many hundred must have died for want of assistance through the night, who were not able of themselves to crawl away. I was wounded by a musket-ball, which passed through my right arm and breast, and lodged in my back, from whence it was extracted by a surgeon in the hospital of this place. Captain M. is most severely wounded, having several shots through his body, and the regiment, in general, are mostly cut off. We have heard, since we came here, that our fine brigade, which entered the field on that eventful day, consisting of the 3d battalion Royal Scots, 42d, 44th, and 92d regiments, are now formed into one battalion, not exceeding in the whole 400 men.

'CW, *a sergeant of the Guards*'[12]

The French behaved very ill to our prisoners on the 16th; several of our wounded the bloodthirsty cowards ran through with their bayonets and swords. (These were not the old soldiers we used to fight with.) ... I was informed of an officer, belonging to the French, who was wounded and fell, and being unable to make his escape, he ripped out his bowels with his own sword, and beat his head against a grate rather than be taken prisoner.

Private George Farmer, 11th Light Dragoons[25]

... knowing that on the efficiency of my horse my own depended, I resolved at all hazards to fetch him some water. Accordingly, I proposed to my comrade that we should steal away together ... by and by, observing a light in the window of one of the houses, I knocked at the door, and we were admitted. My astonishment may be conceived, when the first object that met my gaze was a French grenadier, fully accoutred, and seated in the chimney corner. It was no time for hesitation, so I cocked my pistol; when up he rose, welcomed us with perfect self-possession, and pointing to his knee, informed us that he was wounded. Perceiving he spoke the truth, I desired him to sit down again, adding an assurance that he had nothing to fear ...

'CW, *a sergeant of the Guards*'[12]

As for Colonel Miller's attention to his company, none excelled. He was continually enquiring what could be done to make them more comfortable. 'I do not care for the expence [*sic*],' he would say. 'Money is no object to me.' ... Before the enemy he was cool and deliberate, vigilant and brave, form and determined; and on the 16th of June, at the head of his company in very close action, he received a wound in his breast, which proved mortal. As he passed to the rear, borne by four men, he said, 'Let me see the colours.' The last office I could do for him was to place the colours in Ensign

Batty's hand, to pay him his funeral honours, while living. He then said, 'I thank you – that will do – I am satisfied.' ... Serjeant Clarke, who attended him, informs me that his last breath was prayer.

Charlotte Eaton, travel writer[22]

It was half-past twelve; and hopeless now of hearing any further news from the army, we were preparing to retire to rest but rest was a blessing we were not destined to enjoy in Brussels. We were suddenly startled by the sound of the rapid rolling of heavy military carriages passing at full speed through the Place Royale: a great tumult instantly took place among the people below; the baggage waggons, which we knew were not to set off, except in a case of emergency, were harnessed in an instant, and the noise and tumult became every instant more alarming. For some minutes we listened in silence: faster and faster, and louder and louder, the long train of artillery continued to roll through the town: the cries of the affrighted people increased. I hastily flew out to inquire the cause of this violent commotion. The first person I encountered was a poor, scared fille de chambre, nearly frightened out of her wits.

'Ah, madame!' she exclaimed, 'les Francois sont tout pres ...' As I flew down stairs the house seemed deserted. The doors of the rooms ... were all wide open; the candles were burning upon the tables, and the solitude and silence which reigned in the house formed a fearful contrast to the increasing tumult without. At the bottom of the staircase a group of affrighted Belgians were assembled, all crowding and talking together with Belgic volubility. They cried out that news had arrived of the battle having terminated in the defeat of the British; that all the artillery and baggage of the army were retreating; and that a party of Belgians had just entered the town, bringing intelligence that a large body of French had been seen advancing through the woods to take Brussels, and that they were only two leagues off ...

I sent for our cocher, and most reluctantly we began to think that we must set off; when we found, to our inexpressible joy, that the long trains of artillery, which still continued to roll past with the noise of thunder, were not flying from the army, but advancing to join it. It is impossible to conceive the blessed relief this intelligence gave us. From that moment we felt assured that the army was safe, and our fears for ourselves were at an end.

'Extract of a letter from a private of the 42d Regiment'[11]
I have given you as full an account of affairs, principally what I witnessed on the 16th. Nothing can exceed the kindness and attention of the inhabitants of this city to our wounded men; the hospital is constantly filled with ladies and gentlemen, who, although speaking a different language, personally administer to our wants with the kindest attention, distributing clean shirts, bread, wine, coffee, tea, milk, and fruit of all sorts, with every requisite for our comfort and accommodation.

Lt John Kincaid, 95th Rifle Brigade[18]
As last night's fighting only ceased with the daylight, the scene, this morning, presented a savage unsettled appearance; the fields were strewed with the bodies of men, horses, torn clothing, and shattered cuirasses; and though no movement appeared to be going on on either side, yet, as occasional shots continued to be exchanged at different points, it kept every one wide awake. We had the satisfaction of knowing that the whole of our army had assembled on the hill behind in the course of the night. About nine o'clock, we received the news of Blucher's defeat, and of his retreat to Wavre. Lord Wellington, therefore, immediately began to withdraw his army to the position of Waterloo.

'Extract of a letter from an officer in the Guards'[11]
We had fought till dark; the French became less impetuous, and after a little cannonade they retired from the field. Alas! when we met after the action, how many were wanting among us; how

many who were in the full pride of youth and manhood, had gone to that bourn, from whence they could return no more! I shall now close my letter; and in my next, will endeavour to give you some description of the 18th; for, to add to this account now, would be but to harrow up your mind with scenes of misery, of which those only who have been witnesses, can form an adequate idea.

Part III

WATERLOO: THE CALM BEFORE THE STORM

On 17 June, Ney failed to follow up his attacks on Quatre Bras and Napoleon spent part of the day in a sort of stupor whose causes have been debated ever since, and which have been variously ascribed to physical illness, fatigue, depression and perhaps a combination of the three. (It's surprising how few authorities seem to take into account, when discussing episodes like this and his eventual unexplained death on St Helena, the possible long-term effects on Napoleon's constitution of his genuine attempt to commit suicide by poison just the previous year.) Wellington was busy moving his army north to the vicinity of the village of Mont St Jean, about eleven miles south of Brussels. Here, he deployed most of the infantry on the opposite side of a ridge to offer them some protection from the expected artillery bombardment. Contingents were posted to defend two farms: Hougoumont in front of his right wing, and La Haye Sainte closer to his centre. (A sandpit just across the road from the latter was also occupied by riflemen).

Wellington moved on to the hamlet of Waterloo itself, where he established his headquarters in an inn. He wanted to be certain of Blucher's support before offering battle, and, upon receiving reassurances that the Prussians were committed to joining him, the die was cast for a final showdown.

7

THE DAY BEGINS

Corporal Dickson, Scots Greys[33]
In a drenching rain we were told to halt and lie down away in a hollow to the right of the main road, among some green barley. Yes, how we trampled down the corn! The wet barley soon soaked us, so we set about making fires beside a cross-road that ran along the hollow in which we were posted. No rations were served that night. As we sat round our fire we heard a loud, rumbling noise about a mile away, and this we knew must be the French artillery and waggons coming up. It went rolling on incessantly all night, rising and falling like that sound just now of the wind in the chimney.

'Extract from a letter by an officer of the Guards'[11]
The morning of the 18th dawned full of expectation of something decisive being done.

Sergeant Major Edward Cotton, 7th Hussars[3]
The field of Waterloo is an open undulating plain; and, on the day of the battle, was covered with splendid crops of rye, wheat, barley, oats, beans, peas, potatoes, tares and clover; some of the grains were of great height. There were a few patches of ploughed ground.

The field is intersected by two high-roads which branch off at Mont-St.-Jean; these are very wide: the one on the right, leading to Nivelles and Binche, since planted with trees, is straight as an arrow for miles; that on the left, lying in the centre of both armies, leading south to Genappe, Charleroi and Namur, is not so straight as the former: about eleven hundred yards in advance of the junction, is a gently elevated ridge which formed a good natural military position.

General Miguel Alava, Spanish Commissioner, Wellington's field staff[9]

On the right of the position, and a little in advance, was a country house [Hougoumont], the importance of which Lord Wellington quickly perceived, because without it the position could not be attacked on that side, and it might therefore be considered as its key. The Duke confided this important point to three companies of the English guards, under the command of Lord Saltoun, and laboured during the night of the 17th in fortifying it as well as possible, lining its garden, and wood which served as its park, with Nassau troops as sharp-shooters.

Private George Farmer, 11th Light Dragoons[25]

Before morning broke, we were in our saddles; and immediately the horizon put on a hue of coming day, we shifted our ground to the brow of the hill ... When I reached the ground, my companions were all busily engaged rubbing down their horses and cleaning their accoutrements. I took care to feed my charger first, and then groomed him; nor had I finished buckling up the neatly rolled cloak, when a gun was discharged from some point near us, and in an instant the whole of affairs underwent a change. Drums beat, trumpets brayed, while salvoes of artillery from either side told of a battle begun; and, while we mounted and closed our ranks, peal after peal of musketry warned us that ere long their consistency would be tried ... And never have these eyes of mine rested on a more imposing scene than, for a brief space, was spread out before them. As far as the eye could reach I beheld endless columns of the French – the infantry in front interlaced, as it were, with the cavalry, in comparison with which, as far as numbers go, we appeared as nothing. Then, again, as on our side, I beheld horse, foot, and guns, all in admirable order, hidden in some degree from the enemy by the swell of the ground ... while, both on our side and that of the French, staff-officers in groups, and orderlies one by one, were galloping hither and thither ...

Soldier of the 71st, or Glasgow Regiment, Highland Light Infantry[23]
Two hours after daybreak ... we got half an allowance of liquor, which was the most welcome thing I ever received. I was so stiff and sore from the rain, I could not move with freedom for some time. A little afterwards, the weather clearing up, we began to clean our arms and prepare for action. The whole of the opposite heights were covered by the enemy. A young lad, who had joined but a short time before, said to me, while we were cleaning: 'Tom, you are an old soldier, and have escaped often, and have every chance to escape this time also. I am sure I am to fall.' – 'Nonsense, be not gloomy.' – 'I am certain,' he said: 'All I ask is, that you tell my parents, when you get home, that I ask God's pardon for the evil I have done, and the grief I have given them. Be sure to tell I died praying for their blessing and pardon.' I grew dull myself, but gave him all the heart I could. He only shook his head: I could say nothing to alter his belief.

Corporal Dickson, Scots Greys[33]
After I had eaten my ration of 'stirabout' oatmeal and water I was sent forward on picket to the road two hundred yards in front, to watch the enemy. It was daylight, and the sun was every now and again sending bright flashes of light through the broken clouds. As I stood behind the straggling hedge and low beech-trees that skirted the high banks of the sunken road on both sides, I could see the French army drawn up in heavy masses opposite me. They were only a mile from where I stood; but the distance seemed

greater, for between us the mist still filled the hollows. There were great columns of infantry, and squadron after squadron of Cuirassiers, red Dragoons, brown Hussars, and green Lancers with little swallow-tail flags at the end of their lances. The grandest sight was a regiment of Cuirassiers dashing at full gallop over the brow of the hill opposite me, with the sun shining on their steel breastplates. It was a splendid show. Every now and then the sun lit up the whole country. No one who saw it could ever forget it.

John Booth, editor of The Battle of Waterloo[11]
The Cuirassiers of the French Imperial Guard are all arrayed in armour, the front cuirass is in the form of a pigeon's breast, so as effectually to turn off a musket shot, unless fired very near, owing to its brightness; the back cuirass is made to fit the back; they weigh from nine to eleven pounds each, according to the size of the man, and are stuffed inside with a pad: they fit on by a kind of fish-scaled clasp, and are put off and on in an instant. They have helmet the same as our Horse Guards, and straight long swords and pistols, but no carbines. All the accounts agree in the great advantage that the French cuirassiers derived from their armour. Their swords were three inches longer than any used by the Allies, and in close action the cuts of our sabres did no execution, except they fortunately came across the neck of the enemy. The latter also feeling themselves secure in their armour, advanced deliberately and steadily, until they came within about twenty yards of our ranks, as a musket-ball could not penetrate the cuirasses at a greater distance. The cuirass, however, was attended with one disadvantage; the wearer, in close action, cannot use his arm with perfect facility in all directions; he chiefly thrusts, but cannot cut with ease. They are all chosen men, must be above six feet high, have served in three campaigns, twelve years in the service, and of a good character; and if there is a good horse to be found, they have them. It is to be observed that a wound through a cuirass mostly proves mortal.

Sergeant Major Edward Cotton, 7th Hussars[3]
Sunday the 18th June, 1815, which cast such a brilliant lustre on the military annals of Britain, broke but slowly through the heavy clouds. The rain descended in torrents, succeeded, as the morning advanced, by a drizzling shower which gradually ceased. Soon after break of day, all who were able were on the move. Many, from cold and fatigue, could not stir for some time; fortunately, on most of us the excitement was too powerful to allow this physical inconvenience to be much felt; although, in after-years, many suffered most severely from it. Some were cleaning arms; others fetching wood, water, straw, etc., from Mont-St.-Jean, (my present place of abode); some trying, from the embers of our bivac, to light up fires, most of which had been entirely put out by the heavy rain. At this time there was a continual irregular popping along the line, not unlike a skirmish, occasioned by those who were cleaning their fire-arms, discharging them, when practicable; which was more expeditious and satisfactory than drawing the charges. Our bivac had a most unsightly appearance: both officers and men looked blue with cold; our long beards, and wet and dirty clothing drying upon us, were anything but comfortable. As morning advanced and all were in motion, one might imagine the whole plain itself to be undergoing a movement. Imagine seventy thousand men huddled together. The buzzing resembled the distant roar of the sea against a rocky coast.

An officer of the Brigade of Cavalry[11]
On the morning of the 18th, the brigade was formed into a close column of half squadrons, a little in advance of the field they occupied the preceding night, in order to be in momentary readiness, as also to relieve the men and horses from the deep swamp which the incessant raining the night before had occasioned: the brigade remained in that position dismounted.

8

'I HAVE THEM THEN, THESE ENGLISH'

Major Henry Smith, 95th Foot[49]
General Lambert sent me on to the Duke for orders. I was to find
the Duke himself, and receive orders from no other person. About
11 o'clock I found his Grace and all his staff near Hougoumont.
The day was beautiful after the storm, although the country was
very heavy. When I rode up, he said, 'Hallo, Smith, where are
you from last?' 'From General Lambert's Brigade, and they from
America.' 'What have you got?' 'The 4th, the 27th, and the 40th;
the 81st remain in Brussels.' 'Ah, I know, I know; but the others,
are they in good order?' 'Excellent, my lord, and very strong.'
'That's all right, for I shall soon want every man.' One of his staff
said, 'I do not think they will attack to-day.' 'Nonsense,' said
the Duke. 'The columns are already forming, and I think I have
discerned where the weight of the attack will be made. I shall be
attacked before an hour ... '

Sergeant Major Edward Cotton, 7th Hussars[3]
Between nine and ten o'clock, the duke of Wellington, with his
usual firm countenance, passed along the line and was loudly
cheered. His Grace was dressed in his ordinary field costume,

white buckskin pantaloons, hessian boots and tassels, blue frock coat with a short cloak of the same colour, white cravat, sword, a plain low cocked hat without plume or ornament, except the large black cockade of Britain, and three smaller ones of Spain, Portugal and the Netherlands. In his right hand he carried a long field telescope, drawn out, ready for use. His Grace was mounted on his favourite chestnut charger, Copenhagen. He was followed by a numerous staff, several foreign officers, and the Russian, Austrian, Prussian and Spanish ministers, count Pozzo di Borgo, baron Vincent, baron Muffling, and general Alava. I observed several in his train dressed in plain clothes. Their number was much diminished ere the day was over.

The Duke generally rode alone, or rather without having any one by his side, and rarely spoke, unless to send a message or to give orders; sometimes he would suddenly turn round and glide past his followers; halting occasionally, and apparently paying no attention to his own troops, his Grace would observe through his telescope those of the enemy, which the docile Copenhagen appeared perfectly to understand, from his showing no impatience nor getting restive ... The troops had been previously placed in their respective positions, and afterwards the cavalry dismounted ... About this time, the French bands struck up, so that we could distinctly hear them. I have no doubt, this was the moment when Napoleon assembled all his generals, and forming a circle, placed himself in the centre, and gave his orders. This was in the hamlet of La Maison-du-Roi, about a mile in the rear of his centre.

Corporal Dickson, Scots Greys[33]
Between eight and nine there was a sudden roll of drums along the whole of the enemy's line, and a burst of music from the bands of a hundred battalions came to me on the wind. I seemed to recognise the 'Marseillaise,' but the sounds got mixed and lost in a sudden uproar that arose. Then every regiment began to move. They

were taking up position for the battle. On our side perfect silence reigned; but I saw that with us too preparations were being made. Down below me a regiment of Germans was marching through the growing corn to the support of others who were in possession of a farmhouse that lay between the two armies. This was the farm of La Haye Sainte, and it was near there that the battle raged fiercest.

Colonel Augustus Frazer, Royal Horse Artillery[5]
June 18, quarter-past 9 a.m. All quiet on both sides, all getting into order. Ammunition on ours, and doubtless on the enemy's side, coming up. The road from Brussels through the wood cleared. Finding it blocked up last night Dickson and I begged Captain Price, aide-de-camp to Sir Thomas Picton, whom, we met coming up, to report to the adjutant-general the necessity of the road being cleared. In consequence, baggage has been removed, and the waggons which have been broken down have been burnt by General Lambert's brigade (four battalions of infantry and six Hanoverian field-pieces) from Ghent, who wanted fuel to cook their rations ... I expect we shall have some cannonading this afternoon Adieu for the present.

An officer of the Imperial Guard[9]
Our first surprise, as the day broke, was to see that the English had not only not fled, – had not only resumed their position, but seemed moreover resolved to defend it. Buonaparte, who had no apprehension during the night, but that they would escape the punishment which he designed for them was animated with a most sensible joy, at seeing them at their post; he was too fond of the game of war, and thought that he played it too well to have any pleasure in a game only abandoned to him. He could not retain the expression of his feeling to those who were around him. – 'Bravo!' said he, 'the English!' – '*Ah Je les tiens done, – ces Anglois ...* ' 'I have them then, – these English.'

General Miguel Alava, Spanish Commissioner, Wellington's field staff[9]

I joined the army on the morning of the 18th, though I had received no orders to that effect because I believed that I should thus best serve his Majesty, and at the same time fulfil your Excellency's directions; and this determination has afforded me the satisfaction of having been present at the most important battle that has been fought for many centuries, in its consequences, its duration, and the talents of the chiefs on both sides, and because the peace of the world, and the future security of all Europe, may be said to have depended on its result.

Corporal Dickson, Scots Greys[33]

I rode up to a party of Highlanders under the command of Captain Ferrier, from Belsyde, Linlithgow, whom I knew to belong to the Ninety-second or 'Gay Gordons,' as we called them. All were intently watching the movements going on about them. They, with the Seventy-ninth Cameron Highlanders, the Forty-second (Black Watch), and First Royal Scots formed part of Picton's 'Fighting Division.' They began to tell me about the battle at Quatre Bras two days before, when every regiment in brave old Picton's division had lost more than one-third of its men. The Gordons, they said, had lost half their number and twenty-five out of thirty-six officers. Little did we think that before the sun set that night not thirty men of our own regiment would answer the roll-call.

General Miguel Alava, Spanish Commissioner, Wellington's field staff[9]

The position occupied by his Lordship was very good; but towards the centre it had various weak points, which required good troops to guard them, and much science and skill on the part of the general in chief. These qualifications were, however, to be found in abundance in the British troops and their illustrious commander, and it may be asserted, without offence to any one, to them both belongs the chief part of all the glory of this memorable day.

Private French correspondent[9]
As for the English, we shall see now what will become of them. The Emperor is here.

Anonymous account[11]
These details were furnished by an eye-witness of the whole, and may be relied on: 'From two o'clock until a quarter before seven, Buonaparte commanded all the operations and movements from a position where he remained without any danger whatever to his own person: he was at least a cannon-shot and a half off: nothing in short could reach him. When he was at length convinced, that the corps d'armee which he had so long and so obstinately taken for that of Marshal Grouchy, was in reality a Prussian corps, he seemed to think that the affair was desperate, and that he had no other resource than to make a great effort with the reserve of his Guard, composed of 15,000 men. This part he accordingly took. At this moment he assumed an appearance of resolution, which re-animated a little those who surrounded him. He advanced, saying – 'Let every one follow me,' which evidently signified that he wished to be in front. In fact, he made this movement at first, and headed, for about ten minutes, the formidable column which remained to him as his forlorn hope; but when he arrived within 200 toises (1200 feet) from three solid squares of Allied troops which occupied a ridge, with a formidable artillery, (and which ridge it was necessary to carry), he suddenly stopped under the broken ground of a sand-pit, or ravine, and a little on one side, out of the direction of the cannon balls. This fine and terrible column, which he had some time headed, found him here, as it passed and defiled before him in order to advance, taking a demi-tour to the bottom of the hillock, and directly in front of the Enemy's

squares, which Buonaparte himself could not see from the lateral point which he occupied, although it is very true that he was close enough to the Enemy's batteries. As the corps passed him, he smiled, and addressed to them expressions of confidence and encouragement. The march of these old warriors was very firm, and there was something solemn in it. Their appearance was very fierce. A kind of savage silence reigned among them. There was in their looks a mixture of surprise and discontent, occasioned by their unexpected meeting with Buonaparte, who, as they thought, was at their head.'

'CW, *a sergeant of the Guards*'[12]

I addressed my company in a few words, to 'be steady and attentive to orders – keep perfect silence – and put your whole trust in God's help, for he is with us – be strong and determined – use all your skill in levelling – make sure of your mark – and in the charge, use all your strength – and you will see, by the close of this day's sun, your enemies fly, and the shout of victory shall be yours'.

Anonymous account[11]

Capt. Erskine, who was made prisoner in the battle of the 16th, was brought before Buonaparte for examination. Being asked by Buonaparte 'Who commands the cavalry?' he was answered, 'Lord Uxbridge.' 'No, Paget,' replied Buonaparte. The officer then explained that they meant the same person, and Buonaparte nodded assent. He was then asked, 'Who commanded in chief!' and was answered, 'the Duke of Wellington;' upon which he observed, 'No, that cannot be, for he is sick.' It seems that his Grace had received a fall from his horse, on the 14th, and was reported to be indisposed in consequence, and Buonaparte had received intelligence to that effect. The conversation continued in this line for a considerable time, during which Buonaparte showed himself perfectly acquainted with the strength and position of the several divisions of the Allied

Armies, and the names of their several Commanders. As they were successively mentioned, Buonaparte occasionally remarked, 'Oh! yes, this division cannot be up in time. This division cannot be up in a day,' and so on ... On the conversation being ended, a surgeon was ordered to give his attention, and was placed, with another officer, under three guards – on retiring, they were put to quarters, which happened to be the cock-loft of a house; from hence, on the following morning, they looked secretly, and saw the whole of the French army march to their positions: knowing the disparity of force, he trembled to think of the result; and noticing particularly the enthusiasm and devotion of the troops – in this state of anxiety, they silently waited some hours, fearing every moment to hear the crisis ...

Major Arthur Rowley Heyland[38]
My Mary, let the recollection console you ... that I die loving only you, and with a fervent hope that our souls may be reunited hereafter and part no more. What dear children, my Mary I leave you. My Marianna, gentlest girl, may God bless you. My Anne, my John, may Heaven protect you. My children may you all be happy and may the reflection that your father never in his life swerved from the truth and always acted from the dictates of his conscience, preserve you, virtuous and happy, for without virtue there can be no happiness. My darling Mary I must tell you again how tranquilly I shall die, should it be my fate to fall, we cannot, my own love, die together – one or other must witness the loss of what we love most. Let my children console you, my love. My Mary. My affairs will soon improve and you will have a competency – do not let too refined scruples prevent you taking the usual Government allowance for Officers' children and widows. The only regret I shall have in quitting this world will arise from the sorrow it will cause you and your children and my dear Marianne Symes. My mother will feel my loss yet she possesses a kind of resignation to these inevitable events which will soon

reconcile her. I have no desponding ideas on entering the Field, but I cannot help thinking it almost impossible I should escape either wounds or death.

Ensign the Hon. Samuel S. Barrington, 1st Regiment of Foot Guards[47]
I have nothing to say for myself, but that I am as well and happy as ever I was in my life and if I escape with a whole skin, shall think myself well off and be thankful. If on the other hand some unlucky ball finishes me, I trust I shall not be wholly unprepared to face danger and death.

Wellington[39]
There is one thing certain, Uxbridge. That is, that whatever happens, you and I will do our duty.

Part IV

THE BATTLE BEGINS

It will become apparent from reading the following accounts that there was a lack of agreement among those involved as to when the Battle of Waterloo actually started, but there is something of a modern consensus of around 11.30 a.m. Hougoumont, closer to the French than any other Allied troop disposition, was an early target. This was initially intended as a diversion from the main French attack, but a desperate and bloody 'Rourke's Drift' type battle for the farm was to continue till darkness fell. La Haye Sainte, which still stands today, was also considered a key position. It was guarded by German troops, supported by British reinforcements: in particular Lieutenant-General Picton's infantry and Major General Ponsonby's heavy cavalry.

Napoleon's overall battle plan was uncomplicated – an overwhelming frontal assault intended to bludgeon through the Allied line.

9

GENERAL SIR JAMES SHAW KENNEDY'S DESCRIPTION OF THE BATTLEFIELD

The Overall Picture

- A valley, commencing higher up than Hougoumont and the Nivelles road, continues down past La Haye Sainte, and from that to and below Smohain
- All those three places were situated in this continuous hollow
- The French army was drawn up in order of battle on one side of the valley, and the Allied army on the other
- The ground on each side of the valley was of easy access, and of such a moderate ascent as to allow charges of cavalry up it, at all points, at full gallop.

La Haye Sainte

The farmhouse of La Haye Sainte stood immediately on the west side of the Charleroi road ... On the south of the buildings was an orchard ... The enclosures of the orchard and garden were hedges ... The buildings of La Haye Sainte, which formed the north and west sides of the quadrangle, consisted of the farmhouse, stable, and cow-houses, forming one continuous building ... the south side of the quadrangle consisted chiefly of a barn ... From the great solidity of the buildings of La Haye Sainte ... it is at once obvious and certain that those buildings could, in the course of the night, have been rendered so strong that, had they been properly occupied ... and proper defensive measures adopted, there would have been scarcely a possibility of their falling into the hands of the enemy. But it did ... The garrison was insufficient, the workmen were taken away, the place was declared sufficiently strong ... The impracticable attempt of defending the orchard and garden ... which ended – and could only end in – the defeat of, and great loss to, the defenders; these enclosures were merely hedges, and they were exposed to ... the greatest force of the French army – and to the fire of 74 French guns ...

Hougoumont

The buildings of Hougoumont were also of substantial masonry, and capable of a good defence. Intimation was given on the evening of the 17th that it was to be defended to the utmost; the workmen and tools from La Haye Sainte were sent to it ... and the works and loopholing were carried on with energy. The general enclosure of Hougoumont was a quadrangle, the enclosure being a hedge ... The great enclosure had within it the following subordinate enclosures, viz ... a wood ... two open fields ... a large orchard ... another small orchard immediately north of the wood, and a third orchard on the west of the wood ... The Garden was enclosed ... by walls of masonry in brick. These walls were loopholed by the British, and benches were placed behind them, which enabled the defenders to fire both through and over these walls ... The buildings of the chateau ... formed two enclosed courts.

The distance between the enclosures of Hougoumont and La Haye Sainte is 1000 yards.

10

'THE MOST TREMENDOUS FIRE THAT WAS EVER HEARD'

An officer of the 18th Hussars[11]
At four o'clock in the morning, a Prussian officer arrived, who informed Major General Vivian that he left Ohain at 12 o'clock, and came with the utmost speed possible, with orders to inform the Duke of Wellington, that Marshal Blucher had commenced his march at 12, and that he hoped to be up by one p.m. and that General Bulow was marching from Ohain on our left, to operate agreeably to the promise made to Lord Wellington by Marshal Blucher

Account by an unnamed friend of Goddard[30]
Sergt. Goddard was with an advanced party of skirmishers of the 14th, and about four o'clock the reflux wave of some French cuirassiers passed through them. They were, of course, fired at by the 14th skirmishers, and several bit the dust. One poor wounded Frenchman was thrown from his horse, and a comrade nobly returned and offered the soldier the help of his stirrup. An active light infantry man of the 14th, Whitney by name, who had shot one cuirassier, having reloaded, was about to fire at the mounted

Frenchman, who was then rescuing his comrade, when Goddard interfered and said, 'No, Whitney, don't fire; let him off, he is a noble fellow.'

Sergeant Charles Ewart, Scots Greys[11]
The Enemy began forming their line of battle, about nine in the morning of the 18th: we did not commence till ten. I think it was about eleven when we were ready to receive them. They began upon our right with the most tremendous firing that ever was heard, and I can assure you, they got it as hot as they gave it; then it came down to the left, where they were received by our brave Highlanders. No men could ever behave better; our brigade of cavalry covered them.

Gunner John Edwards, Royal Horse Artillery[1]
The 16th and 17th it rained verrey hard and wee were at camp with our Horses in our hands and nothen in our aversackes. At 8 o'clock on the 18th of Jun the genneral action begun on our right flank. our troop was posted in the senter right and left of the main road. 3 guns one side and 8 on the other. wee been old hands at the tread they put us whare they thought there would be more danger. At about 9 o'clock the french brought 28 gunnes opposite our gunnes and then the game began ... Every man that never seed a bullet would a thought that the world was at a end.

Anonymous French soldier[9]
At half past ten, a movement was observed in the enemy's line, and many officers were seen coming and going to a particular point, where there was a very considerable corps of infantry, which we afterwards understood to be the Imperial Guard; here was Buonaparte in person, and from this point issued all the orders. In the mean time the enemy's masses were forming, and every thing announced the approaching combat ... The Nassau troops found it

necessary to abandon their post but the enemy met such resistance in the house, that though they surrounded it on three sides, and attacked it most desperately, they were compelled to desist from their enterprise, leaving a good number of killed and wounded on the spot. Lord Wellington sent fresh English troops, who recovered the wood and garden, and the combat ceased for the present on this side. The enemy then opened a horrible fire of artillery from more than 200 pieces, undercover of which Buonaparte made a general attack from the centre to the right with infantry and cavalry, in such numbers, that it required all the skill of his Lordship to post his troops, and all the good qualities of the latter, to resist the attack.

Captain Archibald Leach, 95th Rifles[24]

As I did not happen to consult my watch, I shall not be positive as to the exact moment at which the battle commenced; but I should say, that between ten and eleven o'clock our attention was first attracted by a heavy cannonade on the right of the army, followed by an exceedingly sharp fire of light troops, which proved to be the commencement of a desperate attack, made by a large force under Jerome Bonaparte, on the chateau of Hugomont [*sic*].

Ensign Edmund Wheatley, King's German Legion[26]

About ten o'clock, the order came to clean out the muskets and fresh load them. Half an allowance of rum was then issued, and we descended into the plain, and took our position in solid Squares. When this was arranged as per order, we were in our position but, if we like, to lay down, which the battalion did [as well as] the officers in the rere [*sic*] ... A Ball whizzed in the air. Up we started simultaneously. I looked at my watch. It was just eleven o'clock, Sunday (Eliza just in church at Wallingford or at Abingdon) morning. In five minutes a stunning noise took place and a shocking havoc commenced.

Gunner John Edwards, Royal Horse Artillery[1]

About half past 10 o'clock the french Emperial Guardes dressed in steel armour back and brest plates, [Here, the editor of the account has added 'evidently Cuirassiers, not Imperial Guard'] they way about 32 pounds, charged up the maine road till thay came within 600 yardes they extended rite and left of the road. Wee fired case shot at them and swep them of like a swathe of grass before a syth. The ground was cuvvered with men and horses in 5 minutes. wee limbered up but before wee could move one yard the french was all round us. Me and four more of our Gunners left the gun and formed up with the 1st German Horse and charged the french cavallery, wee swept through them four times. with a good horse and a sharpe sord I caused 5 of them to fall to the ground. my horse reseved 4 cuts as I could not guard my horse and my self at one time. wee soon got our gun in action againe, only 4 men to man her and up to our knees in mud. Colonel Ross lost 5 horses shot under him. My gun was struck several times with the french shots.

Private Thomas Hasker, 1st Kings Dragoon Guards[16]

We were in a position behind a rising ground, which concealed from our view the French army before us, and stood there a considerable time dismounted, with the horses' bridles in our hands. About eleven o'clock, the balls came whistling over the hills, occasionally striking one or other of our men or horses. This was Sunday Morning; and I thought how many thousands of my countrymen are at this moment assembling to worship God!

William Gavin, 1st Battalion, 71st Highland Light Infantry[13]

The men were ordered to dry their clothes and accoutrements and put their firelocks in order, and the writer was sent with a party to a farm house, to seize on all the cattle that could be found about it. This was soon performed. Cows, bullocks, pigs, sheep and fowls were put into requisition and brought to camp. Butchers set to work, fires made by pulling down houses for the wood, camp kettles hung on, and everything in a fair way for cooking, when the word 'fall in' put everything to the route. Men accoutring, cannon roaring, bugles sounding and drums beating, which put a stop to our cooking for that day. Our Brigade were ordered to advance to the brow of a hill and lie down in column.

Wellington's report to Earl Bathurst, Secretary of State for the War Department[9]

The enemy collected his army, with the exception of the third corps which had been sent to observe Marshal Blucher, on a range of heights in our front, in the course of the night of the 17th and yesterday morning; and at about ten o'clock he commenced a furious attack upon our post at Hougoumont. I had occupied that post with a detachment from General Byng's brigade of Guards, which was in position in its rear ... and I am happy to add, that it was maintained, throughout the day, with the utmost gallantry by these brave troops, notwithstanding the repeated efforts of large bodies of the enemy to obtain possession of it.

Corporal Dickson, Scots Greys[33]

I noticed, just in front of me, great columns of infantry beginning to advance over the brow of the hill on their side of the valley, marching straight for us. Then began a tremendous cannonade from two hundred and fifty French guns all along the lines. The noise was fearful; but just then a loud report rent the air, followed by a rolling cheer on our side, and our artillery got into action.

Soldier of the 71st, or Glasgow Regiment, Highland Light Infantry[61]

About twelve o'clock we received orders to fall in for attack. We then marched up to our position, where we lay on the face of a brae, covering a brigade of guns. We were so overcome by the fatigue of the two days' march that, scarce had we lain down, until many of us fell asleep [*sic*]. I slept sound, for some time, while the cannon-balls, plunging in amongst us, killed a great many. I was suddenly awakened. A ball struck the ground a little below me, turned me heels-over-head, broke my musket in pieces, and killed a lad at my side. I was stunned and confused, and knew not whether I was wounded or not. I felt a numbness in my arm for sometime ... The young man I lately spoke of lost his legs by a shot at this time. They were cut very close: he soon bled to death. 'Tom,' said he, 'remember your charge: my mother wept sore when my brother died in her arms. Do not tell her how I died; if she saw me thus, it would break her heart: farewell, God bless my parents!' He said no more, his lips quivered, and he ceased to breathe.

Corporal Dickson, Scots Greys[33]
Then, suddenly, a great noise of firing and hisses and shouting commenced, and the whole Belgian brigade, of those whom I had seen in the morning, came rushing along and across the road in full flight. Our men began to shout and groan at them too. They had bolted almost without firing a shot, and left the brigade of Highlanders to meet the whole French attack on the British left centre.

Anonymous British correspondent in Antwerp[11]
It is impossible to imagine the strong overpowering anxiety of being so near such eventful scenes, without being able to learn what is really passing. To know that within a few miles such an awful contest is deciding – to hear even the distant voice of war – to think that in the roar of every cannon, your brave countrymen are falling, bleeding, and dying – to dread that your friends, even those dearest to you, may be the victims – to endure the long and protracted suspense – the constant agitation – the varying reports – the incessant alarms – the fluctuating hopes, and doubts, and

fears – no – none but those who have felt what it is, can conceive or understand it.

William Gavin, 1st Battalion, 71st Highland Light Infantry[13]
The sun rose beautifully. The artillery of both armies had commenced the work of death.

Ensign Edmund Wheatley, King's German Legion[26]
One could almost feel the undulation of the air from the multitude of Cannon shot. The first man who fell was five files on my left. With the utmost distortion of feature he lay on his side and shriveling up every muscle of the body he twirled his elbow round and round in acute agony, then dropped lifeless, dying as it's called a death of glory, heaving his last breath on the field of fame.

Sergeant Critchley of the 1st or Royal Dragoons[11]
Our brigade was the first that charged, and great havoc we made; broke their lines and columns; took two stands of colours, two eagles, and made them fly before us a mile or more; but the loss of the brigade was severe; yet it surprised me that so many escaped as did, for their guns and small arms were playing upon us on every side, pouring like hail, and men falling, and horses, as thick as possible.

Ensign Edmund Wheatley, King's German Legion[26]
A black consolidated body was soon seen approaching and we distinguished by sudden flashes of light from the sun's rays, the ironcased cavalry of the enemy. Shouts of 'Stand fast!' were heard from the little squares around and very quickly these gigantic fellows were upon us. No words can convey the sensation we felt on seeing these heavy armed bodies advancing at full gallop against us, flourishing their sabres in the air, striking their armour with the handles, the sun, gleaming on the steel. The long horse

hair, dishevelled by the wind, bore an appearance confounding the senses to an astonishing disorder. But we dashed them back as coolly as the sturdy rock repels the ocean's foam. The sharp-toothed bayonet bit many an adventrous [*sic*] fool, and on all sides we presented our bristly points like the peevish porcupines assailed by clamorous dogs. The horse guards then came up and drove them back.

II

THE BATTLE INTENSIFIES

Private George Farmer, 11th Light Dragoons[25]
From the instant that the firing became general, all was to me dark and obscure beyond a distance of a few hundred yards ... indeed, it was only by the ceaseless roar, or the whistling of shot and shell around me, that I knew at times that I and those near me were playing a part in the grave game of life and death. For the cavalry, unlike the infantry, come into play only by fits and starts, and they have patiently to sustain the fury of the cannonade, to which they can offer no resistance ... the French, perceiving us, opened upon our columns a battery of howitzers and light mortars, one shell from which falling into the very centre of the 16th, created terrible havoc ... an aide-de-camp rode up at this moment, and two squadrons, one from the 12th, and another from our regiment, were ordered to drive back some lancers which had threatened our guns. We went at them with good will, but not, perhaps, with prefect judgement. We did not consider that, when the ground is soft and heavy, a charge down hill is, of all operations to which cavalry can be put, the most unsafe; and the consequence was, that rushing over the ridge at speed, very many of our horses came down, and we lost all order. The result need hardly be stated. The

squadron of the 12th, which led, was almost cut to pieces, and we with great difficulty, and in great disorder, recovered to the brigade.

Lt-Colonel Stanhope[40]

We heard the action raging hotly at Hougoumont and soon after the roll of musketry from the left announced the main attack on our centre at La Haye Sainte. A number of Staff officers were soon killed and wounded who were at first alone exposed to the cannonade. General Cooke lost his arm, shells began to fall in our squares and though many men were blown up and horribly mangled I never saw such steadiness. As the poor wounded wretches remained in the square it was a horrid sight in cold blood. Soon after a cry of cavalry was heard on the crest of the hill and we saw the artillerymen run from their guns & seek protection in our squares. The men stood up; we advanced a few yards and saw a mass of cuirassiers close to us with thousands of forked pennons waving behind them in all their vanity of colours.

Lt John Kincaid, 95th Rifle Brigade[18]

From the moment we took possession of the knoll, we had busied ourselves in collecting branches of trees and other things, for the purpose of making an *abatis* to block up the road between that and the farm-house, and soon completed one, which we thought looked sufficiently formidable to keep out the whole of the French cavalry; but it was put to the proof sooner than we expected, by a troop of our own light dragoons, who, having occasion to gallop through, astonished us not a little by clearing away every stick of it. We had just time to replace the scattered branches, when the whole of the enemy's artillery opened, and their countless columns began to advance under cover of it.

Captain Archibald Leach, 95th Rifles[24]

We perceived our adversaries bringing into position, on the heights opposite, gun after gun; and ere much time had elapsed, there were, at a moderate computation, fifty pieces of artillery in battery, staring us in the face, and intended to particularly salute our division, the farm of La Haye Sainte, and the left of Baron Alten's division ... In an instant this numerous and powerful artillery opened on us, battering at the same moment the farm-house of La Haye Sainte. Under cover of this cannonade several large columns of infantry, supported by heavy bodies of cavalry, and preceded by a multitude of light infantry, descended at a trot into the plain, with shouts of 'Vive l'Empereur!' some of them throwing up their caps in the air, and advancing to the attack with such confidence and impetuosity, as if the bare possibility of our being able to withstand the shock was out of the question, fighting as they were under the immediate eye of the Emperor. But Napoleon was destined, in a few minutes after the commencement of this hubbub, to see his Imperial Legions recoil in the greatest confusion, with dreadful carnage, and with great loss in prisoners ... The fire of our two companies posted in the excavation near the road, and from the remainder of the battalion on the hillock, as also that from the windows and loop-holes, by the Germans, in La Haye Sainte, had already inflicted a severe loss on the enemy. In spite of it they pressed boldly and resolutely on, until met by our first line, which delivered such a fire, when they approached the thorn hedge, as shattered their ranks and threw them into disorder; and this was increased by the cheers, and an attempt of our line to close them. At this instant the household brigade of cavalry came up to our support, rushed gallantly amongst the infantry and the cavalry which were endeavouring to retrieve matters for them, and drove them back, man and horse, in terrible confusion and dismay, and with immense loss.

Sergeant Major Edward Cotton, 7th Hussars[3]

Shortly after we had taken up our ground, some columns, from the enemy's left, were seen in motion towards Hugoumont, and were soon warmly engaged with the right of our army. A cannon ball, too, came from the Lord knows where, for it was not fired at us, and took the head off our right hand man. That part of their position, in our own immediate front, next claimed our undivided attention. It had hitherto been looking suspiciously innocent, with scarcely a human being upon it; but innumerable black specks were now seen taking post at regular distances in its front, and recognising them as so many pieces of artillery, I knew, from experience, although nothing else was yet visible, that they were unerring symptoms of our not being destined to be idle spectators ...

Not long after, the enemy's skirmishers, backed by their supports, were thrown out; extending as they advanced, they spread over the whole space before them. Now and then, they saluted our ears with well-known music, the whistling of musket-balls ... Their columns, preceded by mounted officers to take up the alignments, soon began to appear; the bayonets flashing over dark masses at different points, accompanied by the rattling of drums and the clang of trumpets ... Could any one behold so imposing a spectacle without awe, or without extreme excitement? Could any one witness the commencement of the battle with indifference? Can any one forget the impressions that are made upon the mind at such a moment? What a magnificent sight! Napoleon the Great, marshalling the chosen troops of France, against those of Britain and her allies under the renowned Wellington! Here, on one side, were the troops that had held nearly all Europe in bonds, and by whom kings and princes had been humbled and deposed; and although it was not the first time that many of us had faced them, yet, on the present occasion, they were under the immediate command of their idolized Napoleon. It was impossible to contemplate so formidable a power in battle array, without a feeling of admiration towards such noble antagonists ... It presented altogether a sight that must be seen and felt to be duly appreciated, a sight that survivors recollect in after-years ... Such a scene fires the blood of the brave, and excites feelings and hopes, compared with which, all other emotions are cold and powerless ...

Sergeant Thomas Morris, 73rd Foot[20]

It was some time before I got our allowance of hollands; and we had scarcely received it, when a cannon-shot went through the cask, and man too. While waiting here, Shaw the fighting-man, of the Life Guards, was pointed out to me; and we little thought then that he was about to acquire such celebrity. He drank a considerable portion of the raw spirit; and under its influence, probably, he soon afterwards left his regiment, and running 'a-muck' at the enemy, was cut down by them as a madman.

Anonymous account[11]

Shaw in the Horse Guards, of pugilistic fame, was fighting seven or eight hours, dealing destruction to all around him; at one time he was attacked by six of the French Imperial Guard, four of whom he killed, but at last fell by the remaining two. A comrade who was by his side a great part of the day, and who is the relater of this anecdote, noticed one particular cut, which drove through his opponent's helmet, and with it cut nearly the whole of his face at the stroke.

Sergeant Thomas Morris, 73rd Foot[20]

As the enemy's artillery was taking off a great many of our men, we were ordered to lie down, to avoid the shots as much as possible; and I took advantage of this circumstance to obtain an hour's sleep, as comfortably as ever I did in my life, though there were at that time upwards of three hundred cannon in full play. But our services were now soon to be required. A considerable number of the French cuirassiers made their appearance on the rising ground just in our front, took the artillery we had placed there, and came at a gallop down upon us. Their intrepid bearing was well calculated, in an enemy, to inspire a feeling of dread, – none of them under six feet; defended by steel helmets and corslets, made pigeon-breasted to throw off the balls. Thus armed and accoutred they looked so truly formidable, that I thought we could not have the slightest chance with them. They came up rapidly until within about ten or twelve paces of the square, when our rear ranks poured into them a well-directed fire, which put them into confusion, and they retired; the two front ranks, kneeling, then discharged their pieces at them. Some of the cuirassiers fell wounded, and several were killed; those dismounted by the death of their horses, immediately unclasped their armour to facilitate their escape. The next square to us was charged at the same time, and being unfortunately broken into, retired in confusion, followed by the cuirassiers; but the Life Guards coming up, the French in their turn were obliged to retrograde, and the 33rd and 69th resumed their position in square on our right, and maintained it during the rest of the day.

The Duke of Wellington came up to us after this, and while speaking to General Halkett, the cuirassiers again advanced. The Duke rode into the square, and we again sent them to the right about: the Horse Guards came out at the intervals, and followed the cuirassiers some distance; but did not then come actually in contact with them. The Duke rode out of the square and paid a visit to the Guards, on the right, after expressing himself satisfied with our conduct. My comrade, whom I have already spoken of as being quartered with me at the village near Soignes, was on my right hand, in the front face of the square in the front rank, kneeling; he had a trifling defect in his speech, and at every charge the cavalry made, he would say, 'Tom, Tom; here comes the *calvary*.' The same body of the enemy, though baffled twice, seemed determined to force a passage through us; and on their next advance they brought some artillery-men, turned the cannon in our front upon us, and fired into us with grape-shot, which proved very destructive, making complete lanes through us; and then the horsemen came up to dash in at the openings. But before they reached, we had closed our files, throwing the dead outside and taking the wounded inside the square, when they were again forced to retire. They did not, however, go further than the pieces of cannon – waiting there to try the effect of some more grapeshot. We saw the match applied, and again it came thick as hail upon us. On looking round, I saw my left-hand man falling backwards, the blood gushing from his left eye; my poor comrade on my right, by the same discharge, got a ball through his right thigh, of which he died a few days afterwards.

Lt-Colonel William Tomkinson, 16th Light Dragoons[42]
We were told very early in the day that a corps of Prussians were on their march to join us. Being on the left, we were constantly looking out for them.

Sergeant Thomas Morris, 73rd Foot[20]
Our situation now was truly awful; our men were falling by dozens every fire. About this time a large shell fell just in front of us, and while the fuze was burning out, we were wondering how many of us it would destroy. When it burst, about seventeen men were either killed or wounded by it; the portion which came to my share was a piece of rough cast-iron, about the size of a horse-bean, which took up its lodging in my left cheek; the blood ran copiously down inside my clothes, and made me rather uncomfortable. Our poor old captain was horribly frightened, and several times came to me for a drop of something to keep his spirits up. Towards the close of the day he was cut in two by a cannon-shot ... One of our poor fellows having received a desperate wound in the forehead, left us, and thought he was going to the rear; but, blinded by the

blood which was streaming down his face, he was actually rushing into the thickest of the battle, calling out loudly and most piteously for relief. He met the cuirassiers who were again advancing, and the foremost of them cutting the poor fellow down with the sword, the rest of them rode over him.

Colonel Augustus Frazer, Royal Horse Artillery[5]
This declination of ground was most favourable to the infantry, who, under a tremendous cannonade, were in a great measure sheltered by the nature of the ground – in great measure, too, by their lying down, by order. On the approach – the majestic approach – of the French cavalry, the squares rose and, with a steadiness almost inconceivable, awaited, without firing, the rush of the cavalry, who, after making some fruitless efforts, sweeping the whole artillery of the line, and receiving the fire of the squares as they passed, retired, followed by, and pell-mell with our own cavalry, who, formed behind our squares, advanced on the first appearance (which was unexpected) of the enemy's squadrons. The enemy rushed down the hill, forming again under its shelter, and in a great measure covered from the fire of our guns, which, by recoiling, had retired so as to lose their original and just position. But in a deep stiff soil, the fatigue of the horse artillerymen was great, *and* their best exertions were unable to move the guns again to the crest without horses; to employ horses was to ensure the loss of the animals ...

The repeated charges of the enemy's noble cavalry were similar to the first: each was fruitless. Not an infantry soldier moved; and on each charge, abandoning their guns, our men sheltered themselves between the flanks of the squares. Twice, however, the enemy tried to charge in front; these attempts were entirely frustrated by the fire of the guns, wisely reserved till the hostile squadrons were within twenty yards of the muzzles. In this the cool and quiet steadiness of the troops of horse artillery was very creditable ... The obstinacy of these attacks made our situation critical: though never forced, our ranks were becoming thin. The second line, therefore, was chiefly ordered across the valley, and formed in masses behind the first, the broken intervals of which, where necessary, it filled up. Some time before this the Duke ordered me to bring up all the reserve horse artillery, which at that moment were Mercer's and Bull's troops, which advanced with an alacrity and rapidity most admirable.

Sergeant Major Edward Cotton, 7th Hussars[3]
Our position was scarcely free from the enemy's cavalry, before their numerous artillery began to ply us again with shells and round-shot. After the first cavalry charges, our infantry squares, finding the odds in their favour, gained confidence, and it was soon evident they considered the enemy's cavalry attacks as a relief, and far more agreeable than their furious cannonade, which was invariably suspended on their attacking force crowning our ridge. I am confident, from what I saw and heard, as well during as after the battle, that our British infantry would rather, when in squares, have the enemy's cavalry amongst them than remain exposed to the fire of artillery. The 1st foot-guards had the enemy's cavalry on every side of their squares several times, and beat them off. Our squares often wheeled up into line, to make their fire more destructive on the French cavalry when retiring: on this, the cuirassiers would suddenly wheel round to charge; but our infantry were instantly in square, and literally indulged in laughter at the disappointment and discomfiture of their gallant opponents. Throughout the day our squares presented a serried line of bristling bayonets, through which our enemy's cavalry could not break. Had the French made their attacks throughout with infantry and cavalry combined, the result must have been much more destructive; for, although squares are the best possible formation against cavalry, there can be nothing worse to oppose infantry. I am not aware of any parallel to the extraordinary scene of warfare which was now going forward: most of our infantry were in squares, and

the enemy's cavalry of every description riding about amongst them as if they had been our own; for which, but for their armour and uniforms, they might have been mistaken ... An ammunition waggon in a blaze passed about this time in full gallop close to our rear, and one of our men, I think Fowler, afterwards the sergeant sadler, drew his pistol and fired at the horses, but without taking effect: the waggon shortly after blew up.

Colonel Augustus Frazer, Royal Horse Artillery[5]
Passing Sir Thomas, and riding to the left of the position, whither I understood the Duke to have gone, the enemy's lancers were observed gaily stretching to their right; and the heads of their infantry columns just appearing. This was about 10 a.m.

Sergeant William Lawrence, Grenadier Guards[8]
During this movement a shell from the enemy cut our deputy-sergeant-major in two, and having passed on to take the head off one of my company of grenadiers named William Hooper, exploded in the rear not more than one yard from me, hurling me at least two yards into the air, but fortunately doing me little injury beyond the shaking and carrying a small piece of skin off the side of my face. It was indeed another narrow escape, for it burnt the tail of my sash completely off, and turned the handle of my sword perfectly black. I remember remarking to a sergeant who was standing close by me when I fell, 'This is sharp work to begin with, I hope it will end better' and even this much had unfortunately so frightened one of the young recruits of my company, named Bartram, who had never before been in action and now did not like the curious evolutions of this shell so close to him, that he called out to me and said he must fall out of rank, as he was taken very ill. I could easily see the cause of his illness, so I pushed him into rank again, saying, 'Why, Bartram, it's the smell of this little powder that has caused your illness; there's nothing

else the matter with you;' but that physic would not content him at all, and he fell down and would not proceed another inch. I was fearfully put out at this, but was obliged to leave him, or if he had had his due he ought to have been shot. From this time I never saw him again for at least six months, but even then I did not forget him for this affair of cowardice, as I shall have occasion to show hereafter.

Colonel Augustus Frazer, Royal Horse Artillery[5]
The howitzer troop came up, and came up handsomely; their very appearance encouraged the remainder of the division of the Guards, then lying down to be sheltered from the fire. The Duke said, 'Colonel Frazer, you are going to do a delicate thing; can you depend upon the force of your howitzers? Part of the wood is held by our troops, part by the enemy,' and his Grace calmly explained what I already knew. I answered that I could perfectly depend upon the troop; and, after speaking to Major Bull and all his officers, and seeing that they, too, perfectly understood their orders, the troop commenced its fire, and in ten minutes the enemy was driven from the wood.

Wellington's report to Earl Bathurst, Secretary of State for the War Department[9]
This attack upon the right of our centre was accompanied by a very heavy cannonade upon our whole line, which was destined to support the repeated attacks of cavalry and infantry occasionally mixed, but sometimes separate, which were made upon it. In one of these, the enemy carried the farm house of La Haye Sainte ...

'CW, a sergeant of the Guards'[12]
The enemy fired round shot, and shell – grape and canister – and new horse nails, tied up in bundles, nine bundles in a gun; I saw these and handled on the 19th. Unlawful carnage ...

William Gavin,1st Battalion, 71st Highland Light Infantry[13]
A brigade of the enemy's artillery got our range and annoyed us very much. One shot made an avenue from the first company to the tenth, which killed and wounded sixty men.

'*CW, a sergeant of the Guards*'[12]
My eyes have seen much. Sir; I have the happiness to serve in the third battalion of the Guards, who in a particular manner distinguished themselves ... Our third battalion and a battalion of rifle of the KGL (say 1200 men) advanced 300 paces in front of the whole line, into a valley which lay between the two positions, and within 100 yards of about 600 cavalry and 300 infantry of the enemy. They viewed us with astonishment; and to prove that God had filled them with fear, they formed square, and neither charged nor fired upon us, except from the heights of their positions; but we suffered much from those guns. We remained firing at them for half an hour, and then retired to our post in the line ... We never fired at the cavalry till they came within about 30 yards of us.

Lt John Kincaid, 95th Rifle Brigade[18]
When the heads of their columns showed over the knoll which we had just quitted, they received such a fire from our first line, that they wavered, and hung behind it a little; but, cheered and encouraged by the gallantry of their officers, who were dancing and flourishing their swords in front, they at last boldly advanced to the opposite side of our hedge, and began to deploy. Our first line, in the mean time, was getting so thinned, that Picton found it necessary to bring up his second, but fell in the act of doing it. The command of the division, at that critical moment, devolved upon Sir James Kempt, who was galloping along the line, animating the men to steadiness. He called to me by name, where I happened to be standing on the right of our battalion, and desired 'that I would

never quit that spot.' I told him that he might depend upon it: and in another instant I found myself in a fair way of keeping my promise more religiously than I intended; for, glancing my eye to the right, I saw the next field covered with the cuirassiers, some of whom were making directly for the gap in the hedge where I was standing. I had not hitherto drawn my sword, as it was generally to be had at a moment's warning; but, from its having been exposed to the last night's rain, it had now got rusted in the scabbard, and refused to come forth! I was in a precious scrape! Mounted on my strong Flanders mare, and with my good old sword in my hand, I would have braved all the chances without a moment's hesitation; but I confess that I felt considerable doubts as to the propriety of standing there to be sacrificed, without the means of making a scramble for it. My mind, however, was happily relieved from such an embarrassing consideration, before my decision was required; for the next moment the cuirassiers were charged by our household brigade; and the infantry in our front giving way at the same time, under our terrific shower of musketry, the flying cuirassiers tumbled in among the routed infantry, followed by the Life Guards, who were cutting away in all directions. Hundreds of the infantry threw themselves down, and pretended to be dead, while the cavalry galloped over them, and then got up and ran away. I never saw such another scene in all my life.

General Miguel Alava, Spanish Commissioner, Wellington's field staff[9]

General Picton, who was with his division on the road from Brussels to Charleroi, advanced with the bayonet to receive them; but was unfortunately killed at the moment when the enemy, appalled by the attitude of this division, fired, and then fled. The English Life Guards then charged with the greatest vigour, and the 49th and 105th French regiments lost their eagles in this charge, together with from 2 to 8,000 prisoners. A column of cavalry, at whose head were the cuirassiers, advanced to charge the Life Guards, and thus save their infantry, but the Guards received them with the greatest valour, and the most sanguinary cavalry fight, perhaps, ever witnessed, was the consequence. The French Cuirassiers were completely beaten, in spite of their cuirasses, by troops who had nothing of the sort, and lost one of their eagles in this conflict, which was taken by the heavy English cavalry called the Royals.

'JH', Scottish soldier[27]

I saw the Duke of Picton fall. He was leading us like a hero when he was struck down. A friend of mine, who entered the regiment when I did, fell just after the Duke: a ball entered his left breast and tore away the whole of his side. Poor fellow, I never saw him afterwards – for, as soon as a man falls, he's no more thought of. Our square was broken, and recovered over, and over again during the afternoon, and not a man of us would have escaped if the divisions of Cooke, Maitland, and Alten, had not come up and saved us.

An officer of the Imperial Guard[9]

It was now nearly two o'clock in the afternoon, and we had been engaged about an hour, when the English army, evidently yielding before the impetuous gallantry of the French, was sensibly retreating. The combat had indeed been murderous, and the cannonade and musquetry were but too well served on both sides. Our front lines advanced as the enemy retreated, and our rear closed up towards it. The artillery was brought in advance along the whole line. Our troops were thus gradually all engaged, and were fighting in the midst of the greatest obstacles and difficulties; the soil under our feet having no tenacity, and the surface of it being hilly, abrupt, and intersected with dikes, ravines, and hollows, in the gorges and channels of which we were momentarily opposed by troops whose existence we did not suspect, and who were hidden in them till the moment in which they rose up to meet us. We had to make our way inch by inch. The enemy never yielded a spot till they had exhausted every means of defence. The most inconsiderable hillock, or hollow, was taken and retaken repeatedly. The fire, instead of relaxing, only increased to universality; both sides fought with the most inconceivable gallantry, and the defence was as obstinate as the attack was impetuous.

Letter from an officer to his friend in Cumberland'[11]
Our lines were formed behind a hedge, with two companies of the 95th extended in front, to annoy the Enemy's approach. For some time we saw that Buonaparte intended to attack us; yet as nothing but cavalry were visible, no one could imagine what were his plans. It was generally supposed, that he would endeavour to turn our flank. But all of a sudden, his cavalry turned to the right and left, and showed large masses of infantry, who advanced up in the most gallant style, to the cries of '*Vive l'Empereur!*' while a most tremendous cannonade was opened to cover their approach. They had arrived at the very hedge behind which we were – the muskets were almost muzzle to muzzle, and a French mounted officer had seized the colours of the 32d regiment, when poor Picton ordered the charge of our brigade, commanded by Sir James Kempt. When the French saw us rushing through the hedge, and heard the tremendous huzza which we gave, they turned; but instead of running, they walked off in close columns with the greatest steadiness, and allowed themselves to be butchered without any material resistance.

Part V

THE CHARGE OF THE HEAVY CAVALRY

One of the key actions of the early stages of the battle was the charge of the British heavy cavalry: Somerset's Life Guards, Royal Horse Guards, 1st Dragoon Guard; Ponsonby's 1st Royal Dragoons, 2nd Dragoons (Scots Greys) and 6th Dragoons.

'Charge' is something of a misnomer, however. Initially at least, owing to the cavalry having to pick its way through the British ranks and there being very little distance between them and the French, most of the horsemen advanced at walking pace.

I2

EWART AND THE EAGLE

'*Extract of a letter from an officer in the Horse Guards*'[11]

About 11 o'clock, the grand action commenced. We were very soon called into action, and charged the French Cuirassiers of the Imperial Guard, whom we almost cut to pieces. A second charge of the same kind, left but few of them; but we suffered very much: we have with the regiment at present about 40 men. We know of 49 wounded, so that the rest must be either killed or prisoners. Lieut. Col. Fitzgerald was killed soon after the first charge. Capt. Irby was taken prisoner, as his horse fell with him in returning from the charge: he has since made his escape, and joined us; but they have stripped him of his sword, watch, and money, and had nearly taken his life. The heaviest fire was directed against the Household brigade the whole of the day; and it is astonishing how any of us escaped ...

Officer of the Brigade of Cavalry[11]

About half past eleven o'clock, three heavy masses of infantry, supported by artillery, and a numerous body of cuirassiers, were formed, and appeared to threaten the left of the British line. The Belgic light infantry were almost immediately driven in upon their support; and as these heavy columns of infantry advanced, the greater part of the Belgic infantry, after a short opposition, gave way, and, although in good order, retreated, leaving the Highland brigade, which was about four hundred yards in front of the 2nd heavy brigade of cavalry, to evince a glorious and very different example. These fine fellows, although they had suffered so severely on the 16th, with the most undaunted courage received the enemy's columns in line, taking up their line in rear of a cross road, somewhat protected by a small bank of earth, which formed a sort of hedge to the road, and with a most steady and well-directed fire presented a most decided check to the enemy. At this critical and awful moment, Lord Uxbridge galloped up; the three regiments of cavalry were in the most masterly style wheeled into line, and presented a most beautiful front of about thirteen hundred men: as his Lordship rode down the line, he was received by a general shout and cheer from the brigade. After having taken a short survey of the force, and threatening attitude of the enemy, and finding the Highland brigade, although still presenting an unbroken front, upon the point of being on both sides outflanked by an immense superiority of numbers, his Lordship determined upon a charge, which, for the wonderful intrepidity of its execution, and its complete success, has rarely been equalled, and certainly never surpassed.

The Royals appeared to take the lead, while the Greys preserved a beautiful line at speed, more to the left, over the cross road, near which spot their brave chief, Colonel Hamilton, fell, together with his horse, pierced with wounds. After considerable resistance, the Eagle of the 45th Regiment was seized by a serjeant of the Greys, of the name of Ewart, a man of most gigantic stature, whose right arm well did its duty on that day. The Royals on the right appeared not to be outdone by the Greys, and amidst the loud and hearty cheers of the Highlanders, two squadrons under Col. Dorville rushed into the second column of the enemy, consisting of about 4000 men, which had kept in reserve, when, after the most desperate individual exertion, the Eagle of the 105th Regiment was seized by a serjeant of the name of Styles ...

This terrible carnage of infantry and cavalry, where almost every thing was left to individual courage, and where every officer and man exerted every nerve to deserve well of his country, lasted about three-quarters of an hour; and after the complete destruction of this formidable mass of infantry, every endeavour was made to collect the fortunate remains of the brigade, under cover of a small wood to the left, which was speedily effected. If any thing could have damped the ardour of the officers and men after they were collected, it was to find that their gallant leader, to whom so much of the success was due, was no more! Sir William, just before the charge, had mounted a fresh horse: after heading the brigade with the most conspicuous valour, and having cut through the first column, he passed on to where Colonel Dorville was so thickly engaged; he here found himself outflanked by a regiment of Polish Lancers, who had come forward to the support of the infantry; finding his fate inevitable, he rushed upon the enemy's infantry to endeavour to join the Royals, and fell together with his horse, pierced with wounds ... Lieut. Col. Clarke, who succeeded to the command of the regiment, was afterwards severely wounded, and had four horses shot under him.

From The History of the Second Dragoons 'Royal Scots Greys'[43]
The battle of Waterloo being accidentally mentioned, Dr H. amused myself and the rest of the party after supper with various anecdotes of the gallantry and success of Sergeant Ewart of the Scots Greys ... The only exploit ... of which Ewart appears to be proud, is the summary revenge which he had an opportunity of taking for the death of Mr Kinchant, who was the Cornet of his own troop ... On the morning of the 18th, a little before 12 o'clock the Scots Greys were ordered to charge a body of French infantry at some distance, which order they instantly proceeded to execute in a

column two deep. Sergeant Ewart in this charge being the front man of Cornet Kinchant. Ewart, on reaching the enemy, immediately singled out a French Officer whom, from being a very expert swordsman, he soon disarmed and was on the point of cutting him down, when Mr Kinchant, on hearing the Officer cry out: *'Ah, mercy, mercy, Angleterre,'* said, *'Sergeant, Sergeant, spare his life and let us take him prisoner'*. Ewart considering that moment as a period for slaughter and destruction and not the proper time for taking prisoners, replied: *'As it is your wish, Sir, it shall be done.'*

Mr K. to whom the French Officer had delivered up his sword, addressed him in French and ordered him to move to the rear. Ewart was preparing to proceed in the charge when he heard the report of a pistol behind him, and turning round, from a suspicion of some treachery, the first object which met his eye was Mr K. falling backwards over his horse apparently in a lifeless state, and the French Officer attempting to hide his pistol under his coat. Indignant at such a dastardly act. Ewart instantly wheeled round, and was again entreated by this villain for mercy in the some supplicating terms as before. The only answer to which he returned was: *'Ask mercy of God, for the de'il a bit will ye get it at my hands,'* and with one stroke of his sabre, severed his head from his body, leaving it a lifeless trunk on the field of battle.

Corporal Dickson, Scots Greys[33]
Then I saw the Brigadier, Sir Denis Pack, turn to the Gordons and shout out with great energy, 'Ninety-second, you must advance! All in front of you have given way.' The Highlanders ... instantly, with fixed bayonets, began to press forward ... They uttered loud shouts as they ran forward and fired a volley at twenty yards into the French. At this moment our General and his aide-de-camp rode off to the right by the side of the hedge; then suddenly I saw De Lacy Evans wave his hat, and immediately our Colonel, Inglis Hamilton, shouted out 'Now then, Scots Greys, charge!'

and, waving his sword in the air, he rode straight at the hedges in front, which he took in grand style. At once a great cheer rose from our ranks, and we too waved our swords and followed him. I dug my spurs into my brave old Rattler, and we were off like the wind. Just then I saw Major Hankin fall wounded ... It was a grand sight to see the long line of giant grey horses dashing along with flowing manes and heads down, tearing up the turf about them as they went. The men in their red coats and tall bearskins were cheering loudly, and the trumpeters were sounding the 'Charge' ... All of us were greatly excited, and began crying 'Hurrah, Ninety-Second! Scotland for ever!' As we crossed the road. For we heard the Highlander pipers playing among the smoke and firing below, and I plainly saw my old friend Pipe-Major Cameron standing apart on a hillock coolly playing 'Johnny Cope, are ye waukin' yet?' in the din ...

The French were uttering loud, discordant yells. Just then I saw the first Frenchman. A young officer of Fusiliers made a slash at me with his sword, but I parried it and broke his arm ... The French were fighting like tigers. Some of the wounded were firing at us as we raced past; and poor Kinchant, who had spared one of these rascals, was himself shot by the officer he had spared. As we were sweeping down a steep slope on the top of them, they had to give way. Then those in front began to cry out for 'quarter', throwing down their muskets and taking off their belts. The Gordons at this point rushed in and drove the French to the rear. I was now in the front rank, for many of ours had fallen ... We now came to an open space covered with bushes, and then I saw Ewart, with five or six infantrymen about him, slashing right and left at them. I cried to Armour to 'Come on!' and rode at them. Ewart had finished two of them, and was in the act of striking a third man who held the Eagle; next moment I saw Ewart cut him down, and he fell dead. I was just in time to thwart a bayonet-thrust aimed at the gallant sergeant's neck. Armour finished another of them.

13

'SCOTLAND FOREVER!'

'Extract of a letter from a private of the 42d Regiment, to his father'[11]

In the afternoon of the 18th, the regiment, which was then reduced to about 200 men, found it necessary to charge a column of the Enemy which came down on them, from 2 to 3000 men: they broke into the centre of the column with the bayonet; and the instant they pierced it, the Scotch Greys dashed in to their support, when they and the 92d cheered and huzza'd 'Scotland forever.' By the effort which followed, the Enemy to a man were put to the sword or taken prisoners; after which the Greys charged through the Enemy's second line, and took the eagles.

Anonymous account[11]

Until we came up with our heavy horses, and our superior weight of metal, nothing was done with the Cuirassiers, unless one got Bow [*sic*] and then a cut at their faces, not one of them gave way; we therefore galloped at them, and fairly rode them down; when they were unhorsed, we cracked them like lobsters in their shells, and by the coming up of the cannon afterwards, thousands of them were squeezed as flat as pancakes. One man of the Scots Greys, from Ayrshire, has eighteen sword and sabre wounds, the greater number of which were inflicted by those savages after he was on the ground, dismounted. His name is Laurie, and a few days previous to the battle, he had accounts of his father's death, by which this gallant private soldier became possessed of £12,000. He says, that he saved his life in the end only by calling out in French, as the Enemy were charging over him – '*Oh! mon Dieu! mon Dieu! mes amis! mes amis!*' by which contrivance he was taken for one of their own men.

Sergeant Major Edward Cotton, 7th Hussars[2]
It was about noon (when, as I have said, we were in advance of the British position with our Brigade) that the French columns crowned the opposite heights, and they now again got into motion and, making a rapid and simultaneous push forward, both infantry and cavalry, neared our whole line and instantly the battle was commenced. The artillery of both armies maintained a terrible cannonade. At the centre right the French brought into action a line of 70 or 80 guns. Supported by this battery a column of Infantry advanced with loud shouts of *Vive l'Empereur* and drove back one of our divisions from its position. They were then charged by our Cavalry and completely routed with great loss of life. The same Cavalry then advanced against a body of French Cavalry, which approached, supported by another column of their Cavalry, to save or sustain their broken and retiring Infantry. As the two lines of Cavalry neared each other the French rather hesitated or at least slackened their pace. The English increased theirs. They met and the French were instantly overthrown, and the ground, which had before been clear, was now covered with wrecks of the charge.

A letter from a Life Guardsman[11]
The Irish howl set up by the Inniskilling [*sic*] Dragoons, and other Irish Regiments, is reported to have carried almost as much dismay into the ranks of the Enemy, as their swords. The stubborn bravery

and conduct of these regiments contributed much to the success of the day, it having been their lot to find themselves in the hottest part of the action, innumerable opportunities were afforded them of showing their devotion to their country's honour, and exalted sense of gallantry and duty. An officer of the Inniskilling says, 'Our brigade charged, upset and completely destroyed three large columns of infantry; at least 9000.' The old Inniskillings behaved most gallantly ... after the action they mustered about 100, some however were sent to escort prisoners.

Sergeant Major Edward Cotton[3]

During the cavalry charges, a man, named Gilmore, of Captain Elphinstone's troop, and belonging to my regiment, was lying under his wounded grey horse, about two hundred yards in our front. The cuirassiers were advancing; and as I was aware they spared none who fell into their hands, I sprang from the saddle, soon reached the spot, and seizing the bridle raised the horse's head; when the animal making a struggled [*sic*], Gilmore was enabled to extricate himself, and to reach our line just before the enemy's cavalry came up.

Sergeant Charles Ewart, Scots Greys[11]

Owing to a column of foreign troops giving way, our brigade was forced to advance to the support of our brave fellows, and which we certainly did in style; we charged through two of their columns, each about 5,000; it was in the first charge I took the Eagle from the Enemy; he and I had a hard contest for it; he thrust for my groin – I parried it off, and cut him through the head; after which I was attacked by one of their lancers, who threw his lance at me, but missed the mark, by my throwing it off with my sword by my right side; then I cut him from the chin upwards, which went through his teeth; next I was attacked by a foot soldier, who, after firing at me, charged me with his bayonet – but he very soon lost the combat, for I parried it and cut him down through the head;

so that finished the contest for the Eagle. After which I presumed to follow my comrades, Eagle and all, but was stopped by the General, saying to me, 'You brave fellow, take that to the rear: you have done enough until you get quit of it;' which I was obliged to do, but with great reluctance. I retired to a height, and stood there for upwards of an hour, which gave a general view of the field; but I cannot express the horrors I beheld: the bodies of my brave comrades were lying so thick upon the field, that it was scarcely possible to pass, and horses innumerable. I took the Eagle into Brussels amidst the acclamations of thousands of the spectators that saw it.

Private Thomas Hasker, 1st Kings Dragoon Guards[16]
About two o'clock we were ordered to mount and ascend the acclivity, sword in hand. There we found French cuirassiers cutting down our infantry. We charged them; on which they turned about and rode off, we following them, and as many as were overtaken were cut down. I observed, however, that many of them on our right flank got behind us, and thus we were at once pursuing and pursued. The regiment then took a direction to the left, and I found myself opposed to one man. We made several ineffectual passes at each other, and he then rode off. I turned to follow the regiment, but had not proceeded far when my horse fell. Before I had well recovered my feet, one of the cuirassiers rode up and began cutting and slashing at my head with his sword. I soon fell down with my face to the ground. Presently a man rode by, and stabbed me with a lance. I turned around, and was then stabbed by a sword by a man who walked past me. Very soon another man came up with a firelock and bayonet, and, raising both his arms, thrust his bayonet (as he thought) into my side near my heart. The coat I had on was not buttoned, but fastened with brass hooks and eyes. Into one of these eyes the point of the bayonet entered, and was thus prevented penetrating my body. One of my fingers was

cut off before I fell; and there I lay bleeding from at least a dozen places, and was soon covered with blood. I was also at that time plundered by the French soldiers of my watch, money, canteen, haversack, and trousers, notwithstanding the balls from the British army were dropping on all sides as I lay there.

Corporal Dickson, Scots Greys[33]

We now reached the bottom of the slope. There the ground was slippery with deep mud. Urging each other on, we dashed towards the batteries on the ridge above, which had worked such havoc on our ranks. The ground was very difficult, and especially where we crossed the edge of a ploughed field, so that our horses sank to the knees as we struggled on. My brave Rattler was becoming quite exhausted, but we dashed ever onwards. At this moment, Colonel Hamilton rode up to us crying, 'Charge! Charge the guns!' and went off like the wind up the hill towards the terrible battery that had made such deadly work among the Highlanders. It was the last we saw of our poor colonel, poor fellow! His body was found with both arms cut off. His pockets had been rifled ... Then we got among the guns, and had our revenge. Such slaughtering! We sabred the gunners, lamed the horses, and cut their traces and harness [sic]. I can hear Frenchmen yet crying 'Diable!' when I struck at them ... and the long-drawn hiss through their teeth as my sword went home. Fifteen of their guns could not be fired again that day. The artillery drivers sat on their horses weeping aloud as we went among them; they were mere boys, we thought.

Captain Alexander Clark, 1st Dragoons[14]

When I first saw it [the Eagle of the French 105th regiment] it was perhaps about forty yards to my left and a little in my front. The officer who carried it, and his companions, were moving with their backs towards me, and endeavouring to force their way through the crowd. I gave the order to my squadron 'Right shoulders forward! Attack the colour!' ... On reaching it, I ran my sword into the officer's right side, a little above the hip-joint. He was a little to my left side, and fell to that side, with the Eagle across my horse's head. I tried to catch it with my left hand, but could only touch the fringe of the flag, and it is probable that it would have fallen to the ground had it not been prevented by the neck of Corporal Styles' horse ... On taking up the Eagle, I endeavoured to break [it] from the pole with the intention of putting it into the breast of my coat; but I could not break it. Corporal Styles said, 'Pray, sir, do not break it,' on which I replied, 'Very well, carry it to the rear as fast as you can, it belongs to me.'

Corporal Dickson, Scots Greys[33]

But you can imagine my astonishment when down below, on the very ground we had crossed, appeared at full gallop a couple of regiments of Cuirassiers on the right, and away to the left a regiment of Lancers ... Behind us we saw masses of French infantry with tall fur hats coming up at the double, and between us and our lines these cavalry. There being no officers about, we saw nothing for it but to go straight at them and trust to Providence to get through. There were half-a-dozen of us Greys and about a dozen of the Royals and Enniskillens on the ridge. We all shouted, 'Come on, lads; that's the road home!' and, dashing our spurs into our horses' sides, set off straight for the Lancers. But we had no chance.

I saw the lances rise and fall for a moment, and Sam Tar, the leading man of ours, go down amid the flash of steel. I felt a sudden rage at this, for I knew the poor fellow well; he was a corporal in our troop. The crash as we met was terrible; the horses began to rear and bite and neigh loudly, and then some of our men got down among their feet, and I saw them trying to ward off the lances with their hands. Cornet Sturges of the Royals he joined our regiment as lieutenant a few weeks after the battle came up and was next me on the left, and Armour on the right. 'Stick together, lads!' we cried, and went at it with a will, slashing about us right and left over our horses' necks. The ground around us was very soft, and our horses could hardly drag their feet out of the clay. Here again I came to the ground, for a Lancer finished my new mount, and I thought I was done for. We were returning past the edge of the ploughed field, and then I saw a spectacle I shall never forget. There lay brave old Ponsonby [Sir William], the General of our Union Brigade, beside his little bay, both dead. His long, fur-lined coat had blown aside, and at his hand I noticed a miniature of a lady and his watch; beyond him, our Brigade-Major, Reignolds of the Greys. They had both been pierced by the Lancers a few moments before we came up. Near them was lying a lieutenant of ours, Carruthers of Annandale. My heart was filled with sorrow at this, but I dared not remain for a moment. It was just then I caught sight of a squadron of British Dragoons making straight for us. The Frenchmen at that instant seemed to give way, and in a minute more we were safe! The Dragoons gave us a cheer and rode on after the Lancers.

Lt-Colonel Sir Frederick Ponsonby[41]
At one o' clock, observing, as I thought, unsteadiness in a column of French infantry, fifty by twenty or thereabouts, which were advancing with an irregular fire, we resolved to charge them. As we descended, we received from our own line on the right a fire much more destructive than theirs; theirs having begun long before it could take effect, and slackening as we drew nearer. When we were within fifty paces of them, they turned, and much execution was done among them, as we were followed by some Belgians, who had seen our success; but we had no sooner passed through them, than we were ourselves attacked before we could form, by about three hundred Polish lancers, who had hastened to their relief, the French artillery pouring in among us a heavy fire of

grape, though for one of our men they killed three of their own. In the melee I was almost instantly disabled in both of my arms, losing first my sword, and then my rein, and followed by a few of my men who were presently cut down, no quarter being asked or given, I was carried on by my horse, till receiving a blow from a sabre, I was fell senseless on my face to the ground. Recovering, I raised myself a little to look round, being, I believe, at that time, in a condition to get up and run away, when a lancer passing by, cried out, 'Tu n'es pas mort, coquin?' and struck his lance through my back; my head dropped, the blood gushed into my mouth, a difficulty of breathing came on, and I thought all was over.

Not long afterwards (it was then impossible to measure time, but I must have fallen in less than ten minutes after the onset) a tirailleur stopped to plunder me, threatening my life. I directed him to a small side-pocket, in which he found three dollars, all I had; but he continued to threaten, and I said he might search me: this he did immediately, unloosing my stock and tearing open my waistcoat, and leaving me in a very uneasy posture. But he was no sooner gone, than an officier bringing up some troops, to which the tirraileur probably belonged, and happening to halt where I lay, stooped down and addressed me, saying, he feared I was badly wounded: I answered that I was, and expressed a wish to be removed into the rear: he said it was against their orders to remove even their own men, but that if they gained the day, (and he understood that the Duke of Wellington was killed, and that six of our battalions had surrendered), every attention in his power should be shown me. I complained of thirst, and he held his brandy-bottle to my lips, directing one of the soldiers to lay me straight on my side, and place a knapsack under my head: he then passed on into the action, soon perhaps to want, though not receive, the same assistance; and I shall never know to whose generosity I was indebted as I believe for my life. Of what rank he was I cannot say: he wore a great coat.

By and by another tirailleur came up, a fine young man, full of ardour: he knelt down and fired over me, loading and firing many times, and conversing with me very gaily all the while: at last he ran off, saying, 'Vous serez bien aise d'apprendre que nous allons nous retirer; bon jour, mon ami'. It was dusk, when two squadrons of Prussian cavalry, each of them two deep, came across the valley, and passed over me in full trot, lifting me from the ground, and tumbling me about cruelly: the clatter of their approach, and the apprehensions they excited, may be imagined; a gun taking that direction must have destroyed me. The battle was at an end or removed to a distance. The shouts, the imprecations, the outcries of 'Vive l'Empereur', the discharges of musketry and cannon were over, and the groans of the wounded all around me, became every instant more and more audible. I thought the night would never end.

Much about this time, I found a soldier of the Royals lying across my legs; he had probably crawled thither in his agony; and his weight, his convulsive motions, his noises, and the air issuing through a wound in his side, distressed me greatly; the latter circumstance most of all, as I had a wound of the same nature myself. It was not a dark night, and the Prussians were wandering about to plunder ... Several stragglers looked at me as they passed by one after another, and at last one of them stopped to examine me. I told him as well as I could, for I spoke German very imperfectly, that I was a British officer, and had been plundered already: he did not desist, however, and pulled me about roughly. About an hour before midnight, I saw a man in an English uniform walking towards me; he was, I suspect, on the same errand, and he came and looked in my face. I spoke instantly, telling him who I was, and assuring him of a reward if he would remain by me. He said he belonged to the 40th, and had missed his regiment: he released me from the dying soldier, and being unarmed, took up a sword from the ground, and stood over me, pacing backwards and forwards. Day broke, and at six o'clock in the morning some English were seen at a distance and he ran to them. A messenger was sent off to Harvey, a cart came for me, and I was placed in it, and carried to the village of Waterloo, a mile and a half off, and laid in the bed from which poor Gordon, as I understood afterwards, had been just carried out. I had received seven wounds: a surgeon slept in my room, and I was saved by excessive bleeding.

Part VI

MID-AFTERNOON

Around 3 p.m. the ferocity of the battle slackened, as both sides gathered themselves for the final onslaught. But barely an hour had passed before the French threw themselves at the Allies once more. Napoleon, who was now receiving messages that the Prussians were closing in, ordered Ney to make another attack on La Haye Sainte, while French cavalry charged the main Allied lines again and again – up to ten thousand riders. This was followed by a French infantry advance up the hill. Still the Allies held on.

14

'SOLDIERS, WE MUST NEVER BE BEAT'

Anonymous account[11]
Col. Harvey of the 14th was in a charge of the Light Cavalry, when he found himself opposed to a French officer, who was proceeding to make a cut at him, when perceiving the Colonel had but one arm, he dropped his sword, exclaiming he would never use his sword against a man thus situated. In this instance also, the gallant Colonel has been unable to find his noble opponent [to thank him, after the battle].

'Extract of a letter from an officer of the 18th Hussars'[11]
I must name to you an individual occurrence which happened in our regiment. Serjeant Taylor, on coming up with the Cuirassiers, made a cut at the head of one of them, which had no other effect on the Frenchman, than to induce him to cry out in derision, 'Ha! ha!' and to return a severe blow at the Serjeant, which was admirably parried, and Taylor then thrust his sabre into the mouth of the Cuirassier, who instantly fell, and the conqueror cried, 'Ha! ha!' in his turn; which circumstance much increased the ardour of the other men.

Lt-Colonel William Tomkinson, 16th Light Dragoons[42]
Lieutenant Colonel Hay, commanding 16th Light Dragoons, was shot through the body. The shot entered his back, coming out the front. It was, at the time, supposed he could not live. He has recovered. I think he was shot by our own infantry firing to check the enemy, and not perceiving our advance to charge. There is little doubt of it.

Anonymous account[11]
Col. Colquitt, of the Guards, having taken refuge in a square, took up a shell that had just fallen within it, and with the utmost *sang-froid* threw it over the men's heads, down a kind of bank; by which the effect of the explosion was saved.

Lt-Colonel William Tomkinson, 16th Light Dragoons[42]
An officer of cuirassiers rode close up to one of our squares with a detachment of men. He saw he had no chance of success, and by himself alone rode full gallop against the square, was shot and killed. Our men and officers regretted his fate.

Anonymous account[11]
A Life-guardsman, who, from being bald, was known among his comrades by the appellation of the Marquis of Granby, had his horse shot under him; in the charge, his helmet fell off, and on foot he attacked a cuirassier, whom he killed, and rode off with his horse, his comrades cheering him with – 'Well done, Marquis of Granby.'

'Letter from an officer to his friend in Cumberland'[11]
All our army was formed in solid squares – the French cuirassiers advanced to the mouth of our cannon – rushed on our bayonets: sometimes walked their horses on all sides of a square to look for an opening, through which they might penetrate, or dashed madly on, thinking to carry every thing by desperation. But not a British

soldier moved; all personal feeling was forgotten in the enthusiasm of such a moment. Each person seemed to think the day depended on his individual exertions, and both sides vied with each other in acts of gallantry.

Sergeant Major Edward Cotton, 7th Hussars[3]
The battle appeared now to rage at every point, and though the day continued drizzling wet and the dullness of the atmosphere was increased along the line by the smoke of the musketry and cannon so as occasionally to render everything momentarily invisible or obscured, yet as the wind blew fresh and rolled it away, one could clearly distinguish other continual charges of the Cavalry of both sides, and the alternate formations of the troops into squares and lines or masses. Twice or thrice a Prussian officer appeared to announce the approach of their army, and at his request we actually cleared the road on which we were standing in order to have firm footing for our horses and guns, to make way for them. The Duke of Wellington on the other hand sent more than once to ascertain if they had arrived, or to enquire if they were in sight, but we could give no account whatever of them. The French were at length formed on a sort of plain or flat, below and in front of the height from which they had commenced their attack, but though nearer, had acquired no part of our position, and they were evidently greatly reduced in numbers, while at the same time the ranks of our Infantry immediately on our right were thinned, as was apparent from the increased space caused by closing the files, between its left and our right.

Lt John Kincaid, 95th Rifle Brigade[18]
Some one asking me what had become of my horse's ear, was the first intimation I had of his being wounded; and I now found that, independent of one ear having been shaved close to his head, (I suppose by a cannon shot,) a musket ball had grazed across his

forehead, and another gone through one of his legs; but he did not seem much the worse for either of them.

Lt John Kincaid, 95th Rifle Brigade[18]

We saw Buonaparte himself take post on the side of the road, immediately in our front, surrounded by a numerous staff, and each regiment as they passed him rent the air with shouts of 'Vive l'Empereur!' Backed by the thunder of their artillery and carrying with them the *rubidub* of drums and the *tantara* of trumpets ... it looked at first as if they had some hopes of scaring us off the ground.

Sergeant Thomas Morris, 73rd Foot[20]

At the next charge the cavalry made they deliberately walked their horses up to the bayonet's point; and one of them, leaning over his horse, made a thrust at me with his sword. I could not avoid it, and involuntarily closed my eyes. When I opened them again, my enemy was lying just in front of me, within reach. In the act of thrusting at me, he had been wounded by one of my rear-rank men, and whether it was the anguish of the wound, or the chagrin of being defeated, I know not, but he endeavoured to terminate his existence with his own sword: this being too long for his purpose, he took one of our bayonets, which was lying on the ground, and raising himself up with one hand, he placed the point of the bayonet under his cuirass, and fell on it.

Sergeant John Douglas, 3rd Battalion, The Royal Scots[15]

The slaughter was great on both sides, and would have been greater, but for the ground, which, being so soft, the balls which struck it never rose again.

Lt William Bates Ingilby, Royal Horse Artillery[2]

Some of our Dragoons we could see individually or in small parties pushing on, and they had actually possession of the right of the large battery of French guns, while on the left their guns continued to fire. Sir H. Vivian was extremely anxious to do something with his Brigade at this charge, but I know that he was restrained by his instructions, which were by no means to quit his position and expose the left flank of the army. As both Cavalries charged obliquely to the left and the French Cavalry was part of their centre right, and did not move, it brought the charge nearly opposite the position of our Brigade. Sir H. Vivian therefore took a couple of guns of the Troop and proceeded with them to assist General Ponsonby and his Cavalry. These were my division (section), but we became so completely within range of the enemy's numerous battery of superior calibre that one of the first shots directed against us blew up a limber, killed the sergeant, and passed through the shoulders of my charger exactly above my knees, and Sir H. Vivian immediately withdrew them, lest, knowing his orders, he might attract the notice of the Commander-in-Chief. The French, on seeing the limber blow up, gave some loud cheers, but that could not compensate for defeat with great loss of both attacks by the Infantry and Cavalry. General [Sir William] Ponsonby was killed and Colonel [Frederick] Ponsonby very badly wounded and left on the enemy position.

Anonymous account[11]

During the charge made by the Royal Horse Guards Blue, against the French Cuirassiers on the 18th, Lieut. Tathwell of that regiment rushed on the Eagle-bearer, and in a most gallant style tore the eagle from his grasp, and was bearing it away in triumph, when unfortunately his horse received a shot, and his rider in consequence fell into the hands of the enemy, from whom, however, he effected his escape, and rejoined his corps the following morning.

Lt William Bates Ingilby, Royal Horse Artillery[2]

The French supporting column of Cavalry, on seeing the overthrow of its leading columns, instantly put about and retired at a trot to its original ground on the extreme right of the French position; they were clothed in red. In these charges (excepting at the great charge between the two large bodies of Cavalry) and repulses, the sight was perpetually interrupted by the smoke of the cannon and musketry, and it was difficult at the distance to affix to each Corps or Regiment the part or share it took in them. Our Infantry that appeared driven back were the Highlanders, and the Cavalry that immediately charged were the Scotch Greys. The great charge was made by Heavy Cavalry supported by Light.

'Extract of a letter from an officer in the Guards'[11]

The French opened upon us [at Hougoumont] a dreadful cross-fire, from three hundred pieces of artillery, which was answered with a most uncommon practice from our guns; but to be just, we must own that the French batteries were served in a manner that was terrible. During this period, the Enemy pushed his troops into the orchard, &c. &c, and after its being contested for some hours, he succeeded in reducing our men to nothing but the house itself. Every tree, every walk, every hedge, every avenue had been fought for with an obstinacy almost unparalleled; and the French were killed all round, and at the very door of the house, to which, as well as a hay-stack, they succeeded in setting fire; and though all in flames over their heads, our brave fellows never suffered them to penetrate beyond the threshold; the greatest part of the wounded on both sides were, alas, here burned to death! – In consequence of this success on the part of the French, the Coldstream and third regiment were ordered into the wood, from whence they drove the Enemy; and every subsequent struggle they made to re-possess themselves of it, proved abortive. The places of these two battalions of guards were supplied by two of our gallant friends, the Black Brunswickers, who seemed, like salamanders, to revel in the smoke and flames.

'Extract of a letter from an officer in the Guards'[11]
Unfortunately for us, during the cannonade the shot and shells which passed over the artillery, fell into our squares, and I assure you I never was in a more awful situation. Col. Cook (who commanded the battalion) [possibly Colonel Richard Harvey Cooke] was struck with a grape shot as he sat on the ground next to me. The Enemy now made an attack with infantry and cavalry on the left, in hopes of carrying the chaussee to Brussels; but the artillery guns cut them to pieces every time they advanced. They then attempted to charge the guns with cavalry; but the squares of infantry kept up so smart a fire that they could never reach our guns, though the artillerymen were obliged to leave them to get out of our fire.

Soldier of the 71st, or Glasgow Regiment, Highland Light Infantry[11]
The noise and smoke were dreadful. At his time I could see but a very little way from me; but, all around, the wounded and slain lay very thick. We then moved on, in column, for a considerable way, and formed line; gave three cheers and fired a few volleys, charged the enemy, and drove them back ... At this moment a squadron of cavalry rode furiously down upon our line. Scarce had we time to form. The square was only complete in front when they were upon the points of our bayonets. Many of our men were out of place. There was a good deal of jostling, for a minute or two, and a good deal of laughing. Our quarter-master lost his bonnet, in riding into the square; got it up, put it on, back foremost, and wore it thus all day ... A French General lay dead in the square. He had a number of ornaments upon his breast. Our men fell to plucking them off, pushing each other as they passed, and snatching at them.

Private George Farmer, 11th Light Dragoons[25]

The wounded horses, of which multitudes wandered all over the field, troubled us. They would come back, some with broken legs, others trailing after them their entrails, which the round-shot had knocked out, and forcing themselves between our files, seemed to solicit aid which no one had time to afford, and which, if afforded, would have been useless.

Private George Farmer, 11th Light Dragoons[11]

A square of Brunswick Infantry had, it appeared, begun to waver, and, as a failure at that point might have proved fatal, we were brought up to stop it if we could. We drew our swords, cheered, and made our horses prance, and the desired end was gained. The Brunswickers, perceiving that there was support, took up their arms, which some of them had thrown away, and they throughout the remainder of the action behaved with all the gallantry for which their countrymen have in every age and country been remarkable.

Anonymous account[11]

When the British and French cavalry encountered each other, the sound of the British swords upon the armour and helmets of the Cuirassiers, was compared by a private in the action to numberless tinkers at work upon their pots and kettles.

Colonel Augustus Frazer, Royal Horse Artillery[5]

I now returned to the first line, and the action becoming more general, the fire hotter, and nothing pressing on our right, I ordered Ramsay's troop to the centre of the second line. To this centre it became at one time necessary to send Bull's troop to refit and repair disabled carriages. The wood, from the front of which it went, was taken and retaken three times. At a quarter before three the large building burst out in a volume of flame, and formed a striking feature in the murderous scene. Imagining that this fire might oblige our troops to quit a post most material, and that it would have an effect, and possibly a great one, on the day, I remarked the time by my watch. The Guards, however, held the post, and maintained themselves in the lesser buildings, from which the enemy could never dislodge them. To our right of the burning buildings, a troop of horse artillery, galled by the superior fire of the enemy's artillery, was forced to give way; but the point being essential, ordered it up again at all hazards. By this time the infantry were entirely formed into squares, the cavalry generally in solid columns, the crest of our position crowned with artillery. It was now that the French cavalry, advancing with an intrepidity unparalleled, attacked at once the right and centre of our position, their advance protected by a cannonade more violent than ever.

Anonymous account[11]
The Duke of Wellington, in riding up to a regiment, which was hard pressed, called to them – 'Soldiers, we must never be beat; what will they say in England?' How this appeal was answered, it is needless to recapitulate.

Charlotte Eaton, travel writer[22]
The ground occupied by Sir Thomas Picton's division, on the left of the road from Brussels, is lower than any other part of the British position. It is divided from the more elevated ridge where the French were posted by a very gentle declivity. To the right the ground rises, and the hollow irregularly increases, until at Chateau Hougoumont it becomes a sort of small dell or ravine, and the banks are both high and steep. But the ground occupied by the French is uniformly higher, and decidedly a stronger position than ours. Nothing struck me with more surprise than the confined space in which this tremendous battle had been fought; and this, perhaps, in some measure contributed to its sanguinary result. The space which divided the two armies from the farm-house of La Haye Sainte,

which was occupied by our troops, to La Belle Alliance, which was occupied by theirs, would, I think, scarcely measure three furlongs. Not more than half a mile could have intervened between the main body of the French and English armies; and from the extremity of the right to that of the left wing of our army, I should suppose to be little more than a mile. The hedge along which Sir Thomas Picton's division was stationed, and through which the Scots Greys, with the Royals and the Inniskillens, headed by Lord Uxbridge, made their glorious and decisive charge at the close of the action, is almost the only one in the field of battle.

Private Smithies, 1st Dragoons[14]
On we rushed at each other, and when we met the shock was terrific [La Haye-Sainte]. We wedged ourselves between them as much as possible, to prevent them from cutting, and the noise of the horses, the clashing of swords against steel armour, can be imagined only by those who have heard it. There were some riders who caught hold of each other's bodies – wrestling fashion – and fighting for life, but the superior physical strength of our regiment soon showed itself.

Ensign Edward Macready, 30th Regt of Foot[34]
As soon as they quickened their trot to a gallop the Cuirassiers bent their heads so that the peaks of their helmets looked like visors and they seemed cased in armour from the plume to the saddle. Not a shot was fired till they were within thirty yards when the word was given ... The effect was magical. Thro' the smoke we could see helmets falling – cavaliers starting from their seats with convulsive springs as they received our balls, horses plunging & rearing in the agonies of fright and pain, and crowds of the soldiery dismounted; part of their squadron in retreat, but the more daring remainder backing their horses to force them on our bayonets. Our fire soon disposed of these gentlemen. The main body reformed in our front

were reinforced and rapidly and gallantly repeated their attacks, In fact from this time (about four o'clock) till near six we had a constant repetition of these brave but unavailing charges ... The best cavalry is contemptible to a steady and well supplied infantry regiment – even our men saw this and began to pity the useless perseverance of their assailants and as they advanced would growl out 'here come those damned fools again'.

Corporal Dickson, Scots Greys[33]

I never saw horses become so ferocious, and woe betide the blue coats that came in their way! But the noble beasts were now exhausted and quite blown, so that I began to think it was time to clear away to our own lines again. But you can imagine my astonishment when down below, on the very ground we had crossed, appeared at full gallop a couple of regiments of cuirassiers on the right, and away to the left a regiment of lancers. I shall never forget the sight. The cuirassiers, in their sparkling steel breastplates and helmets, mounted on strong black horses, with great blue rugs across the croups, were galloping towards me, tearing up the earth as they went, the trumpets blowing wild notes in the midst of the discharges of the grape and canister shot from the heights. Around me there was one continuous noise of clashing arms, shouting of men, neighing and moaning of horses. What were we to do?

Sergeant Major Edward Cotton, 7th Hussars[3]

At one time during that memorable afternoon, the ridge and rear slope of our position were literally covered with every description of horsemen, lancers, cuirassiers, carabineers, horse grenadiers, light and heavy dragoons and hussars; during which our guns stood in position, abandoned by the artillerymen, who took refuge in and around the squares: when at length the enemy's gallant but fruitless efforts became exhausted, our cavalry appeared and cleared the allied position. On one occasion a body of cuirassiers passed along the Nivelles road, closely followed by a party of my regiment, under captain Verner. Upon the high bank on the right of the Nivelles road, a party of the 51st regiment, under Lieutenant Kennedy, was firing upon the enemy, and our advanced files narrowly escaped being shot. As the cuirassiers neared the avenue between the Nivelles road and Hougoumont, they came upon an *abuttis,* or barricade, near which was a party of the 51st, under captain Hoss, who fired upon them; about a hundred and fifty were killed, wounded or taken prisoners.

15

DE LANCEY IS HIT

Lady Magdalene, wife of Colonel Sir William Howe De Lancey[4]
When Sir William was riding beside the Duke, a cannon ball struck
him on the back, at the right shoulder, and knocked him off his
horse to several yards distance. The Duke at first imagined he was
killed; for he said afterwards, he had never in all the fighting he
had ever been in seen a man rise again after such a wound. Seeing
he was alive (for he bounded up again and then sank down), he
ran to him, and stooping down, took him by the hand. Sir William
begged the Duke, as the last favour he could have it in his power
to do him, to exert his authority to take away the crowd that
gathered round him, and to let him have his last moments in peace
to himself. The Duke bade him farewell, and endeavoured to draw
away the Staff, who oppressed him; they wanted to take leave of
him, and wondered at his calmness. He was left, as they imagined,
to die; but his cousin, Delancey Barclay, who had seen him fall,
went to him instantly, and tried to prevail upon him to be removed
to the rear, as he was in imminent danger of being crushed by the
artillery, which was fast approaching the spot; and also there was
danger of his falling into the hands of the enemy. He entreated to
be left on the ground, and said it was impossible he could live; that

they might be of more use to others, and he only begged to remain on the field. But as he spoke with ease, and Colonel Barclay saw that the ball had not entered, he insisted on moving him, and he took the opinion of a surgeon, who thought he might live, and got some soldiers to carry him in a blanket to a barn at the side of the road, a little to the rear ...

Anonymous French soldier[9]

It was now reported amongst us, that some strong columns were about to make a charge of bayonets upon the position of Mont St. Jean whilst the cavalry was to make a charge upon some detached points which seemed to be little supported. We expected the result of this great movement, but it was foiled by the obstinate gallantry with which the English defended the farms of Hougoumont and La Haye upon their wings. They every moment reinforced their battalions which were posted in these positions; our cavalry, increasing in the same proportion, made successive charges, but the English, like a flux and reflux wave, though one time receding, yet advanced again, and maintained their ground. Never did I behold a finer spirit of gallantry, – a more resolute and soldier-like steadiness. If for a moment these brave troops (for let them have what is due to them) were pushed from this position, it seemed only by the effect of our superior weight from our superior numbers brought against them; and the moment which restored the equality by the coming up of a reinforcement, restored at the same time the ground they had lost ...

An officer of the Imperial Guard[9]

The English artillery now made the most frightful havoc in our ranks; we stood in fact point-blank aim for them, and the balls perforated from front to rear through our columns and ranks. Our own artillery answered with the same vivacity, but the enemy were better covered from our fire by means of some eminences which sheltered them. The unbroken thunder of 600 pieces of cannon, all roaring at the same moment, the fire along both lines of at least one hundred thousand musquets, discharged twice or thrice in a minute; the bursting of shells, the blowing up of ammunition waggons, – the hissing of balls, and the groans of the dying, added to the heaps of wounded and killed (the mud being absolutely coagulated with blood), altogether composed a most horrible spectacle; and the more so as the stage upon which so many horrors were acted, was so narrow as to be wholly beneath the eye.

'*Extract of a letter from an officer in the Guards*'[11]
The 2d and 3d battalions of the first regiment were formed with the two battalions of Brunswickers into hollow squares, on the slope and summit of the hill, so as to support each other; and in this situation we all lay down, till between three and four o'clock P. M., in order to avoid the storm of death, which was flying close over our heads, and at almost every moment carrying destruction among us: and it is, you will allow, a circumstance highly creditable to those men, to have lain so many hours under a fire, which for intensity and precision was never, I believe, equalled; with nothing else to occupy their attention, save watching their companions falling around them, and listening to their mournful cries. It was about the time I have just named, that the Enemy, having gained the orchard, commenced their desperate charges of cavalry, under cover of the smoke which the burning houses, &c. had caused; the whole of which the wind drifted towards us, and thus prevented our observing their approach.

'*Extract of a letter from an officer in the Guards*'[11]
At this period the battle assumed a character beyond description interesting, and anxiously awful. Buonaparte was about to use against us an arm, which he had never yet wielded but with

success. Confidently relying upon the issue of this attack, he charged our artillery and infantry, hoping to capture the one, and break the other, and, by instantly establishing his own infantry on the heights, to carry the Brussels road, and throw our line into confusion. These cavalry, selected for their tried gallantry and skill (not their height or mustachios), who were the terror of Northern Europe, and had never yet been foiled, were first brought up by the 3d battalion of the 1st regiment. Never was British valour and discipline so pre-eminent as on this occasion; the steady appearance of this battalion caused the famous Cuirassiers to pull up; and a few of them, with a courage worthy a better cause, rode out of the ranks, and fired at our people and mounted officers, with their pistols, hoping to make the face of the square throw its fire upon them, and thus become an easy prey: but our men, with a steadiness no language can do justice to, defied their efforts, and did not pull a single trigger. The French then made a sudden rush, but we received in such a manner, and with a volley so well directed, as at once to turn them; they then made an attempt on the 2d battalion, and the Brunswickers, with similar success; and, astonished at their own failure, the cool intrepidity of their opponents, and the British cheers, they faced about. This same game was played in succession by the Imperial Horse Guards, and Polish Lancers, none of whom could at all succeed in breaking our squares, or making the least impression upon them whatever. During their attacks, our cavalry rushed out from between the squares, and carried havock through the Enemy's ranks, which were nearly all destroyed.

'*Extract of a letter from an officer of the 18th Hussars*'[11]
At three o'clock p.m. Major Percy was sent by the Duke of Wellington to General Bulow, to inquire how long it would be before he could come up; he returned in a short time, saying, that he would arrive in an hour; but, as I before observed, the roads prohibited the possibility of his doing so.

'Extract of a letter from an officer in the Guards'[II]

I cannot here resist relating an anecdote of Major Lloyd, of the Artillery, who, with another officer, (whose name I could not learn) was obliged to take refuge in our square at the time these charges were made, being unable to continue longer at their posts. There was a gun between our battalion and the Brunswickers, which had been drawn back; this, Major Lloyd with his friend discharged five or six times at the French cavalry, alternately loading it and retiring to the square, as circumstances required. We could see the French knocked off their horses as fast as they came up, and one cannot refuse to call them men of singular gallantry; one of them, indeed, an officer of the Imperial Guards, seeing a gun about to be discharged at his companions, rode at it and never suffered its fire to be repeated while he lived. He was at length killed by a Brunswick rifleman, and certainly saved a large part of his regiment by this act of self-devotion.

Anonymous account[II]

A regimental colour belonging to the 25th French Regiment, was then seized upon by private Fry of the 28th Regiment, and the whole were repulsed; the cavalry pursued and took the Eagles. Lieut. Deares behaved in the bravest manner, advancing to the charge with his company; but when the cavalry continued the pursuit, that officer was led on in the moment of enthusiasm, and accompanied the cavalry on foot, attacking sword in hand every Frenchman that came in his way. He had already cut down two and wounded three others, when being overpowered by a body of infantry, he was seized and made prisoner. In a short time he was stripped of all his appointments, his coat, and shoes: nothing was left him but his shirt and pantaloons, and they were nearly torn off. In this state he made his escape to his regiment during the night.

1. Wellington by Jan Willem Pieneman, 1821. (Rijksmuseum)

2. *An Episode at the Battle of Waterloo* by Wm Heath, 1817. (Yale Center for British Art)

3. *Chelsea Pensioners Receiving the Gazette Announcing the Battle of Waterloo* by Sir D. Wilkie, *c.* 1819. (Yale Center for British Art)

4. A Highlander, Black Watch, attending a General of Hussars, possibly Lord Uxbridge: a study for *The Battle of Waterloo*, G. Jones, 1815. (Yale Center for British Art)

5. Studies for the Duke of Wellington by Sir Geo. Hayter, *c.* 1820. (Yale Center for British Art)

6. *The Battle of Waterloo* by Jan Willem Pieneman, 1824. Depicting Wellington, and the wounded Prince of Orange being carried away. (Rijksmuseum)

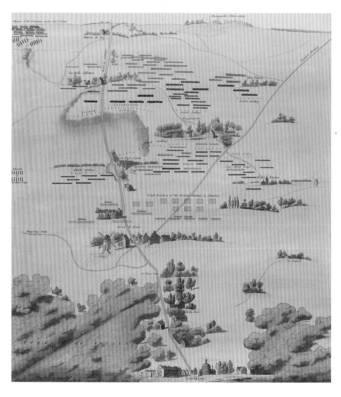

7. Plan of Waterloo Battlefield by C. Smith, 1815. (Rijksmuseum)

8. General von Blucher. Despite a recent defeat at Ligny, his timely arrival at Waterloo was the turning point for the battle. (The British Library Board)

9. General Blucher, leading the charge of the Prussian troops at Waterloo. Despite his advanced age (seventy-two at the time of Waterloo), Blucher was often in the thick of the battle. (The British Library Board)

10. Hougoumont & La Haye Saint, 1816. (Rijksmuseum)

11. Quatre Bras & La Belle Alliance, 1816. (Rijksmuseum)

Above left: 12. Napoleon with his staff. (Rijksmuseum)

Above right: 13. Marshall Ney *c.* 1805. Executed after Waterloo despite his deserved reputation for bravery. (Courtesy of Havang)

Below: 14. The Caillou (Pebble) Farm, Napoleon's HQ at Waterloo. (Courtesy of Kelisi)

15. Napoleon Bonaparte, depicted here as Emperor of France. (Rijksmuseum)

16. *Napoleon Fleeing the Field of Battle*. (Rijksmuseum)

17. The Prince of
Orange. (Rijksmuseum)

18. Mont-Saint-Jean, the hamlet on the reverse slope where Wellington placed his
army. (Rijksmuseum)

19. Marshal Grouchy, who took command of the French retreat to Paris in the aftermath of the battle. (Rijksmuseum)

20. Lion's Mound, Waterloo. Marks where the Prince of Orange was wounded. Provides excellent views of the battlefield, but ironically the earth moved to create it actually altered the shape of the original terrain, to Wellington's dismay. (Courtesy of Myrabella)

21. The north gate of Hougoumont, assaulted by the 1st Légère. (Courtesy of Paul Hermans)

22. South portal of Hougoumont. (Courtesy of Jean-Pol Grandmont)

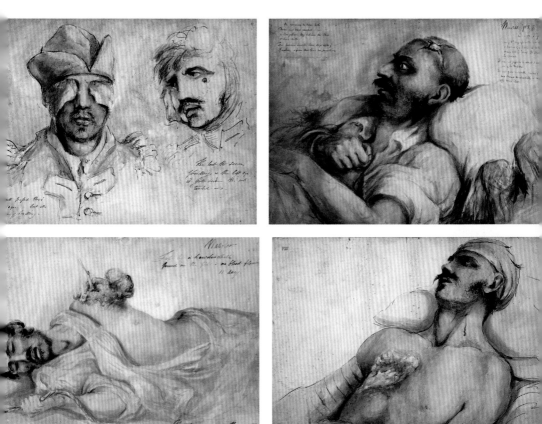

23–26. A number of illustrations made by Charles Bell, showing injuries sustained by soldiers during the Battle of Waterloo. (Wellcome Library, London)

Left: 27. Captured French 6-pounder field gun at the Tower of London. (Courtesy of Uploadalt)

Right: 28. Lord Raglan, taken in the Crimea in 1855. Already suffering from dysentery, he died just weeks after the photograph was taken, aged sixty-six. (Digital image courtesy of the Getty's Open Content Program)

Left: 29. A Waterloo re-enactor in British uniform with a British standard. (Courtesy of Pixar)

Right: 30. Napoleonic re-enactors fire and reload muskets, the standard firearm issued to light infantry on both sides of the Battle of Waterloo. (Courtesy of Pixar)

31. Waterloo re-enactors in British uniform fire their muskets. (Courtesy of Dennis Jarvis)

32. Waterloo re-enactors in the uniform of French Grenadiers march forward. (Courtesy of Dennis Jarvis)

Above: 33. A Waterloo re-enactor in the uniform of a French Cuirassier, with French troops in the background. (Courtesy of Myrabella)

Below: 34. Waterloo re-enactors in front of the wood of Hougoumont. (Courtesy of Myrabella)

William Gavin, 1st Battalion, 71st Highland Light Infantry[13]
At one time we had only the front of the square formed when a squadron charged us, but we soon had it complete, with Lord Wellington in the centre. In the confusion my hat fell off, and on recovering it put it on front part to the back, and wore it like this for the remainder of the day, not knowing it was so. In this charge Ensign Todd was killed, also Lieutenant Elwes mortally wounded. Lieutenant Lawe, who acted as adjutant to the left wing, and was mounted, was hit by a cannon ball, which passed through the calf of his right leg, through the horse's body, and wounded his left leg.

Captain Alexander Kennedy Clarke-Kennedy, 1st Dragoons[14]
From the nature of the ground we did not see each other until we were very close, perhaps eighty or ninety yards. The head of the column appeared to be seized with a panic, gave us a fire which brought down about twenty men, went instantly about and endeavoured to regain the opposite side of the hedges; but we were upon them before this could be effected, the whole column getting into one dense mass, the men between the retiring parts getting so jammed together that the men could not bring down their arms, or use them effectively, and we had nothing to do but continue to press them down the slope, the right of the squadron of the Royals naturally outflanking them as the centre one (which I commanded) also did to a certain degree.

Part VII

CRISIS

Repeated French attacks were repulsed by the Allies, who mostly stood firm despite heavy losses. The British cavalry came into its own, mounting devastating counter-charges – but also at great cost to man and horse.

When the first Prussian units arrived and began to engage the French right, Napoleon ordered a last push against Wellington before Blucher's army could affect the course of the battle. La Haye Sainte was battered once more and the centre of Wellington's line was thinned and stretched to breaking point.

La Haye Saint was finally over-run at around 6.30 p.m. Out of the 400 who had defended it, only forty-two or forty-three escaped. If Napoleon had had reserves to throw into the mix at this time he may have overcome Wellington – but the need to meet the growing Prussian presence meant the troops needed to tip the balance were no longer available.

Napoleon had initially tried to persuade his men that the blue uniforms of the distant Prussians were in fact French, but as it gradually became clear that a new and powerful enemy was arriving on the scene alarm began to spread through French ranks. He gambled everything on a final attack by his feared Old Guard against Wellington's centre. In the past these elite troops had always been let loose to finish off a demoralised or depleted enemy. Their reputation and the mere sight of them could cause panic and flight. In response, Wellington ordered up the British Guards. Their accurate volleys halted the French advance, which was then routed by British cavalry. Wellington could see that the tide had finally turned. After having fought a defensive battle all day, he rose in his stirrups and raised his hat aloft to signal an advance against the retreating enemy.

16

THE FALL OF LA HAYE SAINTE

Major Henry Smith, 95th Foot[49]
The Battle of Waterloo has been too often described, and nonsense enough written about the Crisis for me to add to it. Every moment was a crisis, and the controversialists had better have left the discussion on the battle-field. Every Staff officer had two or three (and one four) horses shot under him. I had one wounded in six, another in seven places, but not seriously injured. The fire was terrific, especially of cannon.

'CW, a sergeant of the Guards'[12]
When the French 105th advanced ... our line at two different times was so shattered that I feared they could not stand: in fact I was for a moment really afraid they would give way ... Our Officers exerted themselves to the very uttermost, as also the Serjeants ... Our loss at this time was tremendous. It was at this juncture that I picked up Ensign Purdo's coat, which was covered with his blood, lying on a horse. The Ensign belonged to our battalion; he was killed and stripped by the plunderers during some of our manoeuvres. I stepped about twenty-five paces before the line and waved the coat, cheering the men, and telling them that while our

Officers bled we should not reckon our lives dear. (I did this a second time when the Imperials came up against us, and I believe it had the desired effect.)

Sergeant William Lawrence, 40th Foot[8]
We did not lose a single inch of ground the whole day, though after these successive charges our numbers were fearfully thinned; and even during the short interval between each charge the enemy's cannon had been doing some mischief among our ranks besides ... The men in their tired state were beginning to despair, but the officers cheered them on continually throughout the day with the cry of 'Keep your ground, my men!' It is a mystery to me how it was accomplished, for at last so few were left that there were scarcely enough to form square.

Colonel Augustus Frazer, Royal Horse Artillery[5]
I have escaped very well. Maxwell's horse, on which I rode at first, received a ball in the neck, and I was afterwards rolled over by a round of case shot, which wounded my mare in several places, a ball grazing my right arm, just above the elbow, but without the slightest pain; and I now write without any inconvenience. In a momentary lull of the fire I buried my friend Ramsay, from whose body I took the portrait of his wife, which he always carried next his heart. Not a man assisted at the funeral who did not shed tears. Hardly had I cut from his head the hair which I enclose, and laid his yet warm body in the grave, when our convulsive sobs were stifled by the necessity of returning to renew the struggle.

Private George Farmer, 11th Light Dragoons[25]
Many wounded men passed us while thus resting; but of the case of only one I shall make mention, because it struck me at the moment as being a remarkable one. An infantry soldier approached, and

asked me for a cup of water. I saw that he was wounded; and, recollecting that a canteen of beer was at my back ... I handed it to him, and desired him to quench his thirst without scruple. The poor fellow drank, thanked me heartily, told me that almost all his regiment – the 28th – was destroyed; and then, lifting himself from my horse, on which he had been leaning, tottered towards the rear. I watched him, and saw that he had not gone twelve yards when he fell. Almost immediately afterwards his limbs gave a convulsive stretch, and he was a corpse ...

Ensign Edmund Wheatley, King's German Legion[26]
The attacks on La Haye Sainte and Hougoumont were continued, but not with much violence, and the cannonade was moderate. But at about four o'clock the cannonade became violent in the extreme, probably as much so as has been witnessed in any open field of battle. This was evidently the prelude to some serious attack. To our surprise we soon saw that it was the prelude to an attack of cavalry upon a grand scale. Such an attack we had fully anticipated would take place at some period of the day; but we had no idea that it would be made upon our line standing in its regular order of battle, and that line as yet unshaken by any previous attack by infantry ... The French force which we saw advancing to the attack was the whole of Milhaud's corps, consisting of forty squadrons of heavy cavalry. That corps, being on the French right of the Charleroi road, had to cross the road before making this attack, and had consequently to oblique considerably to its left. This was effected in beautiful order, and the formation and advance of that magnificent and highly disciplined cavalry had, as a spectacle, a very grand effect. These splendid horsemen were enthusiastic in the cause of Napoleon – full of confidence in him and in themselves – thirsting to revenge the reverses which had been suffered by the French armies – led by most experienced and able cavalry commanders – and they submitted to a rigid

discipline. Their advance to the attack was splendid and interesting in the extreme. Our surprise at being so soon attacked by this great and magnificent force of cavalry was accompanied with the opinion that the attack was premature, and that we were perfectly prepared and secure against its effects, so far as any military operation can be calculated upon ... The French cavalry advanced upon the oblongs, the fire from the front faces of which was given at about thirty yards' distance. This caused the attacking cavalry to swerve to the right and left of the front faces of the squares, as usually has been the case in attacks of cavalry against infantry; but although they did not gallop in mass right on the bayonets of the infantry, they made every other effort to enter the oblongs, by firing into them, cutting aside the bayonets, and surrounding the oblongs to obtain a point of entrance.

Those who were not immediately opposite to the faces of the oblongs passed the first and attacked the oblongs of the second line, showing great gallantry and persevering obstinacy to win; but all their efforts failed, and they had received the artillery fire, and were exposed to the fire of the front, flank, and rear faces of the oblongs: thus their numbers became fearfully diminished, and this splendid body of cavalry became a wreck, surrounded by the immovable masses of infantry within the formations of which it had become entangled. While in this hopeless condition, it was driven down the exterior slope by the Anglo-Allied cavalry. Colonel Ompteda ordered us instantly into the line to charge, with a strong injunction to 'walk' forward, until he gave the word to charge. When within sixty yards he cried 'Charge', we ran forward huzzaing. The trumpet sounded and no one but a soldier can describe thrill one instantly feels in such a awful moment. At the bugle sound the French stood until we just reached them. I ran by Colonel Ompteda who cried out, 'That's right, Wheatley!' I found myself in contact with a French officer but ere we could decide, he fell by an unknown hand. I then ran at a drummer, but he leaped over a ditch through the hedge in which he stuck fast. I heard a cry of 'The Cavalry! The Cavalry!' But so eager was I that I did not mind it at the moment, and when on the eve of dragging the Frenchman back (his iron-bound hat having saved him from a Cut) I recollect no more.

On recovering my senses, I look'd up and found myself bareheaded, in a clay ditch with a violent head-ache. Close by me lay Colonel Ompteda on his back, his head stretched back with his mouth open, and a hole in his throat. A frenchman's arm across my leg [*sic*]. So confused was I that I did not remember I was on the field of Battle at the moment. Lifting up a little, I look'd over the edge of the ditch and saw the backs of a french Regiment and all the day's employment instantly suggested itself to my mind. Suddenly I distinguished some voices and heard one say 'En voici En voici!' I lay down as dead, retaining my breath, and fancied I was shot in the back of my head. Presently a fellow cries, 'Voici un autre.' And a tug at my epaulette bespoke his commission. A thought struck me – he would turn me round to rifle my pockets. So starting up, I leaped up the ditch, but a swimming seized me and I was half on the ground when the fellow thrust his hand in my collar, grinning, 'Ou va's tu, chien?' I begged of him to let me pick up my cap and he dragged me into the house. The inside of La Haye Sainte I found completely destroyed, nothing but the rafters and props remaining. The floor, covered with mortar bricks and straw, was strewed with bodies of the German Infantry and French Tirailleurs. A Major in Green lay by the door. The carnage had been very great in this place. I was taken over these bodies out of the door on the right, through a garden to the back of the house where I found several and men standing. [They] instantly crowded round me. One of my wings and the other half off. My oil skin haversac [was] across my shoulder, and my cap fastened to my waist, by running my sash through the internal lining. A multitude of questions was put to me by the men and Officers while I fastened on my Cap: '*Vous êtes de Battalion, Monsieur?*'

Sergeant William Lawrence, Grenadier Guards[8]
About four o'clock I was ordered to the colours. This, although I was used to warfare as much as any, was a job I did not at all like; but still I went as boldly to work as I could. There had been before me that day fourteen sergeants already killed and wounded while in charge of those colours, with officers in proportion, and the staff and colours were almost cut to pieces. This job will never be blotted from my memory: although I am now an old man, I remember it as if it had been yesterday. I had not been there more than a quarter of an hour when a cannon-shot came and took the captain's head clean off. This was again close to me, for my left side was touching the poor captain's right, and I was spattered all over with his blood. One of his company who was close by at the time, cried out, 'Hullo, there goes my best friend,' which caused a lieutenant, who quickly stepped forward to take his place, to say to the man, 'Never mind, I will be as good a friend to you as the captain.' The man replied, 'I hope not, sir;' the officer not having rightly understood his meaning, the late captain having been particularly hard on him for his dirtiness, giving him extra duty and suchlike as punishment.

Private George Farmer, 11th Light Dragoons[25]
By this time the dusk was closing fast; and, as the battle continued to rage with unabated fury, the magnificence of the scene received, from minute to minute, a perpetual increase to its intensity. Over the surface of the ground, shells, with their burning fuses, rolled, bursting here and there with terrible effect. From the mouths of the cannon fire seemed to be poured, while the ceaseless glare of musketry was terrific. By degrees, however, the sounds and sight of fire-arms began to be distinguishable where neither had before been observed; and the rumour ran from rank to rank among us, that the Prussians were come, and had fallen upon the right and rear of the enemy. Moreover, that the news was not without foundation,

was soon apparent, from the altered state of things both near and far away. Our infantry, which up till this moment had fought in squares, formed all at once into line. There was a heart-stirring cheer begun, I know not where, but very soon audible over the whole of our front; and we, too, were ordered to leap into the saddle and move forward ... On we went at a gallop, dashing past weary yet gallant footmen, and, shouting as we went, drove fiercely and without check up to the very muzzles of a hostile battery. A furious discharge of grape met us, and thinned our ranks. Before it man and horse went down; but the survivors, never pulling bridle or pausing to look back, scattered the gunners to the winds, and the cannon were our own. Just at this moment, Serjeant [*sic*] Emmet of the 11th, whom I covered, received a shot in the groin, which made him reel in his saddle, from which he would have fallen, had I not caught him; while at the same time a ball struck me on the knee, the bone of which was saved by the interposition of my unrolled cloak ... terribly bruising, yet not disabling the limb ... By this time it was too dark to distinguish one corps from another. I therefore attached myself to the first body of horse which I overtook, and in three minutes found myself in the middle of the enemy. There was a momentary check, during which the men demanded one of another, what regiment this was ... an officer called aloud, 'Never mind your regiments, men, but follow me.' In an instant I sprang to his side, and, seeing a mass of infantry close upon us, who, by the blaze of musketry, we at once recognised to be French, he shouted out, 'Charge!' and nobly led the way. We rushed on: the enemy fired and eight of our number fell, among whom was our gallant leader. A musket-ball pierced his heart: he sprang out of his saddle, and fell dead to the ground ... Another check was the consequence, and almost instinctively we recoiled; neither, indeed, was the movement inopportune, for the impetuosity of a mere handful of men had carried them into the middle of a retreating column, and their destruction, had they lingered there, must have been inevitable.

Anonymous French soldier[9]

At length the instant was arrived, when, all his [Napoleon's] attempts having completely failed, it was announced to him, that some Prussian columns were debouching on our right flank, and threatened our rear. He would give no credit to these reports, and answered several times that they had made wrong observations, and that these pretended Prussians were only the corps of Grouchy. He even abused, and sent back in discontent, several of the aides-de-camp, who successively came to bring him this intelligence. 'Away,' said he; 'you have been affrighted; approach without fear these debouching columns, and you will be convinced that they are Grouchy's.'

Lt-Colonel William Tomkinson, 16th Light Dragoons[42]

While in this situation, my coverer (Sergeant Flesh) was hit by a spent ball. It struck him on the chest, and with such violence that he said he was killed. I fancied the ball had gone through him. In a few minutes I saw the ball drop from his overalls at his feet on to the ground, and on desiring him to go to the rear he said he should see it out, and fell in again. He had not been five minutes in the ranks before another spent ball struck him, but not with such violence as the first; he continued with us ... He suffered afterwards from not being bled, and taking no care of himself.

'JH', Scottish soldier[27]

Towards nightfall, whilst rallying after a tremendous shock of the French, which made the very ground shake under our feet, I received these two sabre cuts – at the same time exposing two fearful scars. One extending from the back part of the right shoulder down to the waist; the other, almost the whole length of the hip and thigh on the same side. It was close to the farm-house, and the confusion was so great, that I laid upon a dunghill along with others, who were badly wounded, until early the next morning before we were recognised.

Sergeant Thomas Morris, 73rd Foot[20]

The casualties among our officers at this time was particularly severe; our brave colonel received a musket-ball in the shoulder, which afterwards subjected him to a long and painful confinement. When we were ordered to retire from the French infantry, a young man belonging to us, named Steel, a lad of rare courage, was in the act of firing, when a cannon-shot, in rolling along the ground, took his foot off at the ankle. He did not fall, but advancing a step on his shattered stump, said, 'D—n you, I'll serve you out for that!' and fired his piece among the enemy.

Sergeant Thomas Morris, 73rd Foot[20]

While we were retiring, Sergeant Mure of the grenadiers, a very brave and good soldier, in turning round to have a look at the enemy, received a musket-ball in the forehead, and fell on his back a corpse. A cousin of his, named Morrison, on hearing of his fate, ran back in the face of a most destructive fire, to where his kinsman lay, kissed his cheek, let fall a tear or two, and then joined us again.

Sergeant Major Edward Cotton, 7th Hussars[3]

On one occasion a French horse battery was pushed forward near the south-east angle of the orchard of Hougoumont, where it opened upon the brigade: but our batteries on the ridge concentrated their fire upon it, and drove it off. Our artillerymen cheered. I witnessed the great effect produced by some rockets which were thrown from the valley upon the French horse. Our batteries had been most successful on this part of the line in checking and destroying the enemy's cavalry.

Sergeant Major Edward Cotton, 7th Hussars[3]

The enemy's cavalry, who were now nearly sobered, would come up singly, and fire their carbines at the squares. Their horse artillery often galloped up, unlimbered, when crash! crash! came the grape into

Halkett's squares, making gaps which it was admirable to see the fine fellows fill up, and that without orders. Whenever the Duke came, which at this momentous period was often, there was a low whisper in the ranks, 'Here's the Duke!' and all was steady as on parade. No matter what the havock and destruction might be, the Duke was always the coolest man there: in the words of an eyewitness of this bloody scene, the Duke was coolness personified. It really appeared that the more desperate the fight, the more determined were the few brave fellows that remained to hold their ground; yet often would a murmur escape them, such as, 'This is thundering murderous work! why don't we go into them? Let us give them the cold steel,' etc., etc. But such murmurs were soon hushed, and again were displayed those traits of unyielding passive courage, the grandest, the most sublime characteristics of the British soldier. The troops evinced in their resignation a discipline unparalleled in European armies. Though confident in their chiefs and themselves, their foes were not less so: a French cuirassier officer, a prisoner in Halkett's left square, replied, in a surly and snappish tone, to an officer of the 30th who asked him what force Bonaparte had, 'You will see directly, sir.'

Sergeant Major Edward Cotton, 7th Hussars[3]
The skirmishers in advance of their columns about La Haye-Sainte, the knoll and sand-pit, and along the valley right and left, threw out a rattling fire for the purpose of harassing and weakening our line, in order to clear the way for the grand attack by the Imperial guard; this fire was vigorously replied to by our troops, who were partially covered from the enemy's fire by the hedge-row and banks on this part of the front. Our gallant 27th, upon the bank at the junction of the roads, was still much exposed. Our 95th rifles and the 4th foot were extended along the Wavre road. The 40th, 79th, 28th, and 1st Royals were in line behind the rear hedge. The fire increased, and it appeared as if all would be borne down before it. The banks on the road side, the garden wall, the knoll and sand-pit

swarmed with skirmishers, who seemed determined to keep down our fire in front; those behind the artificial bank seemed more intent upon destroying the 27th, who at this time, it may literally be said, were lying dead in square; their loss after La Haye-Sainte had fallen was awful, without the satisfaction of having scarcely fired a shot; many of our troops in rear of the ridge were similarly situated. A British officer, who was an eyewitness of the gallant conduct of the 27th, says, 'If ever the sovereign give them another motto, it should be, *Muzzle to muzzle;* for so they fought at Waterloo.'

Anonymous account[11]
The artillery attached to Maj.-General Sir J. Kempt's (late Picton's) division, were most distinguished upon this occasion, although at one time the men were entirely routed from their battery. Col. Sir Philip Belson, of the 28th Regiment, who commanded the brigade that was Sir James Kempt's, had his horse shot under him, when he was leading up the 32d Regiment to the support of this battery of artillery. Major General Sir J. Lambert brought up his brigade to this part of the line, and contributed to the success of the day. Sir Denis Pack's brigade was to the left of Sir Philip Belson's: that officer had two horses shot when he was with the 28th Regiment, who were posted along La Haye Sainte, where the French made the most desperate attacks during the day. Capt. Kelly, of the 28th Regiment, seized the Frenchman who carried the colour, of the 25th Regiment, and private Fry coming up to his assistance, they carried it off, and Fry shot him dead.

Sergeant Major Edward Cotton, 7th Hussars[3]
The battle had been now raging for nearly eight hours, and not a square had been broken, nor had the enemy gained more than one advantage, viz. the capture of La Haye-Sainte, which was through one of those mischances in war which often mar the best planned arrangements. But those continued furious attacks had not been

met and repulsed without a most severe loss to the troops who had stood the brunt of the battle, and had been so long exposed to a murderous cannonade.

Lt John Kincaid, 95th Rifle Brigade[18]
The loss of La Haye Sainte was of the most serious consequence, as it afforded the enemy an establishment within our position. They immediately brought up two guns on our side of it, and began serving out some grape to us; but they were so very near that we destroyed their artillerymen before they could give us a second round. The silencing of these guns was succeeded by a very extraordinary scene, on the same spot. A strong regiment of Hanoverians advanced in line, to charge the enemy out of La Haye Sainte; but they were themselves charged by a brigade of cuirassiers, and, excepting one officer, on a little black horse, who went off to the rear, like a shot out of a shovel, I do believe that every man of them was put to death in about five seconds. A brigade of British light dragoons advanced to their relief, and a few on each side began exchanging thrusts: it seemed likely to be a drawn battle between them, without much harm being done, when our men brought it to a crisis sooner than either side anticipated, for they previously had their rifles eagerly pointed at the cuirassiers, with a view of saving the perishing Hanoverians; but the fear of killing their friends withheld them, until the others were utterly overwhelmed, when they instantly opened a terrific fire on the whole concern, sending both sides flying; so that on the small space of ground, within a hundred yards of us, where five thousand men had been fighting the instant before, there was not now a living soul to be seen, It made me mad to see the cuirassiers, in their retreat, stooping and stabbing at our wounded men, as they lay on the ground. How I wished that I had been blessed with omnipotent power for a moment, that I might have blighted them!

Anonymous French soldier[9]
At the same time that they began to be agitated with astonishment and terror, [The French had heard stories of the Allied rear and baggage train 'retreating with precipitation' towards Brussels] the French army was equally struck with hesitation, and the liveliest inquietude. Some dismounted batteries were put in retreat, great numbers of the wounded forsook the columns, and spread the greatest uncertainty for the event of the battle; the acclamations and joyful shouts of soldiers, certain of marching to victory, were followed by a profound silence. All the troops, except the infantry of the guard, were seen in action, and exposed to the most murderous fire; the engagement prolonged itself with the same continued violence, and yet brought forward no result.

Sergeant Thomas Morris, 73rd Foot[20]
The cuirassiers now transferred their favours to some other quarter, leaving us at liberty to contemplate the havock they had made; and the Duke of Wellington riding by, again addressed our general with, 'Well, Halkett, how do you get on?' The general replied, 'My lord, we are dreadfully cut up; can you not relieve us for a little while?' 'Impossible,' said the Duke. 'Very well, my lord,' said the general; 'we'll stand till the last man falls!'

Sergeant Thomas Morris, 73rd Foot[20]
I noticed one of the Guards, who was attacked by two cuirassiers at the same time; he bravely maintained the unequal conflict for a minute or two, when he disposed of one of them by a deadly thrust in the throat. His combat with the other one lasted about five minutes, when the guardsman struck his opponent a slashing back-handed stroke, and sent his helmet some distance, with the head inside it. The horse galloped away with the headless rider sitting erect in the saddle, the blood spouting out of the arteries like so many fountains.

Sergeant Thomas Morris, 73rd Foot[20]

Our sergeant-major was a brave soldier, and had been through the whole of the engagements in the Peninsula with the 43rd regiment. During the day, when our men were falling very fast, he turned deadly pale, and said to the colonel, 'We had nothing like this in Spain, sir.' The worst fault he had was an inveterate habit of swearing, which he could not avoid, even under these awful circumstances. Noticing one of the men, named Dent, stooping every now and then, as the shots came whizzing by, he said, 'D – n you, sir, what do you stoop for? You should not stoop if your head was off!' He had scarcely spoken the word, when a musket-ball struck him full on the nose, killing him on the spot. Dent immediately turned round and said, 'D – n you, sir, what do you lie there for? You should not lie down if your head was off!'

Charlotte Eaton, travel writer[22]

An order had been issued not to fire at the enemy's field-pieces, but at the troops. However, during the latter part of the action, a young officer of artillery, out of patience with the destruction caused among his men, and particularly with the loss of Captain Bolton, his friend and brother officer, from the fire of some guns opposite, levelled his cannon at them, and had the satisfaction to see the French artillerymen, and officers who commanded them, fall in their turn. At that moment he was accosted suddenly by the Duke of Wellington, whom he had no idea was near. 'What are you firing at there?' The artillery officer confessed what he was about. 'Keep a good look out to your left,' said the Duke, 'you will see a large body of the enemy advancing just now; fire at them.' They soon perceived a tremendous number of the Imperial Guards, the elite of the army, advancing with great order and steadiness to attack the British. The moment they appeared in view, the officer to whom the Duke had spoken, directed against them such a tremendous and effective fire, that they were mowed down by ranks.

Sergeant Thomas Morris, 73rd Foot[20]
Whilst thus occupied an order came for us medical officers to shift our quarters, as there was no shelter for us whilst dressing the wounded; indeed, we were exposed to the fire of the French artillery and their infantry, so we were directed to take up our quarters in the village of Mount St Jean ... It was neither an easy or pleasant task to undertake, for the shot were flying about us in every direction, though in a sunken road we were somewhat protected. The huge cannon balls hissing and whistling over our heads, lodging with a terrible thud into the opposite bank, or striking the surface and rebounding, committed havoc and destruction in the most unexpected quarters. Many of these missiles would have done comparatively little damage had the road not been paved, but on striking these stones the shot not only rebounded, but caused large fragments of rocks to fly about, killing and wounding many who would otherwise have escaped ...

Assistant-Surgeon William Gibney[21]
During much of this time I accompanied the regiment, riding by the Colonel's side [This must have been Lt-Col Dalrymple – see Appendix], only quitting them or halting when they were charging, or opposing other cavalry. Again I was directed to return to Mount St Jean ... I had not been ten minutes in the village ... when the colonel of my regiment was brought in desperately wounded, he telling me it had occurred almost immediately after I had left his side. A round shot had shattered his leg, and entering the horse's abdomen, killed it on the spot. As the wounded limb was on the side near which I had been riding, it is not improbable that had I remained I also should have suffered. The leg was only suspended by a few muscles and the bone in splinters. Amputation, and that

at once, was the only chance. I got the Colonel placed in a room where there were several other wounded officers, and separating the foot from its connections, told him he must undergo the operation of amputation ...

An officer of the Imperial Guard[9]

During these movements, the fate of Buonaparte was unknown. Some asserted that he had fallen in the combat. When this intelligence was stated to a well known general officer, he replied in the words of Megret, after Charles the twelfth was killed at Frederickstadt, '*Thus ends the tragedy.*' It was stated by others, that after charging several times at the head of his guards, he was dismounted and taken prisoner.

French officer's letter[9]

The fire of the artillery had been terrible, and destructive all day, but at this moment, no idea can be conveyed of the shock and crush that was now felt from it.

17

NAPOLEON'S FINAL GAMBLE

Colonel Augustus Frazer, Royal Horse Artillery[5]
The French cavalry made some of the boldest charges I ever saw: they sounded the whole extent of our line, which was thrown into squares. Never did cavalry behave so nobly, or was received by infantry so firmly. Our guns were taken and retaken repeatedly. They were in masses, especially the horse artillery, which I placed and manoeuvred as I chose. Poor fellows! many of them – alas, how many! – lie on the bed of honour. Failing in his repeated attacks of cannonading and movements of cavalry, Napoleon at length pierced the left of our centre with the infantry of the Imperial Guard: the contest was severe beyond what I have seen, or could have fancied. I cannot describe the scene of carnage. The struggle lasted even by moonlight.

Sergeant William Lawrence, 40th Foot[8]
But now I must get on to the last charge of cavalry ... Few as we were, when we saw it coming we formed squares and awaited it. Then we poured volley after volley into them, doing fearful execution, and they had to retire at last before the strong dose we administered; not, however, without our losing more men and

so becoming even weaker than before. We were dreading another charge, but all the help we got was the cry of 'Keep your ground, my men, reinforcements are coming!' Not a bit, however, did they come till the setting sun, in time to pursue our retreating enemy; the Prussians under Marshal Blucher having been detained elsewhere, and although long expected, only being able at this period to make their appearance at last.

Colonel Augustus Frazer, Royal Horse Artillery[5]
With all these, however, this last struggle was nearly fatal to us; but our infantry remaining firm, and not only receiving the cavalry in squares, but, on their retiring, darting into line and charging the Imperial Infantry Guards, and again resuming their squares, the enemy was forced to give way. I have seen nothing like that moment, the sky literally darkened with smoke, the sun just going down, and which till then had not for some hours broken through the gloom of a dull day, the indescribable shouts of thousands, where it was impossible to distinguish between friend and foe. Every man's arm seemed to be raised against that of every other. Suddenly, after the mingled mass had ebbed and flowed, the enemy began to yield; and cheerings and English huzzas announced that the day must be ours.

'Extract of a letter from John Marshall, private, 10th Dragoons'[11]
Their attention was then arrested by a large body of Prussians, who came point blank upon their right flank, and opened a very heavy fire of artillery upon them. This for a little time put them in a consternation; but even this they recovered, and, altering their lines, seemed to suffer but little from this our new reinforcement. This was about five in the evening, and victory was still doubtful.

Anonymous French soldier[9]
The hour of seven was near. Buonaparte, who till now had remained on the eminence where he had placed himself, and from which he

had an excellent view of all which occurred, contemplated with a ferocious look the hideous spectacle of so frightful a butchery. The more obstacles increased, the greater appeared his obstinacy. He became impatient of these unforeseen difficulties, and far from fearing to push to extremities an army whose confidence in him was unbounded, he did not cease to send fresh troops, and to give orders to advance, to charge bayonets, to assault. Several times was it mentioned to him from different quarters, that the affair was unfortunate, that the troops appeared shaken; 'Forward, forward,' was his reply. A general caused him to be informed, that he was unable to maintain his position which was annoyed by a battery; at the same time he inquired what he should do to withdraw himself from its murderous fire. 'Seize it,' he replied, and turned his back to the aide-de-camp.

'Extract of a letter from John Marshall, private, 10th Dragoons'[11]
The enemy then made one more attempt to vanquish us, by bringing the most of his force at our right flank, trying to force it, and to gain the high road for Brussels, which if he had succeeded, our defeat would have been complete; and here it was that our Commander the Duke of Wellington was put to the test; for they advanced with a vast and numerous body of cavalry, supported by infantry, and covered by artillery, and seemed determined to have this road. The chief of our artillery was then brought to this point, and theirs parallel with ours; such a tremendous peal of thunder did they ring one against the other, as I never knew since my name was Marshall.

General Miguel Alava Spanish Commissioner, Wellington's field staff[9]
At last, about seven in the evening, Buonaparte made a last effort, and putting himself at the head of his guards, attacked the above point of the English position with such vigour, that he drove back the Brunswickers who occupied part of it, and, for a moment, the

victory was undecided, and even more than doubtful. The Duke, who felt that the moment was most critical, spoke to the Brunswick troops with that ascendency which every great man possesses, made them return to the charge, and, putting himself at their head, again restored the combat, exposing himself to every kind of personal danger. Fortunately, at this moment, we perceived the fire of Marshal Blucher, attacking the enemy's right with his usual impetuosity; and the moment of decisive attack being come, the Duke put himself at the head of the English Foot Guards, spoke a few words to them, which were replied to by a general *hurrah,* and his Grace himself guiding them forward with his hat, they marched at the point of the bayonet, to come to close action with the Imperial Guard. But the latter began a retreat, which was soon converted into flight, and the most complete rout ever exhibited by soldiers. The famous rout at Vittoria was not even comparable to it.

Lt John Kincaid, 95th Rifle Brigade[18]
I shall never forget the scene which the field of battle presented about seven in the evening. I felt weary and worn out, less from fatigue than anxiety. Our division, which had stood upwards of five thousand men at the commencement of the battle, had gradually dwindled down into a solitary line of skirmishers. The twenty-seventh regiment were lying literally dead, in square, a few yards behind us. My horse had received another shot through the leg, and one through the flap of the saddle, which lodged in his body, sending him a step beyond the pension list. The smoke still hung so thick about us that we could see nothing. I walked a little way to each flank, to endeavour to get a glimpse of what was going on; but nothing met my eye except the mangled remains of men and horses, and I was obliged to return to my post as wise as I went. I had never yet heard of a battle in which every body was killed; but this seemed likely to be an exception, as all were going by turns

Marshall Michel Ney to the Duke of Otranto[9]

About seven o'clock in the evening, after the most frightful carnage which I have ever witnessed, General Labedoyere came to me with a message from the Emperor, that Marshal Grouchy had arrived on our right, and attacked the left of the English and Prussians united. This General Officer, in riding along the lines, spread this intelligence among the soldiers, whose courage and devotion remained unshaken, and who gave new proofs of them at that moment, in spite of the fatigue which they experienced. Immediately after, what was my astonishment, I should rather say indignation, when I learned that so far from Marshal Grouchy having arrived to support us, as the whole army had been assured, between forty and fifty thousand Prussians attacked our extreme right, and forced it to retire.

Captain Archibald Leach, 95th Rifles[24]

The arrival of the Prussians had long been expected; but the only intimation we had of their approach was the smoke of a distant cannon occasionally seen far on the left. About seven o'clock in the evening a party of their Lancers arrived on the field to announce the approach of their army. It was about this time that the last and desperate attack was made by Napoleon and his guard, to annihilate us before the Prussians should arrive to our assistance.

Marshal Michel Ney to the Duke of Otranto[9]

A short time afterwards, I saw four regiments of the middle guard, conducted by the Emperor, arriving. With these troops he wished to renew the attack, and to penetrate the centre of the enemy. He ordered me to lead them on; Generals, officers, and soldiers, all displayed the greatest intrepidity; but this body of troops was too weak to resist, for a long time, the forces opposed to it by the enemy, and it was soon necessary to renounce the hope which this attack had, for a few moments, inspired. General

Friant had been struck with a ball by my side, and I myself had my horse killed, and fell under it. The brave men who will return from this terrible battle, will, I hope, do me the justice to say, that they saw me on foot with sword in hand during the whole of the evening, and that I only quitted the scene of carnage among the last, and at the moment when retreat could no longer be prevented.

Sergeant Major Edward Cotton, 7th Hussars[3]
The sanguinary drama was now, with the long and trying day, fast drawing to a close. The Emperor's guards, their country's pride, they who had never turned their backs on foe or fled the battle field, were, for the first time, about to attack men who, like themselves, acknowledged no victor.

General Sir James Shaw Kennedy, 3rd Division[7]
The Duke of Wellington stood at this moment [about 7–7.30pm] on the right of the Nivelles road, behind the left of Maitland's brigade of Guards. The Prince of Orange, Count Alten, and so many officers of the 3rd division, had, before this event happened, been killed, or wounded and obliged to leave the field, that I did not then know, nor do I now know, who was, at the moment I allude to, senior officer of the division on the field: I therefore, as the staff-officer present, galloped direct to the Duke, and informed him that his line was open for the whole space between Halkett's and Kempt's brigades. This very startling information he received with a degree of coolness, and replied to in an instant with such precision and energy, as to prove the most complete self-possession; and left on my mind the impressions that his Grace's mind remained perfectly calm during every phase, however serious, of the action; that he felt confident of his own powers of being able to guide the storm which raged around him; and from the determined manner in which he then spoke, it was evident

that he had resolved to defend to the last extremity every inch of the position which he then held. His Grace's answer to my representation was in the following words, or very nearly so: – 'I shall order the Brunswick troops to the spot, and other troops besides; go you and get all the German troops of the division to the spot that you can, and all the guns that you can find.' Of such gravity did Wellington consider this great gap in the very centre of his line of battle, that he not only ordered the Brunswick troops there, but put himself at their head ...

'*CW, a sergeant of the Guards*'[12]
The fight at one time, was so desperate with our battalion, that files upon files were carried to the rear, from the carnage, and the line was held up by serjeants' pikes, placed against the rear: not for want of courage on the men's part (for they were desperate) only for the moment our loss so unsteadied the line ... Some of the men kept up firm in the line, but others fell back to get out ammunition, and others were begging ammunition in the rear as their own was spent, which, with our continual loss, quite unsteadied the line; so the pikes were intended to prevent any from falling back for ammunition, as we wanted the men to use the bayonet ...

'*Extract of a letter from an officer*'[11]
After seven hours dreadful cannonade, and during which we suffered very much from grape and shells, the French cavalry advanced in a gallop, in masses, up the slope of a gentle hill; they were arrested by a continual echelon of squares, whose cross fire cut them to pieces, our men standing like statues. After this succeeded a tiraillade (sharp-shooting) of about half an hour, when we all imagined the fight was over, and that it would die away with the night; but to our surprise, the head of an immense column of the Old Guard appeared trampling down the corn fields in our front: they advanced to within one hundred and fifty yards of our brigade, without attempting to deploy

or fire a shot. Our wings threw themselves immediately forward, and kept up such a murderous fire, that the Enemy retired, losing half their numbers, who, without any exaggeration, literally lay in sections.

Letter from anonymous British officer[9]

The 27th had 400 men, and every officer but one subaltern, knocked down in square, without moving an inch, or discharging one musket; and at that time I mention, both divisions could not oppose a sufficient front to the Enemy, who was rapidly advancing with crowds of fresh troops. We had not a single company for support, and the men were so completely worn out, that it required the greatest exertion on the part of the officers to keep up their spirits. Not a soldier thought of giving ground; but victory seemed hopeless, and they gave themselves up to death with perfect indifference. A last effort was our only chance. The remains of the regiments, were formed as well as the circumstances allowed, and when the French came within about 40 paces, we set up a death-howl, and dashed at them. They fled immediately, not in a regular manner as before, but in the greatest confusion.

18

BLUCHER ARRIVES

Blucher[9]

It was half an hour past seven, and the issue of the battle was still uncertain. The whole of the 4th corps, and a part of the 2d, under General Pvich had successively come up. The French troops fought with desperate fury: however, some uncertainty was perceived in their movements, and it was observed that some pieces of cannon were retreating. At this moment, the first columns of the corps of General Ziethen arrived on the points of attack, near the village of Smonhen, on the enemy's right flank, and instantly charged. This moment decided the defeat of the enemy. His right wing was broken in three places; he abandoned his positions. Our troops rushed, forward at the *pas de charge,* and attacked him on all sides, while, at the same time, the whole English line advanced.

'Extract of a letter from John Marshall, private, 10th Dragoons'[11]
It was now eight in the evening, and still the battle raged with redoubled fury, and still was much to be done, and but little time to do it in, for night was fast approaching; therefore, no time was to be lost. Our brigade was then formed into three lines, each regiment composing its own line, which was the 10th, 18th,

and a regiment of the German Legion Hussars, my own regiment forming the first line. The General then came in front of the line, and spoke in the following manner: 'Tenth,' he said, 'you know what you are going to do, and you also know what is expected of you, and I am well assured it will be done, I therefore shall say no more, only wish you success;' and with that, he gave orders for us to advance. I am not ashamed to say, that, well knowing what we were going to do, I offered up a prayer to the Almighty, that for the sake of my children, and the partner of my bosom, he would protect me, and give me strength and courage to overcome all that might oppose me, and with a firm mind I went, leaving all that was dear to me to the mercy of that great Ruler, who has so often in the midst of peril and danger protected me.

'*Extract of a letter from an officer of the Guards*'[11]
Upon the cavalry being repulsed, the Duke himself ordered our second battalion to form line with the third battalion, and, after advancing to the brow of the hill, to lie down and shelter ourselves from the fire. Here we remained, I imagine near an hour. It was now about seven o'clock. The French infantry had in vain been brought up against our line, and, as a last resource, Buonaparte resolved upon attacking our part of the position with his veteran Imperial Guard, promising them the plunder of Brussels. Their artillery covered them, and they advanced in solid column to where we lay. The Duke, who was riding behind us, watched their approach, and at length, when within a hundred yards of us, exclaimed, 'Up, Guards, and at them again!' Never was there a prouder moment than this for our country or ourselves. The household troops of both nations were now, for the first time, brought in contact, and on the issue of their struggle the greatest of stakes was placed. The Enemy did not expect to meet us so soon; we suffered them to approach still nearer, and then delivered a fire into them, which made them halt; a second, like the first, carried hundreds of deaths

into their mass; and, without suffering them to deploy, we gave them three British cheers, and a British charge of the bayonet. This was too much for their nerves, and they fled in disorder. The shape of their column was tracked by their dying and dead, and not less than three hundred of them had fallen in two minutes to rise no more. Seeing the fate of their companions, a regiment of tirailleurs of the Guard attempted to attack our flank; we instantly charged them, and our cheers rendered any thing further unnecessary, for they never awaited our approach. The French now formed solid squares at their rear, to resist our advance, which, however, our cavalry cut to pieces. The Duke now ordered the whole line to move forward; nothing could be more beautiful. The sun, which had hitherto been veiled, at this instant shed upon us its departing rays, as if to smile upon the efforts we were making, and bless them with success. As we proceeded in line down the slope, the regiments on the high ground on our flanks were formed into hollow squares, in which manner they accompanied us, in order to protect us from cavalry – the blow was now struck, the victory was complete, and the Enemy fled in every direction ...

'Extract of a letter from John Marshall, private, 10th Dragoons'[11]
After advancing about one hundred yards, we struck into a charge, as fast as our horses could go, keeping up a loud and continual cheering, and soon we was amongst the Imperial Guards of France. The 18th Hussars also charging, as soon as we got amongst them, which so galled them, that we slew and overthrew them like so many children, although they rode in armour, and carried lances ten foot long; but so briskly did our lads lay the English steel about them, that they threw off their armour and pikes, and those that could get away, flew in all directions. But still we had not done, for there was two great solid squares of infantry, who had hurt us much, whilst we were advancing, with their fire, and still continued to do so, whilst we were forming again: in short they

were all around us. We therefore formed as well as we could, and at them we went, in spite of their fixed bayonets. We got into their columns, and like birds they fell to the ground. Thus they were thrown into confusion, for it seemed like wild-fire amongst their troops, that the Guards was beaten, and, panic-struck, they flew in all directions. But we had done our part, and left those to pursue, who had seen the onset. We took sixteen guns at our charge, and many prisoners: but it was so dark, we could not see any longer, and at length we assembled what few men we had got left of the regiment, and the General of Brigade formed us in close columns, so that we might all hear him, and he addressed us in the following manner: 'Now, Tenth,' he said, 'you have not disappointed me, you were just what I thought you were. You was the first regiment that broke their lines, and to you it is, that we are indebted for turning the fate of the day, and depend upon it that your Prince shall know it; for nothing but the bravery and good discipline of the regiment could have completed such a work.' We then gave him three cheers ...

General Sir Hussey Vivian[36]
'Eighteenth, will you follow me?': 'Yes, General,' answered Sergeant-Major Jeffs. 'To hell if you will lead us.'

Wellington to General Maitland of the Guards
'Now, Maitland. Now's your time!'

'Extract of a letter from an officer of the Guards'[11]
When they failed in their attacks upon our squares, the cavalry rushed out from between our squares and cut them up most desperately. When he found these efforts vain, he began his attack upon the centre. He first endeavoured to carry the guns with his cavalry, which came up most gallantly; but our squares sent them to the right about three times in great style. I never

saw any thing so fine, the cavalry rushing out and picking up the deserted cannon. After these failures he brought up his *Garde Imperiale,* just opposite to our brigade, which had formed in line on their advancing. We were all lying under shelter of a small bank, as they covered their advance with a most terrible fire of grape and musketry. Buonaparte led them himself to the rise of the hill, and told them 'that was the way to Brussels'. We allowed them to approach very near – when we opened so destructive a fire, that there were soon above 300 of them upon the ground, and they began to waver. We instantly charged, but they ran as fast as possible. The Duke of Wellington, observing this crisis, brought up the 42d and 95th, taking the Enemy in flank, and leading them himself quite close up. The Enemy's column was entirely dispersed. After this, we were again annoyed with grape and musketry, which obliged us to retire. On fronting, we saw another heavy column of the *Chasseurs de la Garde Imperiale.* We immediately started at double quick time to meet them; but they had had such a proper reception just before, that they never let us come near them; and when they turned, the rout became general. We ran on as fast as we could, and the cavalry started after them. We got about two miles that evening, taking ourselves 30 pieces of cannon. Nothing could be more complete and decisive. Most fortunately the Prussians came on the field at this moment, and pursued the Enemy through the night.

Soldier of the 71st, or Glasgow Regiment, Highland Light Infantry[23]
The whole army retired to the heights in the rear; the French closely pursuing to our formation, where we stood, four deep, for a considerable time. As we fell back, a shot cut the straps of the knapsack of one near me: it fell, and was rolling away. He snatched it up, saying, 'I am not to lose you that way, you are all I have in the world;' tied it on the best manner [*sic*] he could, and marched on ... Lord Wellington came riding up ... Shortly

the whole army received orders to advance. We moved forwards in two columns, four deep, the French retiring at the same time. We were charged several times in our advance. This was our last effort; nothing could impede us. The whole of the enemy retired, leaving their guns and ammunition, and every other thing behind. We moved towards a village, and charged right through, killing great numbers, the village was so crowded.

Sergeant Major Edward Cotton, 7th Hussars[3]
The Duke stood on the rise (immediately in front of the Lion) with his hat raised in the air, as a signal to advance. The last parting rays of the beautiful setting sun at this moment (a quarter after eight) shone most resplendently, as if to enliven the scene presented to our view on emerging from the smoke, which had long rendered every object invisible except the flashes of the enemy's batteries. It was a spectacle never to be forgotten by those who witnessed it. Were I to live to the age of Methuselah, never shall I forget that evening. In front might be seen the retiring columns of the enemy, broken and mingled with crowds of fugitives of all arms, mounted and dismounted, mixed pell-mell together. In the right front was a dense smoke, curling upwards, from the smouldering ruins of Hougoumont. Far in the distance to the left front might also be dimly seen the dark columns of the Prussians, many of whom had arrived just in time to witness the overthrow of the French.

Anonymous French soldier[9]
These veteran warriors [the Imperial Guard] attacked the summit with that intrepidity which might be expected from them. The whole army resumed its vigour, and the combat was rekindled along the whole line. The guard made successive charges, but was in all repulsed. Beneath the thunders of a dreadful artillery, which seemed to multiply, these invincible grenadiers perceived their ranks to thin under the shots; they closed them with promptness, and

with coolness; they continued to march without dismay; nothing withstood them but death or severe wounds; but the hour of defeat was come. Enormous masses of infantry, supported by an immense cavalry, to which we had none to oppose, ours being totally cut to pieces, fell upon them with fury, and surrounding them on every side, summoned them to yield. They replied, 'The guard does not yield, it dies.' No quarter was then allowed; they almost all fell, fighting with desperation, under the edge of the sabres, and the bayonets' points. This frightful massacre was continued while they resisted. But at length, oppressed with forces infinitely superior, and wearied besides with fronting in vain certain death, they abandoned their ranks, and fell back in disorder towards their first positions, undoubtedly with the purpose of rallying there.

Anonymous French soldier[9]
While things were thus passing near the centre, the Prussian columns, which had arrived at our right, continued to advance, and ardently to press the few troops which were on that point. The loud roaring of the cannon and musquetry was now distinctly heard in the rear of our line, and gradually approached it. Our troops sustained the fight with all their power, but gradually lost ground. At length our right wing sensibly retrograded, and the Prussians, who were turning it, were on the point of debouching on the road, when a rumour was spread, that the guard had been repulsed, and that its battalions had been dispersed, reduced to a small number, and were retiring in precipitation. A general alarm spread through the army, its ranks broke in every direction, and sought safety in the most speedy flight. Buonaparte in vain desperately collects for a last effort some battalions of the young and old guard, which had not yet been engaged, and conducts them against the enemy, who had already left his positions in a body. This feeble reserve, intimidated by what was passing around, and likewise overwhelmed by numbers, is speedily overthrown. The army now, rushing like an overflowing torrent,

spontaneously and at the same instant forsook its positions. The artillerymen abandoned their guns, the soldiers of the waggon-train cut the harness of their horses; infantry, cavalry, troops of every description, mingled and confused, now present only a misshapen mass, which nothing can retain, and which flies for its safety towards the road, and across the fields. A crowd of carriages, ranged along the sides of the road in a confused mass, encumber it so as to render it impassable.

'*Extract of a letter from an officer*'[11]
At eight o'clock, the Enemy moved forward his old Guard, who were received by the first brigade of Guards, and a Dutch brigade, with Saltoun at their head, with such a fire, that they took to their heels – their whole army fled in the greatest disorder, and was followed in sweeping lines, as fast as the lines could move. Our cavalry cut them to pieces. The abandoned guns, carriages, knapsacks and muskets, choaked up the ground; and for five miles, in which we followed them last night, the field was covered with the bodies of Frenchmen only.

'*CW, a sergeant of the Guards*'[12]
Towards evening, Bonaparte directed against us his choice 105th regiment; and in half an hour we cut them all to pieces, and took one stand of colours. He then sent against us his Grenadier Imperial Guards; they came within 100 yards of us and ported arms to charge; but we advanced upon them in quick time, and opened a brisk file fire by two ranks – they allowed us to come within 30 yards of them – they stood still then, looking at us, as if panic struck, and did not fire – they then, as we approached, faced about and fled for their lives, in all directions ... they ran very fast, but many of them fell, while we pursued, and with them one stand of colours; and I have the honour to wear a Colonel's sword of the French Imperial Guard.

Lt William Bates Ingilby, Royal Horse Artillery[2]

At about half past eight o'clock more of the Prussian Army appeared, and some of their Cavalry and Artillery taking up the ground we had maintained the whole day, Sir Hussey Vivian moved his Brigade towards the right, crossed the *pavé* road and formed in line behind the Brunswick-Oels Infantry, who were in line, advancing firing. The smoke was so dense we could for a time see nothing immediately before us, while thus, at the distance of about 15 paces, supporting what proved to be at length an attack from our side, and a total overthrow of the French. We could, however, perceive that the right of the French was engaged in, and opposed by, a heavy cannonade on their right rear, which could only be another body of Prussians, although from the distance, and dusk, which at this time was commencing, we could discern nothing with the eye but the flashes and smoke of their cannon, and the sound even extended beyond where we could see, and it was evident that the French were engaged in rear of the heights on which they showed their front to us.

Uxbridge to Wellington

'By God, Sir, I've lost my leg' ... 'By God, Sir, so you have.'

Lt John Kincaid, 95th Rifle Brigade[18]

Presently a cheer, which we knew to be British, commenced far to the right, and made every one prick up his ears; – it was Lord Wellington's long wished-for orders to advance; it gradually approached, growing louder as it grew near; – we took it up by instinct, charged through the hedge down upon the old knoll, sending our adversaries flying at the point of the bayonet. Lord Wellington galloped up to us at the instant, and our men began to cheer him; but he called out, 'No cheering, my lads, but forward, and complete your victory!' This movement had carried us clear of the smoke; and, to people who had been for so many hours enveloped in darkness, in the midst of destruction, and naturally anxious about the result of the day, the scene which now met the eye conveyed a feeling of more exquisite gratification than can be conceived. It was a fine summer's evening, just before sunset. The French were flying in one confused mass. British lines were seen in close pursuit, and in admirable order, as far as the eye could reach to the right, while the plain to the left was filled with Prussians. The enemy made one last attempt at a stand on the rising ground to our right of La Belle Alliance; but a charge from General Adams' brigade again threw them into a state of confusion, which was now inextricable, and their ruin was complete. Artillery, baggage, and every thing belonging to them, fell into our hands. After pursuing them until dark, we halted about two miles beyond the field of battle, leaving the Prussians to follow up the victory.

Lt William Bates Ingilby, Royal Horse Artillery[2]
About this time, while crossing the *pavé*, Sir Robert Gardiner and Captain Dyneley both expressed their distrust of present appearances; they did not like them, and, bearing in mind everything I had gathered from what Colonel de Lancey said in my hearing to Sir H. Vivian, as to the time and occasion when his Brigade would move and be brought to support the centre, I held and expressed a contrary opinion, that it was the Duke's turn and that he was now attacking their centre, his time for doing which evidently having depended upon the Prussians making their appearance in force on the right flank of the French. A short while afterwards the Infantry on our front, which had continued steadily to advance, firing along their whole line, halted and ceased firing, and we then perceived the French, both those immediately in our front and those on other parts of their positions, scampering off in full retreat. The Brunswickers broke into open columns and Sir H. Vivian, passing through their intervals, the Cavalry pushed forward and were presently charging the fugitive masses in every direction, while we with the guns alternately unlimbered and advanced, bringing them

to bear on every possible occasion, until it was too dark to fire without danger to our own Cavalry, which continued to press upon the rear of the French, and turned their retreat into a complete rout and confused flight. We then halted to bivouac near what we called the Observatory, a wooden frame erection which was conspicuous in rear of the line of battle of the French in the morning.

Anonymous French soldier[9]
Each person saved himself at chance, – they drive, they hurry, endeavouring each to precede the one before him; groups, more or less numerous, are formed, and follow passively those at the head. Some are afraid to leave the road, and struggle to obtain a passage through the carriages that cover it; others on the contrary think it dangerous, and leave it to the right or the left, accordingly as reasons well or ill founded influence them. Every danger is exaggerated by terror, and the night, which soon comes upon them, although not very dark, contributes to augment the disorder.

Colonel Sir George Wood, Royal Artillery[35]
Damn it, Mercer – you seem to be having a hot time of it here.

Sergeant William Lawrence, 40th Foot[8]
We were indeed glad to see the arrival of these Prussians, who now coming up in two columns on our left flank, advanced on the enemy's right. Lord Wellington, who was ever enticing his army on, now came up to our regiment and asked who was in command. On being told it was Captain Brown, he gave the order to advance, which we received with three cheers, and off we set as if renewed with fresh vigour. The attack was now being made by the whole line, together with the Prussians, who had come up fresh and were therefore more than a match for the harassed French. They soon forced the French into a downright retreat by their fire, and the retreat becoming universal, the whole body of the French

were thrown into disorder and pursued off the field by Blucher's fresh and untried infantry and cavalry.

Captain Alexander Cavalie Mercer, Royal Horse Artillery[35]
An aide-de-camp rode up, crying, 'Forward, sir! Forward! It is of the utmost importance that this movement is supported by artillery!' ... I smiled at his energy, and pointing to the remains of my poor troop, quietly asked, 'How, sir?' A glance was sufficient to show him the impossibility, and away he went.

Private Thomas Hasker, 1st Kings Dragoon Guards[16]
The fighting went on with murderous effect till night, when I heard the bugles sounding to march; and some dragoon regiment passed over the spot where I lay. After that I saw some fires not far off, and endeavoured to rise, but staggered like a drunken man, and soon fell. The dead and dying lay thick about me. Hearing two men talking very near, I called to them as well as I could to come and help me. They said they could not for a while. Soon after this two foreigners passed by, to whom I made signs; they came, and raising me up between them, took me to one of the fires, and brought me a surgeon; they afterwards wrapped a cloak about me, and left me there for the night.

Captain Alexander Cavalie Mercer, Royal Horse Artillery[35]
My recollections of the latter part of this day are rather confused; I was fatigued, and almost deaf. I recollect clearly, however that we had ceased firing – the plain below being covered with masses of troops, which we could not distinguish from each other. Captain Walcot of the horse-artillery had come to us, and we were all looking out anxiously at the movements below, and on the opposite ridge, when he suddenly shouted out, 'Victory! Victory! They fly!' and sure enough we saw some of the masses dissolving, as it were, and those composing them streaming away in confused crowds over the field,

whilst the already desultory fire of their artillery ceased altogether. I shall never forget this joyful moment! This moment of exaltations!

Major Henry Smith, 95th Foot[49]
Late in the day, when the enemy had made his last great effort on our centre, the field was so enveloped in smoke that nothing was discernible. The firing ceased on both sides, and we on the left knew that one party or the other was beaten. This was the most anxious moment of my life. In a few seconds we saw the red-coats in the centre, as stiff as rocks, and the French columns retiring rapidly, and there was such a British shout as rent the air. We all felt then to whom the day belonged. It was time the 'Crisis' should arrive, for we had been at work some hours, and the hand of death had been most unsparing. One Regiment, the 27th had only two officers left – Major Hume, who commanded from the beginning of the battle, and another – and they were both wounded, and only a hundred and twenty soldiers were left with them. At this moment I saw the Duke, with only one Staff officer remaining, galloping furiously to the left. I rode on to meet him. 'Who commands here?' 'Generals Kempt and Lambert, my lord.' 'Desire them to get into a column of companies of Battalions, and move on immediately.' I said, 'In which direction, my lord?' 'Right ahead, to be sure.' I never saw his Grace so animated. The *Crisis* was general, from one end of the line to the other.

Sergeant Major Edward Cotton, 7th Hussars[3]
An arrangement had been previously made by Wellington and Blucher, that the allied army should halt here, and that the Prussians should pursue and harass the routed enemy. The Duke was now, with all his advance, a little beyond Rossomme, upon a particular knoll with a gap where the Charleroi road cuts through it, which can be distinctly seen from most parts of the right of the allied position. As the Prussians passed us, (for I had the honour

and good fortune to be an actor in this scene,) I heard their bands play, 'God save the King!' which soul-stirring compliment we returned by hearty cheers.

Blucher[9]

From that time the retreat became a rout, which soon spread through the whole French army, which, in its dreadful confusion, hurrying away every thing that attempted to stop it, soon assumed the appearance of the flight of an army of barbarians. It was half-past nine. The Field Marshal assembled all the superior officers, and gave orders to send the last horse and the last man in pursuit of the enemy. The van of the army accelerated its march. The French being pursued without intermission were absolutely disorganised. The causeway presented the appearance of an immense shipwreck; it was covered with an innumerable quantity of cannon, caissons, carriages, baggage, arms, and wrecks of every kind. Those of the enemy who had attempted to repose for a time, and had not expected to be so quickly pursued, were driven from more than nine bivouacs. In some villages they attempted to maintain themselves: but as soon as they heard the beating of our drums, or the sound of the trumpet, they either fled or threw themselves into the houses, where they were cut down and made prisoners. It was moonlight, which greatly favoured the pursuit, for the whole march was but a continued chace, either in the corn-fields or the houses.

'Extract of a letter from an officer of the Horse Guards'[11]

At the conclusion of the battle, we were masters of the field; and only one officer of the 2nd Life Guards, with two corporals and 40 privates, remained. There was no officer of the 1st Regiment, all, or most of them having been dismounted. The command of the two regiments for the night was given by Lord Somerset to the remaining officer of the 2d. Col. Lygon had one horse shot under him, towards the conclusion of the battle, and the horses of several of our officers were wounded. Lord Wellington was with the brigade the greater part of the day, during which time I saw him repeatedly. He seemed much pleased; and was heard to observe, to the general officer near him, that it was the hardest battle he had ever fought, and that he had seen many charges, but never any to equal the charges of the Heavy Brigades, particularly the Household.

Sergeant Major Edward Cotton, 7th Hussars[3]
The remains of the allied army bivacked [*sic*] on what had been the French position. The 52d, 71st, and 2d and 3d battalions of the 95th, halted on the ground that had been occupied by the Imperial guard in reserve, near the farm of Rossomme. The remains of my regiment, with Vivian's brigade, went to the vicinity of the farm of Hulencourt: I accompanied general Vivian and colonel Sir E. Kerrison to the farm, acting as orderly, and still mounted on the cuirassier's horse. Thus closed upon us the glorious 18th of June. Fatigue and extreme exhaustion, following such exertions and such excitement has had been our lot that day, left us little power to reflect either upon the completeness of our own triumph, or the extent of the disasters that overtook the remains of our vanquished foes. These fled in utter and hopeless disorder before the Prussians, who dashed into the pursuit, and continued the work of slaughter with a ferocious and avenging spirit, which the conduct of the French two days before had provoked.

Napoleon[9]
At half-past eight o'clock, the four battalions of the middle guard, who had been sent to the ridge on the other side of Mont St. Jean in order to support the cuirassiers, being greatly annoyed by the grape-shot, endeavoured to carry the batteries with the bayonet. At the end of the day, a charge directed against their flank, by several English squadrons, put them in disorder. The fugitives recrossed the ravine. Several regiments, near at hand, seeing some troops

belonging to the guard in confusion, believed it was the old guard, and in consequence were thrown into disorder. Cries of *all is lost, the guard is driven back,* were heard on every side. The soldiers pretend even that on many points ill disposed persons cried out, *sauve qui peut* [loosely, 'Every man for himself']. However this may be, a complete panic at once spread itself throughout the whole field of battle, and they threw themselves in the greatest disorder on the line of communication; soldiers, cannoneers, caissons, all pressed to this point; the old guard, which was in reserve, was infected, and was itself hurried along. In an instant, the whole army was nothing but a mass of confusion; all the soldiers, of all arms, were mixed *pile mile,* and it was utterly impossible to rally a single corps. The enemy, who perceived this astonishing confusion, immediately attacked with their cavalry, and increased the disorder; and such was the confusion, owing to night coming on, that it was impossible to rally the troops, and point out to them their error. Thus a battle terminated, a day of false manoeuvres rectified, the greatest success insured for the next day, all was lost by a moment of panic terror. Even the squadrons of service drawn up by the side of the Emperor were overthrown and disorganised by these tumultuous waves, and there was then nothing else to be done but to follow the torrent. The parks of reserve, the baggage which had not repassed the Sambre, in short every thing that was on the field of battle, remained in the power of the enemy. It was impossible to wait for the troops on our right; every one knows what the bravest army in the world is when thus mixed and thrown into confusion, and when its organization no longer exists.

Wellington's report to Earl Bathurst, Secretary of State for War[9]
I continued the pursuit till long after dark, and then discontinued it only on account of the fatigue of our troops, who had been engaged during twelve hours, and because I found myself on the same road with Marshal Blucher, who assured me of his intention to follow the enemy throughout the night.

Part VIII

AFTERMATH

Even experienced soldiers seem to have been shocked by the intensity and carnage of the day-long battle. Around 15,000 men of Wellington's army were killed or wounded, with over 3,000 listed as missing. The Prussian casualty figure was around 7,000, and the French had about 25,000 killed or wounded and 8,000–9,000 taken prisoner. Thus, even making allowances for walking wounded who had departed, the relatively small battlefield would still have been covered by a shocking 40,000 or more dead and wounded soldiers by the end of the day.

19

'OH DOCTOR, IT WAS A TERRIBLE NIGHT ... '

Therese Roland of Chapelle, aged thirteen[30]
In the evening we heard the booming of great cannon, and from the windows I could see the clouds of smoke rising into the air like trees. I was in the mill, and the windows rattled. All night long we heard the tramp of silent men and the creaking, stumbling guns passing our doors.

Blucher[9]
The English army fought with a valour which it is impossible to surpass. The repeated charges of the Old Guard were baffled by the intrepidity of the Scottish regiments; and at every charge the French cavalry was overthrown by the English cavalry. But the superiority of the enemy in number was too great; Napoleon continually brought forward considerable masses, and, with whatever firmness the English troops maintained themselves in their position, it was not possible but that such heroic exertions must have a limit.

General Sir James Shaw Kennedy, 3rd Division[7]
In the action (18th June) I had one horse killed and one wounded;

and I was disabled for a short time by a shot which, first breaking to pieces the strong steel handle of my sword, struck me on the side.

Anonymous account[11]

Col. Hon. F. C. Ponsonby, in heading gallantly the first charge of the 12th Dragoons, about 11 on the 18th, was disabled successively in both arms by sabre wounds. The reins dropped from one hand, and his sword from the other. While in this situation, he was knocked off his horse, by a violent blow on the head, which stunned him. He then lay for some time on the ground in a state of insensibility. On recovering his senses, he opened his eyes; and raising his head to look about him, he observed a French Lancer standing over him. The wretch seeing him open his eyes, instantly exclaimed: 'Aha! brigand; tu n'es pas mort done!' and, thrusting his lance twice through his body, left him for dead. The weapon having passed through his lungs, he was immediately deprived of speech, so that, on two foreign soldiers coming in succession to plunder him, he could only make a faint noise, to prove that he was still alive. They, however, pursued their object, and took even his segars, and left him to his fate. At length, his situation was noticed by a French Officer, who lay severely wounded, at some distance, and with great difficulty crept towards him, and presented a pocket pistol to his mouth, when he was in nearly an exhausted state, from which he drank some sort of spirit: to this act of humanity he attributes his strength to go through his sufferings. In this state, he remained with seven severe wounds, and suffering great agony particularly from thirst, till late in the evening, when a private soldier of the 40th British regiment came up to him. By this time he had sufficiently recovered his voice to entreat the soldier to remain with him till the morning, being apprehensive that if he once left him he would not be able to find him out again in the dark. The man begged leave to look out for a sword; 'now then, your honour,' said he, 'I'll engage the devil himself won't come near you.' He soon picked up a French sabre, and then sat quietly down by the Colonel till day-light, when he went in search of some men of the 12th Dragoons, who hastened to carry their gallant Commander to a place of greater comfort and security.

Assistant-Surgeon William Gibney[21]
Nothing could exceed the misery exhibited on this road, which being the highpave, or I might say the stone causeway leading to Brussels, was crowded to excess with our wounded and French prisoners, shot and shell meanwhile pouring into them. The hardest heart must have recoiled from this scene of horror; wounded men being re-wounded, many of whom had received previously the most frightful injuries. Here a man with an arm suspended only by a single muscle, another with his head horribly mangled be a sabre cut, or one with half his face shot away, received fresh damage ...

Major Henry Smith, 95th Foot[49]
That evening at dark we halted, literally on the ground we stood on; not a picquet was required, and our whole cavalry in pursuit. Then came the dreadful tale of killed and wounded; it was enormous, and every moment the loss of a dear friend was announced. To my wonder, my astonishment, and to my gratitude to Almighty God, I and my two brothers – Tom, the Adjutant of the 2nd Battalion Rifle Brigade, who had, during the day, attracted the Duke's attention by his gallantry, and Charles, in the 1st Battalion, who had been fighting for two days – were all safe and unhurt, except that Charles had a slight wound in the neck. In the thunderstorm the previous evening he had tied a large silk handkerchief over his stock; he forgot to take it off; and probably owed his life to so trifling a circumstance.

Private George Farmer, 11th Light Dragoons[25]
I shall never forget … the adventures of that extraordinary night. In the first place, the ground … was literally strewn with the wreck of the mighty battle. Arms of every kind – cuirasses, muskets, cannon, tumbrils, and drums … cumbered the very face of the earth. Intermingled with these were the carcasses of the slain, not lying about in groups of four and six, but so wedged together, that we found it, in many cases, impossible to avoid trampling them where they lay under our horses' hoofs … It was indeed a ghastly spectacle, which the feeble light of a young moon rendered, if possible, more hideous than it would have been if looked upon under the full glory of a meridian sun.

Sergeant Thomas Morris, 73rd Foot[20]
We lay on the ground that night. I fell asleep, but awoke again about midnight, almost mad for want of water, and I made up my mind to go in search of some. By the light of the moon I picked my way among the bodies of my sleeping, as well as of my dead comrades; but the horrors of the scene created such a terror in my mind, that I could not muster courage to go by myself, and was turning back to take my brother along with me, when on passing where a horse was lying dead on its side, and a man sitting upright with his back against the horse's body, I thought I heard the man call to me, and the hope that I could render him some assistance overcame my terror. I went towards him, and placing my left hand on his shoulder, attempted to lift him up with my right; my hand, however, passed through his body, and I then saw that both he and his horse had been killed by a cannon-ball.

Captain Alexander Cavalie Mercer, Royal Horse Artillery[35]
Here and there some poor wretch, sitting up amidst the countless dead, busied himself in endeavours to staunch the flowing stream with which his life was fast ebbing away. Many whom I saw so

employed that night were, when morning dawned, lying stiff and tranquil ... From time to time a figure would half raise itself from the ground, and then, with a despairing groan, fall back again. Others, slowly and painfully rising, stronger, or having less deadly hurt, would stagger away with uncertain steps across the field until lost in the obscurity of the distance; but many, alas! After staggering a few paces, would sink again on the ground, probably to rise no more. It was heart-rending – and yet I gazed!

Letter by anonymous officer[11]
For my own part, when we halted for the night, I sunk down almost insensible from fatigue; my spirits and strength were completely exhausted. I was so weak, and the wound in my thigh so painful, from want of attention, and in consequence of severe exercise, that after I got to Nivelles, and secured quarters, I did not awake regularly for 36 hours.

'Extract of a letter from an officer of the Guards'[11]
I cannot better close this than by informing you, that when we halted for the night, which we did close to where Buonaparte had been during a great portion of the battle, and were preparing our bivouac by the road side, a regiment of Prussian lancers coming by, halted, and played *'God save the King,'* than which nothing could be more appropriate or grateful to our feelings; and I am sure I need scarcely add, that we gave them three heartfelt cheers, as the only return we could then offer.

Private Thomas Hasker, 1st King's Dragoons[17]
On perceiving that I had lost time, and that the regiment had left me to settle the question with the French dragoon, I tried to follow; but, in crossing a bad, hollow piece of ground, my horse fell, and before I had well got upon my feet, another of the French dragoons came up, and (sans cérémonie) began to cut at my head, knocked

off my helmet, and inflicted several wounds on my head and face. Looking up at him, I saw him in the act of striking another blow at my head, and instantly held up my right hand to protect it, when he cut off my little finger and half way through the rest. I then threw myself on the ground, with my face downward. One of the lancers rode by, and stabbed me in the back with his lance. I then turned, and lay with my face upward, and a foot soldier stabbed me with his sword as he walked by. Immediately after, another, with his firelock and bayonet, gave me a terrible plunge, and while doing it with all his might, exclaimed 'Sacré nom de Dieu!' No doubt that would have been the finishing stroke, had not the point of the bayonet caught one of the brass eyes of my coat – the coats being fastened with hooks and eyes – and prevented its entrance. There I lay, as comfortably as circumstances would allow – the balls of the British army falling around me, one of which dropped at my feet, and covered me with dirt; so that, what with blood, dirt, and one thing and another, I passed very well for a dead man. I was next plundered of my watch, money, canteen and haversack. I lay till night, the British army marching, some near me, and some over me, in pursuit of the French. At length I was picked up by two Prussian soldiers, and laid beside a fire, when one of their surgeons dressed some of my wounds, and left me for the remainder of the night. Next day I received great kindness from an English regiment, just then arrived. An officer gave me a little rum, and one of the privates carried me in a blanket; the latter, as he pushed the blanket under me, repeatedly said, 'Pray to God, comrade, pray to God, comrade.'

'JH', Scottish soldier[27]

Oh! Doctor, it was a terrible night, for what with the pain and loss of blood and kicking and knocking about, I suspected that every moment would be my last; and, indeed I wished it so, and more than once prayed for some one to put me out of my misery. However, it was not to be so, and, in the course of time, I was so far recovered as to be able to move about with a crutch, but it was after I had been many weeks in the hospital in Brussels.

'Extract of a letter from a private of the 42d Regiment'[11]
You would be astonished how we could have borne the fatigue which we suffered. We marched from Brussels at one in the morning, and arrived at three o'clock in the afternoon at the place of action, having marched nine leagues. We were engaged in five minutes after, and continued so till night.

Unknown soldier of the 3rd Battalion of the Royals[11]
About nine o'clock in the morning of the 18th, the battalion was attacked by the Enemy, and with very little interruption the entire day they formed a line of skirmishing in front of the brigade. I have often seen the battalion engaged; but I must confess, on this trying day, they far excelled any thing I ever witnessed.

Lt John Kincaid, 95th Rifle Brigade[18]
This was the last, the greatest, and the most uncomfortable heap of glory that I ever had a hand in; and may the deuce take me if I think that every body waited there to see the end of it, otherwise it never could have been so troublesome to those who did. We were, take us all in all, a very bad army. Our foreign auxiliaries, who constituted more than half of our numerical strength, with some exceptions, were little better than a raw militia – a body without a soul, or like an inflated pillow, that gives to the touch, and resumes its shape again when the pressure ceases; not to mention the many who went clear out of the field, and were only seen while plundering our baggage in their retreat.

Major Henry Smith, 95th Foot[49]
Captain McCulloch of the 95th Regiment wished to see me. He was a dear friend whom I had not seen since he was awfully wounded at Foz

d'Aruz [Foz de Aronce] on Massena's retreat, after having had seven sabre-wounds at the Coa, in Massena's advance, and been taken prisoner. He was in a cottage near, awfully wounded. I found him lying in great agony, but very composed. 'Oh, Harry, so long since we have met, and now again under such painful circumstances; but, thank God, you and Tom are all right.' I had brought all my remaining tea, which he ravenously swallowed. The ball had dreadfully broken the elbow of the sound arm, and had passed right through the fleshy part of his back, while the broken bone of the arm previously shattered at Foz d'Aruz was still exfoliating, and very painful even after a lapse of years. I got hold of a surgeon, and his arm was immediately amputated. When dressed, he lay upon the stump, as this was less painful than the old exfoliating wound, and on his back he could not lie. He recovered, but was never afterwards able to feed himself or put on his hat, and died, Heaven help him, suddenly of dysentery.

Lt John Kincaid, 95th Rifle Brigade[18]

If Lord Wellington had been at the head of his old Peninsular army, I am confident that he would have swept his opponents off the face of the earth immediately after their first attack; but with such a heterogeneous mixture under his command, he was obliged to submit to a longer day. It will ever be a matter of dispute what the result of that day would have been without the arrival of the Prussians: but it is clear to me that Lord Wellington would not have fought at Waterloo unless Blucher had promised to aid him with thirty thousand men; as he required that number to put him on a numerical footing with his adversary. It is certain that the promised aid did not come in time to take any share whatever in the battle. It is equally certain that the enemy had, long before, been beaten into a mass of ruin, in condition for nothing but running, and wanting but an apology to do it; and I will therefore ever maintain, that Lord Wellington's last advance would have made it the same victory had a Prussian never been seen there.

17

THE MORNING AFTER

Therese Roland of Chapelle, aged thirteen[30]
When I looked out next morning I saw wounded men lying by the roadside. In the distance I could hear a sound like a rough sea breaking against the rocks. There were clouds of smoke, and I saw men galloping, and masses of my brave soldiers moving hurriedly across the fields. Then the doctors came, and took out the bullets from the wounds of the soldiers ... The Prussians came by, and then the English, shouting their cries of victory. Not far away soldiers were digging trenches in our fields to bury the dead. There were so many of them, so many of them ... I saw one woman of Gotarville cut off the fingers of a Prussian officer, sorely hurt but still living, to secure the jewelled rings that he wore.

Lt John Kincaid, 95th Rifle Brigade[18]
The field of battle, next morning, presented a frightful scene of carnage: it seemed as if the world had tumbled to pieces, and three fourths of every thing destroyed in the wreck. The ground running parallel to the front of where we had stood, was so thickly strewed with fallen men and horses, that it was difficult to step clear of their bodies; many of the former still alive, and imploring assistance, which it was not in our power to bestow.

Lt-Colonel Isaac Clarke to the parents of Lt James Carruthers[34]
Brussels, 19th June. By the request of your son I am pained to inform you that in an attack on the enemy yesterday he received a musket shot on his right breast, which incapacitated him from writing to you himself. I have not seen him myself but from those who have, I am led to hope that his wound is not dangerous. The number of letters I have to write prevents my adding more that my most sincere wishes that your son may speedily recover ...

Major Henry Smith, 95th Foot[49]
I had been over many a field of battle, but with the exception of one spot at New Orleans, and the breach of Badajos, I had never seen anything to be compared with what I saw. At Waterloo the *whole* field from right to left was a mass of dead bodies. In one spot, to the right of La Haye Sainte, the French Cuirassiers were literally piled on each other; many soldiers not wounded lying under their horses; others, fearfully wounded, occasionally with their horses struggling upon their wounded bodies. The sight was sickening, and I had no means or power to assist them. Imperative duty compelled me to the field of my comrades, where I had plenty to do to assist many who had been left out all night; some had been believed to be dead, but the spark of life had returned. All over the field you saw officers, and as many soldiers as were permitted to leave the ranks, leaning and weeping over some dead or dying brother or comrade.

Lt John Kincaid, 95th Rifle Brigade[18]
The usual salutation on meeting an acquaintance of another regiment after an action, was to ask who had been hit? but on this occasion it was, 'Who's alive?' Meeting one next morning, a very little fellow, I asked what had happened to them yesterday? 'I'll be hanged,' says he, 'if I know any thing at all about the matter, for I was all day trodden in the mud and galloped over

by every scoundrel who had a horse; and, in short, that I only owe my existence to my insignificance.' Two of our men, on the morning of the 19th, lost their lives by a very melancholy accident. They were cutting up a captured ammunition wagon for firewood, when one of their swords striking against a nail, sent a spark among the powder. When I looked in the direction of the explosion, I saw the two poor fellows about twenty or thirty feet up in the air. On falling to the ground, though lying on their backs or bellies, some extraordinary effort of nature, caused by the agony of the moment, made them spring from that position, five or six times, repeatedly, to an extraordinary height, just as a fish does when thrown on the ground after being newly caught. It appeared to me that of five or six springs made by the two bodies in that manner, that the highest exceeded the height of a man, and the lowest was not less than three or four feet. It was so unlike a scene in real life that it was impossible to witness it without forgetting, for a moment, the horror of their situation. I ran to the spot along with others, and found that every stitch of clothes had been burnt off, and they were black as ink all over. They were still alive, and told us their names, otherwise we could not have recognised them; and, singular enough, they were able to walk off the ground with a little support, but died shortly after. Among other officers who fell at Waterloo, we lost one of the wildest youths that ever belonged to the service. He seemed to have a prophetic notion of his approaching end, for he fore gave the particulars at random, without considering that a foot or two more or less in the description made any difference. In its present shape, however, it may be taken as the avowed opinion, I believe, of every living witness, and rigidly true. Colour-Serjeant Pasket, of the rifles, tells me that he happened to be very near them at the time – that one of the two was his comrade, and that he caught him in his arms while he was yet in the act of springing; and that with the assistance of him and another, the man walked to a house close by, where they left him in the hands of some medical men, who were there dressing the wounded.

Sergeant Thomas Morris, 73rd Foot[20]
Of one of the officers of the 30th, who, when we were laying together at the village near Soignes, I recollected one of our men observing, that 'he would be a decent-sized fellow if his legs were taken off.' I thought of the remark when I saw the officer lying with both legs broke just below the knees by a cannonball. He requested me to cut off his legs, but I had not the heart to do it, though it would have been an act of mercy, for when I saw him next morning he was in the same situation, having received no assistance.

Lt-Colonel William Tomkinson, 16th Light Dragoons[42]
There were three men of the 32nd lying wounded together from grape. They begged a little water from me with such earnestness that I got off and gave them a taste of some brandy I had in a flask. The two first I gave it to were wounded in the leg, and on my putting it to the mouth of the third, who was wounded in the body, one of the others requested me to give him his share, for his comrade was wounded *in the belly,* and brandy would only do *him harm.* I was aware it was not good for any, yet having been out all night, and probably having had nothing on the 18th, I thought a taste could not injure them. They begged me to send their doctor, and were afraid they would remain out a second night.

Lt-Colonel William Tomkinson, 16th Light Dragoons[42]
A man of the Highland regiments was employing himself in carrying water to the wounded on both sides, and had been doing so from daylight.

Lt William Bates Ingilby, Royal Horse Artillery[2]

On being despatched to bring up our ammunition waggons, which had been left behind at our advance, I passed in rear of the guns abandoned by the French and met another body of Prussian Cavalry, apparently quite fresh and proceeding as if to continue the pursuit. The ground and roads were strewed with the dead and wounded, the latter crawling towards the roads with the hope of meeting more speedily with assistance, and it was with difficulty the waggons could be driven clear of the living and dead bodies along a part of the Quatre Bras road, where I saw many of both mangled by the wheels, I suppose, of the French Artillery in their retreat. In the early part of the day, when the battle was about commencing, a calf strayed in among the Troop, which having been instantly slaughtered, for the men and officers both were entirely without provisions, it served us all for a meal. Fires were made and we soon had a fresh dish of veal, which satisfied our hunger, and I for my part had a good night's rest after having been up very early and to Brussels, altogether a long and hard day.

Colonel Augustus Frazer, Royal Horse Artillery[5]

How shall I describe the scenes through which I have passed since morning? I am now so tired that I can hardly hold my pen. We have gained a glorious victory, and against Napoleon himself. I know not yet the amount of killed, wounded, or prisoners, but all must be great. Never was there a more bloody affair, never so hot a fire. Bonaparte put in practice every device of war. He tried us with artillery, with cavalry, and last of all with infantry. The efforts of each were gigantic, but the admirable talents of our Duke, seconded by such troops as he commands, baffled every attempt.

Sergeant William Lawrence, 40th Foot[8]

We followed them [the retreating French] ourselves for about a mile, and then encamped on the enemy's ground; and if ever there was a hungry and tired tribe of men, we were that after that memorable day of the 18th of June. Then the first thing to be thought of was to get a fire and cook some food, which was not so easy, as wood was scarce and what there was was wet through. One of our company, named Rouse, who went out in search of sticks, came across one of the enemy's powder-wagons that we had taken in the battle amongst the rest of the many things, and immediately commenced cutting the cover up for fuel; but his hook coming in contact with a nail or some other piece of iron and striking fire, as a natural consequence the remains of the powder in the wagon exploded and lifted the poor fellow to a considerable height in the air. The most remarkable thing was that he was still alive when he came down and able to speak, though everything had been blown from him except one of his shoes. He was a perfect blackguard, for although he was in a most dangerous state he did not refrain from cursing his eyes, which happened, as it was, to be both gone, and saying what a fool he must have been. He was that night conveyed to Brussels Hospital with the rest of the many wounded, and died in a few days, raving mad.

Colonel Augustus Frazer, Royal Horse Artillery[5]
All now with me is confused recollection of scenes yet passing before me in idea: the noise, the groans of the dying, and all the horrid realities of the field are yet before me. In this very house are poor Lloyd (leg shot off but not yet amputated), Dumaresque (General Byng's aide-de-camp) shot through the lungs and dying; Macdonald, Robe, Whinyates, Strangways and Baynes, wounded.

Sergeant William Lawrence, 40th Foot[8]
About this time I heard a Frenchman groaning under a cannon, where he was lying on a quantity of straw. I thought he was badly wounded, and perhaps as hungry as myself, so I went to him and told him as well as I was able to stop till our supper was cooked,

and then I would bring him some; but when it was ready and I had cut off some bread, fowl, and ham, and taken it to the place where I had seen him, he had gone. For one reason I was not sorry, for he left his straw, which made a very good bed for us three sergeants, the ground itself being unpleasantly wet. I think perhaps this Frenchman must have been a skulker, or he would not have ventured to escape.

An officer of the Imperial Guard[9]
The French army continued its disastrous march through the night, scattering its accoutrements along the road, and assaulted every instant with charges by which its disorganisation was rendered complete. The consternation which prevailed in this rout was so great, that large bodies of well armed cavalry and infantry suffered themselves to be made prisoners, without attempting to defend themselves, by a few miserable lancers, whom they might have driven back by merely turning to face them.

Sergeant William Lawrence, 40th Foot[8]
After that, as the general did not want us for anything, we retired to rest on our straw, but I was too tired to go to sleep for a long time, and lay contemplating the scenes of the day. I was merely scratched on the face myself during the whole day, besides being a little shaken by the bursting of the shell I mentioned; but this scratch had been terribly aggravated by a private who had been standing next to me having overprimed his musket, with the consequence that when he fired, my face being so close, the powder flew up and caught my wound, which though only originally a slight one soon made me dance for a time without a fiddle.

Marshal Michel Ney[9]
As for myself, constantly in the rear guard, which I followed on foot, having all my horses killed, worn out with fatigue, covered with contusions, and having no longer strength to march, I owe

my life to a corporal who supported me on the road, and did not abandon me during the retreat. At eleven at night I found Lieutenant-General Lefebvre Desnouettes, and one of his officers, Major Schmidt, had the generosity to give me the only horse that remained to him. In this manner I arrived at Marchieuneau at four o'clock in the morning, alone, without any officers of my staff, ignorant of what had become of the Emperor, who, before the end of the battle, had entirely disappeared, and who, I was allowed to believe, might be either killed or taken prisoner.

William Prince of Orange[10]
It is impossible to describe to your Majesty the animosity with which the troops fought, especially during the last six hours. I had not the good fortune to be present at the conclusion of this glorious and important battle, having, half-an-hour before the defeat of the enemy, received a shot through the left shoulder, by which I was compelled to leave the field.

Anonymous British correspondent in Antwerp[11]
Unable to rest, we wandered about the Pare the whole evening, or stood upon the ramparts listening to the heavy cannonade, which towards 10 o'clock became fainter, and soon afterwards entirely died away. No further intelligence had arrived – the cannonade had continued five hours since the last accounts came away. The anxiety to know the result of the battle may be imagined. Between twelve and one, we suddenly heard the noise of the rapid rolling of heavy carriages, in long succession, passing through the Place Royale, mingled with the loud cries and exclamations of the people below. For some minutes we listened in silence, – faster and faster, and louder and louder, the long train of carriages continued to roll through the town; the cries of the affrighted people increased. In some alarm Ave hastily ran out to inquire the cause of this tumult: the first person we encountered was a scared Fille-de-Chambre,

who exclaimed in a most piteous tone – 'Les Francois sont tout pres ... ' ['The French are nearby'] ... At length after a considerable interval of terror and suspense, an Aid-de-camp of the Duke of Wellington arrived, who had left the army at four o'clock, and, to our unspeakable joy, this was found to be a false alarm.

Lord William Pitt Lennox[31]
After the battle Wellington rode to Brussels, and the first person who entered his room on the morning of the 19th was Dr Hume. 'He had, as usual,' says the doctor, 'taken off his clothes, but his face was covered with the dust and sweat of the previous day. He extended his hand to me, which I held in mine while I told him of Alexander Gordon's death. He was much affected. I felt his tears dropping fast upon my hand, and, looking towards him, saw them chasing one another in a stream over his dusty cheeks. He brushed them suddenly away with his left hand, and said to me, in a voice tremulous with emotion 'Well, thank God, I don't know what it is to lose a battle, but certainly nothing can be more painful than to gain one with the loss of so many of one's friends.'

Lord William Pitt Lennox[31]
The scene at Brussels surpassed all that imagination could conjure up. Upwards of 40,000 wounded – French, Belgians, Prussians and English – were brought into the town. The wounded were laid indiscriminately on straw throughout the city. Destitute of surgical assistance, the Belgian ladies and females were employed in their humane and indefatigable exertions, bandaging their wounds, serving out nourishment, and soothing and alleviating the pangs of the dying sufferers.

Anonymous British correspondent in Antwerp[11]
We saw a Belgic soldier dying at the door of his own home, and surrounded by his relatives, who were weeping over him;

numerous were the sorrowful groups standing round the dead bodies of those who had died of their wounds in the way home. Numbers of wounded, who were able to walk, were wandering upon every road; their blood-stained clothes and pale haggard countenances, perhaps, giving the idea of sufferings much greater than the reality.

Charlotte Eaton, travel writer[22]
Towards evening a wounded officer arrived, bringing intelligence that the onset had been most terrible, and so immense were the numbers of the enemy, that he 'did not believe it was in the power of man to save the battle.' To record the innumerable false reports we heard spread by the terrified fugitives, who continually poured into the town from Brussels, would be endless. At length, after an interval of the most torturing suspense, a wounded British officer of hussars, scarcely able to sit his horse, and faint from loss of blood, rode up to the door of the hotel, and told us the disastrous tidings, that the battle was lost, and that Brussels, by this time, was in the possession of the enemy. He said, that in all the battles he had ever been engaged in, he had never witnessed anything at all equal to the horrors of this. The French had fought with the most desperate valour, but, when he left the field, they had been repulsed by the British at every point with immense slaughter: the news of the defeat had, however, overtaken him on the road; all the baggage belonging to the army was taken or destroyed, and the confusion among the French at Vittoria, he said, was nothing to this. He had himself been passed by panic-struck fugitives from the field, flying for their lives, and he had been obliged to hurry forward, notwithstanding his wounds, in order to effect his escape. Two gentlemen from Brussels corroborated this dreadful account: in an agitation that almost deprived them of the power of utterance, they declared that when they came away, Brussels presented the most dreadful scene of tumult, horror, and confusion; that intelligence

had been received of the complete defeat of the British, and that the French were every moment expected. The carnage had been most tremendous. The Duke of Wellington, they said, was severely wounded; Sir Dennis Pack killed; and all our bravest officers killed, wounded, or prisoners.

Anonymous British correspondent in Antwerp[11]

At length, between nine and ten in the evening, some wounded British officers arrived on horseback from the field, bringing the dreadful news, that the battle was lost, and that Brussels was actually in the possession of the French! This was corroborated by fugitives from Brussels, who affirmed they had seen the French in the town ... It was then, when fear almost amounted to certainty, when suspense had ended in despair, after a night of misery – that the great, the glorious news burst upon us – that the Allies had gained a complete victory – that the French – defeated – routed – dispersed – had fled from the field of battle – pursued by our conquering troops. No words can describe the feelings of that moment – no eloquence can paint the transport which filled every breast and brought tears into every eye ... A party of wounded Highlanders, who had found their way on foot from the field of battle, no sooner heard the news, than, regardless of their sufferings, they began to shout and huzza with the most vociferous demonstrations of joy; and those who had the use of their arms, threw their Highland bonnets into the air, calling out in broad Scotch, 'Boney's beat! – Boney's beat! – huzza! – huzza! – Boney's beat!'

Anonymous British correspondent in Antwerp[11]

If it was a day of glory, it was likewise a day of sorrow for Britain; if we triumph in it as the proudest, we must also mourn it as the most bloody of all the battles that she has fought or won. Those who witnessed the most sanguinary contests of the Peninsular war, declared they had never seen so terrible a carnage; and the

Prussians acknowledged that even the battle of Leipsic was not to be compared to it. The dead could not be numbered; and by those who visited this dreadful field of glory, and of death, the day after the battle, the spectacle of horror that it exhibited can never be forgotten. The mangled and lifeless bodies were even then stripped of every covering – every thing of the smallest value was already carried off. The road between Waterloo and Brussels, which passes for nine miles through the thick shades of the Forest of Soignies, was choaked up with scattered baggage, broken waggons, and dead horses. The heavy rains and the great passage upon it, had rendered it almost impassable, so that it was with extreme difficulty that the carriages containing the wounded could be brought along. The way was lined with unfortunate men who had crept from the field, and many, unable to go farther, lay down and died: – holes dug by the road side, served as their graves, and the road, weeks after the battle, was strewed with the tattered remains of their clothes and accoutrements. In every village and hamlet, – on every road, – in every part of the country, for thirty miles round, wounded soldiers were found wandering; the wounded Belgic and Dutch stragglers exerting themselves to the utmost to reach their own homes. So great were the numbers of the wounded, that, notwithstanding the most active and unremitting exertions, the last were not removed from the field of battle into Brussels till the Thursday following. It is impossible for words to do justice to the generous kindness, and unwearied care and attention, which the inhabitants of Brussels and Antwerp, and the whole of the Belgic people, exerted towards these poor sufferers. Nor should the humanity shown by the British soldiers themselves be unnoticed. The wounded of our army, who were able to move, employed themselves in tying up the wounds and administering to the wants of their suffering enemies – a striking and noble contrast to the brutality with which the French had treated our prisoners! The desolation which reigned on the scene of action, cannot easily be described. The fields of high standing corn were trampled down, and so completely beaten into the earth, that they had the appearance of stubble.

The ground was completely ploughed up in many places with the charge of the cavalry, and the horses' hoofs, deep stamped into the earth, left the traces where many a deadly struggle had been. The whole field was strewed with the melancholy vestiges of war and devastation – soldiers' caps pierced with many a ball, and trodden under foot – eagles that had ornamented them – badges of the legion of honour – cuirasses – fragments of broken arms, belts and scabbards innumerable – shreds of tattered cloth, shoes, cartridge boxes, gloves, highland bonnets, feathers steeped in mud and gore – French novels, and German Testaments – scattered music belonging to the bands – packs of cards, and innumerable papers of every description, that had been thrown out of the pockets of the dead, by those who had pillaged them. French love-letters, and letters from mothers to their sons, and from children to their parents, were scattered about in every direction. Amongst the thousands that we examined, it was however remarkable, that we found only one English letter. It was from a soldier's wife to her husband.

John Booth, editor of The Battle of Waterloo[11]
It is pleasing to add the testimony of a foreigner. 'The British regiments of infantry, which displayed such intrepid valour in the battle of the 18th, gave, after the action, the most affecting and sublime example ever offered to nations. They were seen forgetting their own wounds, and hardly escaped from the sword of the enemy, proceeding to afford all the succour in their power to those who had just endeavoured to cut them down, and who, in their turn, had fallen on the field of destruction. The conduct of the English army is mentioned with admiration, as uniting the heroism of valour, to the heroism of humanity.'

Anonymous narrative[11]

The General of Infantry, Count Gneisenau, gave personal order to Major Von Keller to pursue the flying enemy without intermission. The hero Gneisenau remained constantly at the head of the pursuers. At eleven o'clock at night the troops arrived at the barricaded town of Jenappe. At the entrance of Jenappe, Major Von Keller met the travelling carriage of Buonaparte with six horses. The postilion, and the two leaders, were killed by the bayonets of the fusileers. The Major then cut down the coachman, and forced open the doors of the carriage. At that moment he observed Buonaparte mounting a horse at the opposite side. In his precipitation, Napoleon let fall his hat, sword, and mantle; which were sent to Prince Blucher the next morning. The Major then took possession of the carriage; and afterwards brought it to England himself. (This carriage, naturally an object of curiosity, was built by Symonds at Brussels, according to Buonaparte's order, for the campaign in Russia, is replete with personal convenience, and is now exhibiting with the contents, identical horses, &c. at the London Museum, Piccadilly, where a sight of it cannot fail to interest a reflective mind, and afford a subject of contemplation ... The captured carriage contained a gold and silver *necessaire,* including above seventy pieces; a large silver chronometer; a steel bedstead with merino mattresses; a pair of pistols; a green velvet cap; a pair of spurs; linen, and many other things for the convenience of travelling. There were also a diamond head-dress, (tiara;) hat, sword, uniform, and an imperial mantle.

Anonymous account[11]

At length they [Captain Erskine and others] heard a great bustle of men and horses; upon coming nearer, they discovered them to be French: – all is now lost, victory is gained, and these are the messengers. On coming to the town, they however found them flying French; then was their joy superior to their former dejection: but in their helpless situation, they dare not show themselves, as they certainly would have been shot – but after an hour, the black Brunswickers came riding through, then they came out of their lurking-places, and joined their comrades; it is to be observed, that their guards had long left them.

Major Henry Smith, 95th Foot[49]
That afternoon we moved forward by the Nivelles road. I had to go into my General's room. I was not aware he was there, and entered abruptly. He was changing his shirt, when I saw he had received a most violent contusion on his right arm. It was fearfully swelled (in those days our coat-sleeves were made very large), and as black as ebony from the shoulder to the wrist. 'My dear General,' I said, 'what an arm! I did not know you had been wounded.' 'No, nor you never would, if accident had not shown you.' He made me promise to say nothing, about which I compromised by saying, 'To no one but to a surgeon, whom you must see. An arm in that state, if inflammation succeed, might slough, and you would lose it.' The General would not see a surgeon, and thank God he got well.

Therese Roland of Chapelle, aged thirteen[30]
No; I did not see Napoleon, and I still regret it. Poor Napoleon! We did not like the English or the Prussians ... The next day we knew that Napoleon's power was broken, by the lines we heard the people singing:

> *Les cannoniers bombardaient à feu et à flamme,*
> *Les cuirassiers, les gardes d'honneur, sont renversés,*
> *Bonaparte, enfin voilà ta fin. Il faut te rendre –*
> *Te voilà battu, convaincu, tu n'en peux plus!*

> *(The gunners bombarded with fire and with flame,*
> *The cuirassiers, the guards of honour, are fallen,*
> *Bonaparte, this at last is the end for you. You must surrender –*
> *Look at you, you're beaten, condemned, finished!)*

Part IX

COUNTING THE COST

It was time for the survivors to lick their wounds and regroup, and secure the victory by marching on Paris. Napoleon still had a sizeable army in the field and a large conscript force to call on, but soon had cause to become more concerned about his own position within France than fighting the invading enemy.

21

THE DREADFUL SCENE OF DEATH

John Sadler to the father of Lt James Carruthers[34]
Antwerp, 24 June. It is with regret I have to inform you of the melancholy event of your son James Carruthers, officer in the Scotch Greys. While engaged in that dreadful battle ... about 5 o'clock in the evening he was killed by a cannon ball.

Charlotte Eaton, travel writer[22]
[Standing on] the heights occupied by the French, upon which, at some distance, and secure from the storm of war, stands the Observatory, where Buonaparte stationed himself at the beginning of the action, and whence he Issued his orders, and commanded column after column to advance to the charge, and rush upon destruction ... From the spot where we now stood I cast my eyes on every side, and saw nothing but the dreadful and recent traces of death and devastation. The rich harvests of standing corn, which had covered the scene of action we were contemplating, had been beaten into the earth, and the withered and broken stalks dried in the sun, now presented the appearance of stubble, though blacker and far more bare than any stubble land. In many places the excavations made by the shells had thrown up the earth all around them; the marks of

horses' hoofs, that had plunged ankle deep in clay, were hardened in the sun; and the feet of men, deeply stamped into the ground, left traces where many a deadly struggle had been. The ground was ploughed up in several places with the charge of the cavalry, and the whole field was literally covered with soldiers' caps, shoes, gloves, belts, and scabbards; broken feathers battered into the mud, remnants of tattered scarlet or blue cloth, bits of fur and leather, black stocks and haversacs, belonging to the French soldiers, buckles, packs of cards, books, and innumerable papers of every description.

I picked up a volume of Candide; a few sheets of sentimental love-letters, evidently belonging to some French novel; and many other pages of the same publication were flying over the field in much too muddy a state to be touched. One German Testament, not quite so dirty as many that were lying about, I carried with me nearly the whole day; printed French military returns, muster rolls, love-letters, and washing bills; illegible songs, scattered sheets of military music, epistles without number in praise of 'L'Empereur, le Grand Napoleon,' and filled with the most confident anticipations of victory under his command, were strewed over the field which had been the scene of his defeat. The quantities of letters and of blank sheets of dirty writing paper were so great that they literally whitened the surface of the earth.

'Extract of a letter from a German officer'[11]
Where the battle was, the fields are completely trodden down for a circuit of about a league. On both sides of the high road, ways are made about 100 feet broad, and you can still follow the march of the battalions in all directions through the fine fields of maize.

Charlotte Eaton, travel writer[22]
We entered the village which has given its name to the most glorious battle ever recorded in the annals of history. It was the Headquarters of the British army on the nights preceding and

following the battle. It was here the dispositions for the action were made on Saturday afternoon. It was here on Monday morning the dispatches were written, which perhaps contain the most brief and unassuming account a conqueror ever penned, of the most glorious victory that a conqueror ever won. Waterloo consists of a sort of long, irregular street of whitewashed cottages, through which the road runs. Some of them are detached, and some built in rows. A small house, with a neat, little, square flower-garden before it, on the right hand, was pointed out to us as the quarters of Lord Uxbridge, and the place where he remained after the amputation of his leg, until well enough to bear removal. His name, and those of 'His Grace the Duke of Wellington,' 'His Royal Highness the Prince of Orange,' and other pompous titles, were written on the doors of these little thatched cottages. We also read the lamented names of Sir Thomas Picton, Sir Alexander Gordon, Sir William de Lancey, and Sir William Ponsonby, who had slept there the night before the battle, and many others who now sleep in the bed of honour. Volumes of sermons and homilies upon the instability of human life could not have spoken such affecting and convincing eloquence to our hearts as the sight of these names, thus traced in chalk, which had been more durable than the lives of these gallant men.

'*Extract of a letter from a German officer*'[11]
At the inn by the cross roads at Quatre Bras, the contest was the hottest. Here are the most graves. The wounded reeled into the inn yard, leaned against the walls, and then sank down. There are still the traces of the blood on the walls, as it spouted forth from the wounds with departing life.

Charlotte Eaton, travel writer[22]
It was not till we arrived at the little village of Mont St. Jean, more than a mile beyond Waterloo, that we finally quitted the

shade of the forest, and entered upon the open field where the battle had been fought. During the whole of the action the rear of the left wing of our army rested upon this little village, from which the French named the battle. We gazed with particular interest at a farm-house, at the farthest extremity of the village nearest the field, on the left side of the road, with its walls and gates and roofs still bearing the vestiges of the cannon-balls that had pierced them. Every part of this house and offices was filled with wounded British officers; and here our friend Major L. was conveyed in excruciating agony, upon an old blanket, supported by the bayonets of four of his soldiers.

Private George Farmer, 11th Light Dragoons[25]
How frightful the whole scene! It was indeed, a field of carnage over which we passed; and the smell of blood, as it rose upon the morning air, wellnigh sickened us ... entering the farm-yard, found it crowded with wounded wretches, some of whom had evidently received their hurts where they now lay, while others seemed to have dragged themselves thither in the hope of shelter. We could not shut our ears to their frightful cries, yet we were powerless to help them ... we could not find so much as a drop of water wherewith to moisten our own lips or those of our horses ... parties were sent out, under non-commissioned officers, to search for and bring in such wounded men as might have fallen in the woods, or on broken ground, where they might not easily be discovered. Scores of human beings, who but for this humane proceeding must have perished, were thus snatched from the jaws of death – among whom were not a few mere boys, the whole of whom appeared to entertain of us, and especially of the surgeons, the most pitiable dread. It required, indeed, in several instances, two or three of us to hold the patient while the balls were extracted from his wounds ...

Charlotte Eaton, travel writer[22]

While I loitered behind the rest of the party, searching among the corn for some relics worthy of preservation, I beheld a human hand, almost reduced to a skeleton, outstretched above the ground, as if it had raised itself from the grave. My blood ran cold with horror, and for some moments I stood rooted to the spot, unable to take my eyes from this dreadful object, or to move away: as soon as I recovered myself, I hastened after my companions, who were far before me, and overtook them just as they entered the wood of Hougoumont. Never shall I forget the dreadful scene of death and destruction which it presented. The broken branches were strewed around, the green beech leaves fallen before their time, and stripped by the storm of war, not by the storm of Nature, were scattered over the surface of the ground, emblematical of the fate of the thousands who had fallen on the same spot in the summer of their days. The trunks of the trees had been pierced in every direction with cannon-balls. In some of them I counted the holes, where upwards of thirty had lodged: yet they still lived, they still bore their verdant foliage, and the birds still sang amidst their boughs.

Anonymous account[11]

We have picked up several wounded. I cannot omit a circumstance that occurred yesterday: while on the field among the wounded, we discovered a French soldier, most dreadfully cut down the face, and one of his legs broken by a musket-ball: common humanity induced me to offer him assistance: he eagerly requested some drink; having a flask of weak gin-and-water I had taken purposely for the wounded, I gave it him, and could not help remarking how many thousand had suffered for the ambition of one man. He returned me the flask, and looking with a savage pride on the dead bodies that lay in heaps around him, he cried as strong as his weakness would allow him, '*Vive Napoleon! la gloire de la France!!*' Such an instance will give you a strong idea of the infatuation of these people.

Charlotte Eaton, travel writer[22]

A poor countryman, with his wife and children, inhabited a miserable shed amongst these deserted ruins. This unfortunate family had only fled from the spot on the morning of the battle. Their little dwelling had been burnt, and all their property had perished in the flames. They had scarcely clothes to cover them, and were destitute of everything. Yet the poor woman, as she told me the story of their distresses, and wept over the baby that she clasped to her breast, blessed heaven that she had preserved her children. She seemed most grateful for a little assistance, took me into her miserable habitation, and gave me the broken sword of a British officer of infantry (most probably of the Guards), which was the only thing she had left; and which, with some other relics before collected, I preserved as carefully as if they had been the most valuable treasures.

22

THE DEATH OF DE LANCEY

Wellington's report to Earl Bathurst, Secretary of State for War[9]
I have not yet got the returns of killed and wounded, but I enclose a list of officers killed and wounded on the two days, as far as the same can be made out without the returns; and I am very happy to add, that Col. Delancy is not dead, and that strong hopes of his recovery are entertained.

Lady Magdalene, wife of Colonel Sir William Howe De Lancey[4]
He said the wound gave him no pain at all, but a little irritating cough caused excessive pain in his chest and side. As far as I could learn, the blow had affected the lungs, which produced inflammation and afterwards water in the chest, which was eventually the cause of his death. I suspect the surgeons had never much hope, but they said there was a chance if the inflammation could have been stopped. By constantly watching him, and gradually day after day observing the progress and increase of suffering and the elevated tone of his mind, along with fatigue and weakness, I was prepared for his final release in a manner that nothing but his firmness and composure could have effected.

Private George Farmer, 11th Light Dragoons[27]
We marched that day some distance on the road to Nivelle, and arriving towards dark at a very pretty village, we halted for the night in an orchard. There we remained the whole of the next day, cleaning our swords and accoutrements, which were covered with rust ... our boots we were obliged to cut from our legs ere we could get them off.

Lady Magdalene, wife of Colonel Sir William Howe De Lancey[4]
On Wednesday he wished to have leeches applied to his side, where the bruise appeared. Mr Powell had no objection, and desired me to send for him when the leeches were brought from Brussels. I did so; but in the meantime, not knowing why he was sent for, I began as a matter of course to apply them. When he came, he apologised, and thanked me. I was not at first aware of how I was obliging him. He said he was very tired, and when he attempted to fix the leeches, he did not do it so well as I did.

Charlotte Eaton, travel writer[22]
Thus the road between Waterloo and Brussels was one long uninterrupted charnel-house: the smell, the whole way through the forest, was extremely offensive, and in some places scarcely bearable. Deep stagnant pools of red putrid water, mingled with mortal remains, betrayed the spot where the bodies of men and horses had mingled together in death ... The melancholy vestiges of death and destruction became more frequent, the pools of putrid water more deep, and the smell more offensive, as we approached Waterloo, which is situated at the distance of about three leagues, or scarcely nine miles, from Brussels.

Private Thomas Hasker, 1st Kings Dragoon Guards[16]
At length we reached Brussels, where we met with all the assistance and sympathy which the kindness of ladies could bestow; and from our weak and critical condition, we were in almost as much

danger, from the abundance of wine, cakes, and fruit, as we had been from the powder and balls of the enemy.

Anonymous account[11]
Brussels presented a melancholy scene: each side of a great number of the streets was laid with straw, on which the wounded were placed till proper places could be obtained for them. The inhabitants certainly behaved very well to them.

Sergeant Edward Costello, 95th Rifles[19]
I remained in Brussels three days, and had ample means here, as in several other places, such as Salamanca, &c., for witnessing the cutting off legs and arms. The French I have ever found to be brave, yet I cannot say they will undergo a surgical operation with the cool, unflinching spirit of a British soldier. An incident which here came under my notice, may in some measure show the difference of the two nations. An English soldier belonging to, if I recollect rightly, the 1st Royal Dragoons, evidently an old weather-beaten warfarer, while undergoing the amputation of an arm below the elbow, held the injured limb with his other hand without betraying the slightest emotion, save occasionally helping out his pain by spitting forth the proceeds of a large plug of tobacco, which he chewed most unmercifully while under the operation. Near to him was a Frenchman, bellowing lustily, while a surgeon was probing for a ball near the shoulder. This seemed to annoy the Englishman more than any thing else, and so much so, that as soon as his arm was amputated, he struck the Frenchman a smart blow across the breech with the severed limb, holding it at the hand-wrist, saying, 'Here take that, and stuff it down your throat, and stop your damned bellowing!'

Lady Magdalene, wife of Colonel Sir William Howe De Lancey[4]
On Friday evening Sir William was very feverish, and the appearance of the blood was very inflammatory. I had learnt now to judge for

myself, as Mr Powell, seeing how anxious I was, sometimes had the kindness to give me a little instruction. About ten at night Mr Powell and Mr Woolriche came. While I told them how Sir William had been since their last visit, and mentioned several circumstances that had occurred, I watched them and saw they looked at each other. I guessed their thoughts. I turned away to the window and wept.

Dr Charles Bell[28]
When I first went round the wards of the wounded prisoners, my sensations were very extraordinary. We had every where heard of the manner in which these men had fought – nothing could surpass their devotedness. In a long ward, containing fifty, there was no expression of suffering, no one spoke to his neighbour. There was a resentful, sullen rigidness of face, a fierceness in their dark eyes, as they lay half-covered in the sheets.

Lady Magdalene, wife of Colonel Sir William Howe De Lancey[4]
After I had brought everything the surgeons wanted, I went into another room. I could not bear to see him suffering. Mr Powell saw a change in his countenance; he looked out, and desired Emma to call me, to tell me instantly Sir William wanted me. I hastened to him, reproaching myself for having been absent a moment. I stood near my husband, and he looked up at me and said, 'Magdalene, my love, the spirits.' I stooped down close to him and held the bottle of lavender to him: I also sprinkled some near him. He looked pleased. He gave a little gulp, as if something was in his throat. The doctor said, 'Ah, poor De Lancey! He is gone.' I pressed my lips to his, and left the room.

Sergeant Edward Costello, 95th Rifles[19]
A singular case of loss of limb here [Antwerp] fell under my notice: a young fellow, a German, one of the drivers to the German Artillery, had lost both his legs by a round shot, which passing

through the horse's belly, had carried away both limbs; while on the ground in this mangled state, he received a dreadful gash in one of his arms, from a French cuirassier, and, a ball in the other; through these he was also obliged to undergo the amputation of both arms, one below the elbow and the other above; here the unfortunate youth (for he was not more than nineteen), lay a branchless trunk, and up to the moment I left, though numbers died from lesser wounds, survived.

Colonel Augustus Frazer, Royal Horse Artillery[5]

Pressing Glose and Bell into the service, we rode to Lillois (between Waterloo and Nivelle), collected all the scattered artillerymen and horses, and proceeded by the burnt house (Hougoumont) and carefully rode over the ground of the action. Before we reached it, the air was tainted with the remains of the dead. It was a moonlit night, frequently dull, and with repeated flashes of lightning. We moved in silence, carefully looking over the ground, which I well knew; we soon reached poor Ramsay's grave; it stands close by a stone 800 yards from the wood, to the left of Hougoumont, and close, too, by a little road crossing from one *pave* to the other; 400 yards to the right, as you look towards the wood, are three remarkable and isolated trees. I enter into this minuteness of detail, since, if I live, the grave of my friend shall have some stone, some mark, to record his worth. I had ordered a hole to be bored through the stone with a bayonet, but the order had been disregarded. Passing by this, and carefully examining the field, we observed few guns; indeed we already knew that most of them were blocked up in the road leading to Genappe, from which they had merely been thrown aside to clear the road. But anticipating that we should find in the field many wretched sufferers dying from neglect and want, I had taken all the spare horse-artillerymen whom I could find at Lillois, where all our broken parts of troops were sent to refit. Soon did we find full occupation for all; we found on every side poor fellows dying in every variety of wretchedness, and had repeatedly to enjoin the strictest silence that we might hear their scarcely audible groans. After doing what we could, (and, thank God, before morning we collected several waggon-loads of brave fellows, friends and foes,) we looked for the guns; but, except a few here and there, could observe none where we knew we had seen them in abundance the night before.

Major W. E. Frye[6]
June 22 – This morning I went to visit the field of battle, which is a little beyond the village of Waterloo, on the plateau of Mont St Jean; but on arrival there the sight was too horrible to behold. I felt sick in the stomach and was obliged to return. The multitude of carcases, the heaps of wounded men with mangled limbs unable to move, and perishing from not having their wounds dressed or from hunger, as the Allies were, of course, obliged to take their surgeons and waggons with them, formed a spectacle I shall never forget. The wounded, both of the Allies and the French, remain in an equally deplorable state ... At Hougoumont, where there is an orchard, every tree is pierced with bullets. The barns are all burned down, and in the court-yard it is said they have been obliged to burn upwards of a thousand carcases, an awful holocaust to the War-Demon ... As nothing is more distressing than the sight of human misery when we are unable to silence it, I returned as speedily as possible to Bruxelles with Cowper's lines in my head:

> *War is a game, which, were their subjects wise,*
> *Kings should not play at.*

I hope this battle will, at any rate, lead to a speedy peace.

Major W. E. Frye[6]
June 28. We have no other news from the Allied Army, except that

they are moving forward with all possible celerity in the direction of Paris. You may form a guess of the slaughter and of the misery that the wounded must have suffered, and the many that must have perished from hunger and thirst, when I tell you that all the carriages in Bruxelles, even elegant private equipages, landaulets, barouches and berlines, have been put in requisition to remove the wounded men from the field of battle to the hospitals, and that they are yet far from being all brought in. The medical practitioners of the city have been put in requisition, and are ordered to make domiciliary visits at every house (for each habitation has three or four soldiers in it) in order to dress the wounds of the patients. The Bruxellois, the women in particular, have testified the utmost humanity towards the poor sufferers. It was suggested by some humane person that they who went to see the field of battle from motives of curiosity would do well to take with them bread, wine and other refreshments to distribute among the wounded, and most people did so. For my part I shall not go a second time.

Charlotte Eaton, travel writer[22]
While my sister was taking a view of the field of battle, and my brother was overlooking and guarding her, I entered the cottage of 'La Belle Alliance,' and began to talk to Baptiste la Coste, Buonaparte's guide, whom I found there. He is a sturdy, honest-looking countryman, and gave an interesting account of Buonaparte's behaviour during the battle. He said that he issued his orders with great vehemence, and even impatience: he took snuff incessantly, but in a hurried manner, and apparently from habit, and without being conscious that he was doing so: he talked a great deal, and very rapidly his manner of speaking was abrupt, quick, and hurried: he was extremely nervous and agitated at times, though his anticipations of victory were most confident. He frequently expressed his astonishment, rather angrily, that the British held out so long at the same time he could not repress

his admiration of their gallantry, and often broke out into exclamations of amazement and approbation of their courage and conduct. He particularly admired the Scotch Greys ... and then he said they would all be cut to pieces. He said 'These English certainly fight well, but they must soon give way;' and he asked Soult, who was near him, 'if he did not think so?' Soult replied, 'He was afraid not.' 'And why?' said Napoleon, turning round to him quickly. 'Because,' said Soult, 'I believe they will first be cut to pieces.' Soult's opinion of the British army, which was founded on experience, coincided with that of the Duke of Wellington. 'It will take a great many hours to cut them in pieces,' said the Duke, in answer to something that was said to him during the action; 'and I know they will never give way.'

Sergeant William Lawrence, 40th Foot[8]
While we were lying there [outside Paris] several of the wounded who had recovered rejoined the army from Brussels, and with some of these Bartram [There appear to have been at least three Bartrams at Waterloo, so this man is difficult to identify with any certainty] made his appearance, the man whom I mentioned as having smelt powder at the beginning of the 18th of June, and having so cowardly fallen out of his rank. As soon as I saw him I put him in the rear-guard as a prisoner, and reported him, as it was my duty to do, to the captain of my company. Next day a court-martial was ordered, I being the chief but not the only evidence against him, and being sentenced to three hundred lashes as a punishment for absenting himself from the field of action, he was tied up and received every lash. This may seem to some a hard case, three hundred lashes for absenting himself, but it must be remembered that had there been many like this man, for I cannot call him a soldier, that day would most decidedly have ended in favour of the French. When taken down he was sent to hospital for three weeks and then came back to us, but even then he was not

quite free, for I had orders from the captain to examine his kit to see if everything was complete, and I found his knapsack completely empty. I then searched his pouch and found all his ammunition gone. I was not much surprised at this, knowing that he did not like the smell of powder; but I reported these circumstances to the captain, who ordered him back to the rear-guard as a prisoner again; and the next day another court-martial was held on him for making away with his kit, and he was sentenced to three hundred more lashes, of which strange to say he received every one without crying out. He seemed to be a man without any feeling, for it may be pretty well taken for granted that the drummers did not fail in their duty towards such a man as this, for there is no one they feel more strongly against than a coward.

Charlotte Eaton, travel writer[22]
Numbers of country-people were employed in what might be called the gleanings of the harvest of spoil. The muskets, the swords, the helmets, the cuirasses all the large and unbroken arms had been immediately carried off; and now the eagles that had emblazoned the caps of the French Infantry, the fragments of broken swords, &c., were rarely to be found ... It was astonishing with what dreadful haste the bodies of the dead had been pillaged. The work of plunder was carried on even during the battle; and those hardened and abandoned wretches who follow the camp, like vultures, to prey upon the corpses of the dead, had the temerity to press forward beneath a heavy fire to rifle the pockets of the officers who fell of their watches and money.

Sergeant William Lawrence, 40th Foot[8]
After this [advance on Paris] we saw no more of Napoleon's army, nor did we want to much, for most of us had had quite enough of it at Waterloo ...

Part X

SCARS OF BATTLE

It goes without saying that medical treatment in 1815 was primitive compared to today – and battlefield medical treatment was necessarily cruder still. Amputation was almost a first, rather than a last resort when a surgeon was confronted with any major limb injury – not because of any brutal or callous attitude, but because overworked, overwhelmed surgeons, fearing the onset of infection and gangrene, often felt they had little time or alternative but to remove arms and legs.

The organisation of the British Army's medical services had a rather poor reputation at this time. General Napier, in his History of the Peninsular War, written just before Waterloo, said, 'Where one soldier died for want of surgical skill, hundreds perished from the absence of medical organisation.'

The retrieval of casualties from the battlefield, and even basic care such as the distribution of water to wounded men who had been lying for hours or even days after battles, seems to have existed as little more than an afterthought if at all. If able-bodied men could be found they were sent to collect the stricken, and carts might be commandeered for transport. A field hospital was set up at Mont St Jean – but not until three days after the battle. Other hospitals were eventually established in Brussels and Antwerp. It's clear from the accounts that many men were left to fend for themselves, and the relatively lucky walking wounded limped towards Brussels and other towns and villages where help might be sought. Many locals took wounded soldiers into their own homes.

There was no anaesthetic in the modern sense, though opiates were used when available. Whether or not it was bravado, peer pressure or simply the fact that times – and thus people – were tougher then, men often behaved with great sang-froid in the face of devastating injury. We have already seen how Uxbridge reacted to having his leg destroyed by a cannonball. Upon having his arm amputated after Waterloo, Lord Raglan famously said, 'Hello. Don't carry away that arm until I have taken off the ring.'

23

ATTENDING TO THE WOUNDED

Dr Charles Bell[28]

... I found that the best cases, that is the most horrid ones, were to be found in the hospital of the French wounded. This hospital was only forming; they were even then bringing these poor creatures in from the woods. It is impossible to convey to you the picture of human misery continually before my eyes. What was heartrending in the day, was intolerable at night; and I rose and wrote, at four o'clock in the morning, to the chief surgeon Gunning, offering to perform the necessary operations upon the French. At six o'clock I took the knife in my hand, and continued incessantly at work till seven in the evening; and so the second day, and again the third day. All the decencies of performing surgical operations were soon neglected: while I amputated one man's thigh, there lay at one time thirteen, all beseeching to be taken next ... It was a strange feeling to feel my clothes stiff with blood, and my arms powerless with the exertion of using the knife; and more extraordinary still, to find my mind calm amidst such a variety of suffering; but to give one of these objects access to your feelings was to allow yourself to be unmanned for the performance of a duty.

Lt-Colonel William Tomkinson, 16th Light Dragoons[42]

The wounded of the British army generally receive more attention than those of other nations. The French system is to run great risks with a man's life in hopes of saving a limb ... With us, the practice is possibly too much in favour of hasty amputation. There have been instances of officers saving their limbs, from not allowing the surgeon to operate, choosing rather to run the risk of losing their life than being cut out of their profession.

Volunteer doctor Charles Bell, on treating an unnamed trooper of 1st Dragoons (Royals)[46]

A portion of the skull ... completely detached by the sabre-cut; the corresponding part of the scalp remains connected by a small isthmus ... On being urged to speak, he makes a painful effort to speak but cannot. He can sit up in a chair without support, but stands languidly and with a vacant and indifferent expression of countenance.

Dr J. Cole, The London Medical Repository[50]

William Peachman, of the 2d battalion of the 1st guards, was wounded by a musket ball at the affair of Quatre Bras, on the 16th June, 1815. He was received into the Minimes General Hospital at Antwerp, on the 18th or 19th, with a compound fracture of the right elbow joint, extending up the humerus; the whole of the arm in a state of extreme tension, and considerable constitutional irritation. From the moment of his admission, no hope was entertained of saving the limb ... and ... a favourable opportunity of removing it did not occur until the 5th of July; even then it was impracticable to save any portion of the humerus, abscesses having extended to the point of the shoulder: its removal from the scapula was therefore determined on ... The patient seated on a chair, supported by orderlies, with a medical assistant so placed as to have his thumb on the subclavian artery, where it emerges from between the scaleni, just above the middle part of the clavicle, I commenced the operation by making diverging incisions with a scalpel, from the point of the acromion anteriorly and posteriorly, though the integuments, and keeping close to their outer edge, through the muscles, down to the bone, leaving the body of the deltoid untouched, thus between them [*sic*]; the capsular ligament was, as far as possible, cut through, as well as the long head of the biceps, with the same instrument. The arm being then brought a little from the side, and an amputating knife substituted for the scalpel, the extreme angles of the two incisions were united by one sweep through the soft parts from within, outwards, and the limb disengaged without loss of blood; a glance of the eye sufficing to inform the assistant *when* to apply the pressure required. The mouths of the two large arteries were seen gaping, of equal proportions, and running close to each other ... they were seized with tenaculums, and separately tied; the only vessels requiring a ligature. The flaps were brought together, which were found to neatly and completely cover the wound: they were retained in apposition by three adhesive strips.

The patient was tranquil after the operation, passed a good night, and the following day every prospect of success was held out. On the 11th, the adhesions had considerably advanced. The pus secreted was healthy, and the strength improved. On the 14th, when the dressings were removed, the appearance of the stump was good, and the wound reduced to a simple line; the ligatures remained; an abscess in the side was opened with a lancet. During the night of the 15th there was considerable haemorrhage from the wound: for some time the patient was impressed with the idea of its being pus trickling down his side, and did not call for assistance until he felt very faint. The bleeding ceased before the orderly medical officer could arrive, but unfortunately not before the quantity lost was so great as to produce death the same morning ... This poor fellow may be considered as particularly unfortunate;

for had his arm been removed on the field of battle, his life, in all probability, would have been preserved: at all events his sufferings would have been, doubtless, immediately arrested by compression, and the patient in all likelihood afterwards been placed out of danger, by the ligature of the subclavian artery.

Dr J. Cole, The London Medical Repository[50]

Benjamin Varender, aged thirty-two, of the 32d regiment, was wounded on the same day (at the affair of Quatre Bras) by a musket ball passing through the elbow joint, fracturing the olecranon and humerus. He likewise was sent to Antwerp, a distance from the field of forty-four miles: and when received into the Minimes General Hospital, on the 21st of June, was in an alarming state of constitutional irritation and the whole of the limb inflamed and tense. By fomentations, poultices, and the strictest antiphlogistic regimen, the high action was reduced: but by this time the general strength was greatly exhausted; hectic fever had declared itself, with rigors approaching in severity the cold stage of ague. On 7th July, generous diet, bark, and mineral acids, were had recourse to, but the strength daily declined; and on the 11th, excision at the humerous scapular articulation was determined on ... The method I adopted was, as nearly as circumstances would allow, the same as the preceding ... A compress and bandage being applied, the patient was removed to his bed, feeling, as he expressed himself, released from a heavy burthen.

   12th – Has passed a better night then he has done since receiving the wound; nevertheless, his exhausted state and tendency to hectic make us not over sanguine in the expectations of recovery ... 19th – His health has rather improved; no untoward symptom his arisen, and union is making rapid progress ... 27th – The stump doing extremely well; but from the constant pressure in so emaciated a frame, the integuments on the sacrum have, spite [sic] of every precaution, ulcerated ... 30th – The ligatures came away, and the stump is nearly healed: the ulcer on the sacrum looks cleaner: he however is obliged, from extreme debility, to keep his bed; and this debility is increased by profuse night sweats ... August 4th – The stump nearly well; the ulcer on the sacrum extensive. ... 6th – In consequence of the concentration of all the British wounded, Varender was removed to the Facon Hospital. The stump nearly healed; yet from his tendency to hectic, his extreme weakness, ulceration of the sacrum, and disposition to phthisis, it required all the zeal and ability of my friend, Staff-Surgeon Bliche (who had charge of that hospital) to complete the cure: which, however, after much labour, was ultimately effected, and he embarked, recovered, for England.

Dr J. Cole, The London Medical Repository[50]
The subject of the following observation must be considered particularly unfortunate. William Goodwin, of the 23d light dragoons, not more than twenty-one years of age, was severely wounded in the shoulder joint by a musket ball, on the 18th of June, 1815, at the battle of Waterloo. From that moment to the 13th of July he had been moved from place to place without any active means being employed. He was received ... into the Minimes General Hospital: his condition was then deplorable: nearly a month had elapsed: extensive abscesses had formed around the shoulder joint, through which the ball had passed from before backward; the discharge was foetid, profuse, and ill-conditioned; the constitutional irritation and general debility were very great.

Every thing was done to ameliorate his situation. On the 15th, the anterior wound, by which the ball had entered, was dilated longitudinally; and the destruction, both of bone and soft parts, was found so considerable, as to make it evident excision of the humerus was the only remedy ... Unfortunately the patient could not be brought to submit to it. He had lost the firmness of character which, doubtless, was his portion. Restless nights and dolorous days had worn him to the bone, and unstrung once high toned nerves. With a mind ill at ease, confirmed hectic, immense discharge, and constant pain, his death was rapidly approaching, when, on the 26th, he gave his reluctant assent to the oft proposed operation ... The patient supported by orderlies in a sitting position, and the subclavian placed, as before, under the control of a steady hospital assistant, with a view of getting rid of diseased parts, I made with scalpel the anterior incision ... In doing this, enormous quantities of foetid pus gushed out ... a head of the humerus was shattered, the glenoid cavity splintered, and the fracture extended along the body of the scapula far beyond our reach: and sinuses, from various diseased quarters, poured out their offensive contents.

The blood-vessels were, however, seized with a tenaculum, and secured; the flaps brought down, the stump dressed, and the poor fellow placed on his bed with as much speed as possible; for I felt disheartened at the misery of the man, and feared that he might expire on the table. This, indeed, was the prevailing sentiment ... In the evening he was found to have rallied amazingly; had taken nourishment and cordials, and walked from a small room (where he had been placed to breathe his last in peace) to his former ward, that he might occupy his own bed, and be in the neighbourhood of his former companions. The first night after the operation he described to be by far the best that he had passed since his admission: his strength seemed for some days to increase, and his spirits greatly improved; but we never indulged the expectation of ultimate recovery. The discharge was profuse: colliquative diarrhoea came on, and death put a period to his sufferings on the 4th of August.

Dr J. Cole, The London Medical Repository[50]
William Rogers, aged only nineteen years, belonging to the 32d regiment, was wounded at Quatre Bras, on the 16th June, 1815, by a musket ball. On the 18th he was admitted into the Minimes General Hospital at Antwerp. The ball had struck the inferior angle

of the left parietal bone, taking a direction upward and forward for nearly two inches between the tables of the cranium: it could be distinctly felt with a probe ... The power of speech was much impaired: but being exhausted with fatigue, he was placed in bed, and was much refreshed by a sound sleep. On waking, he showed no other symptom of either concussion or compression. During his recovery, he told me that on receiving the wound he felt senseless for a few minutes, then recovered his recollection, heard and understood his comrades, but was totally incapable of speaking ... His battalion moved on, leaving him in the charge of a soldier, who, little suspecting he would be ever able to communicate the circumstance, left him for the sake of plunder. He soon recovered sufficiently to retire out of the reach of shot, where he lay down for the night. The following morning ... he fell back ... and by the evening found himself at Bruxelles, where he was superficially dressed. On the 18th he removed to Antwerp, on one of his officer's [sic] horses, where I received him, overwhelmed with fatigue and exhausted by privation. On the morning of the 20th, there was a considerable re-action, with pain in the forehead, increased by light or sound. Thirty ounces of blood were taken from the arm, cold applications kept to the head, and a brisk purgative ordered: stimuli of every kind were avoided ... By these means the pain was relieved, the action moderated, and the wound was nearly healed: the powers of speech had increased, but he still articulated imperfectly. When nearly in a state to be discharged ... on the 16th of July the wound began to re-open. On the 18th the symptoms of compression were alarming. I dilated the wound, and removed a small quantity of splintered bone. On the 22nd symptoms of phrenitis appeared, which were with difficulty got under [sic] by copious bleedings that and the following day. On the 24th he was much relieved: 26th another small piece of bone came away, leaving the dura mater completely exposed. From this period to his recovery no untoward symptoms arose, although the ball was never removed ...

Dr J. Cole, The London Medical Repository[50]

William Kitchen, aged forty, of the 1st regiment, as also wounded by a musket ball on the 18th of June, which fractured the cranium, and depressed a considerable portion of both parietal bones. In this situation he was admitted on the 27th, with the lower extremities only completely paralyzed ... I applied the trephine, raised the depressed portions of bone, and removed the detached. Every bad symptom disappeared; the power of the lower extremities was gradually restored, and on the 28th of July he also embarked for England.

Dr J. Cole, The London Medical Repository[50]

James Beswick, of the fourth regiment of foot, was admitted into the Minimes General Hospital at Antwerp, on the 27th of June 1815, in consequence of a musket-wound received at the affair of Quatre Bras on the 16th. The ball entered at the inferior angle of the lower jaw on the right side, passed across the neck, and made its exit about an inch below the same angle on the opposite side: it was evident that in its passage the pharynx, larynx, and some arteries were wounded ... The food escaped through the wound on the left side; the haemorrhage had been occasionally profuse, and the voice was lost ... The morning after his admission, I was called to his bed-side, and found him covered with blood, which was flowing from his mouth, and filling vessel after vessel, almost as fast as they could be emptied ... Tying the common carotid immediately suggested itself as the only step likely to prolong his life; I therefore determined on it. The patient, readily consenting to my proposition, was placed recumbent on the table, with his head gently inclined towards the right shoulder. I began by making an incision through the incision through the integuments along the inner margin of the sterno-cliedo-mastoideus, about two inches and a half in length, terminating not more than an inch from the junction of the clavicle to the sternum: by dividing some cellular membrane ... My patient lost scarcely any blood by the operation, nor a drop from the original wound after the ligature was made; yet, from previous fasting, fatigue, and haemorrhages since the wound was inflicted, he was removed to his bed in a very exhausted, though collected state.

29th – Seems much relieved; has passed a tranquil night; has lost no blood; nor is there any change manifested in his mental powers. Swallowing being extremely difficult, he is fed with milk and animal broths, through the oesophagus; an anodyne is mixed with his evening potion ... 30th – Seems improving, and gains strength; his respiration is a little oppressed, and the questions put to him by the assistants and occasional visitors are irksome ... July 1st – His progress is satisfactory; he every day rallies; and in spite of the complicated injury he has sustained, we indulge in the expectation of his recovery ... 2d – He has passed a quiet night; pulse distinct, though small; continues to receive his food in the way mentioned without any difficulty ... Eleven P.M. – After some stertorous breathing, he so quietly sunk into the arms of death, that the nurse appointed to attend him for some time was not aware of it.

On examination, the ball was found to have fractured the right angle of the inferior maxillary bone, one of the cornua of the os hyoides [*sic*], and to have wounded in its course the phraynx, larynx, and some large branches of the carotid. The lungs were sound, but the bronchiae and air cells were found choked with fetid pus, precisely of the same appearance and odour as that secreted by the surface of the original wound, and from which it might be traced down the trachea ... The function of respiration was gradually impaired, and ultimately destroyed.

Part XI

NAPOLEON'S FINAL JOURNEY

Napoleon fled to Paris, arriving three days after the battle. Wellington and Blucher were slow to advance on the French capital, and Napoleon felt he still had the troops at his disposal to reverse his recent defeat, but found himself politically outmanoeuvred and retired to Malmaison [the literal translation of which, rather ironically, is 'bad/evil house'] just outside Paris, the chateau where he had once lived with Joséphine. But fearing that his liberty and even his life were in jeopardy, he slipped away on 8 July with the idea that he would take refuge in America.

In the meantime, Captain Frederick Maitland of the Bellerophon *of Trafalgar fame was on blockade duty off Rochefort. He received news of Napoleon's defeat from a captured vessel ten days after the event, and two days later an anonymous letter was delivered by boat stating that*

with a degree of certainty, being informed that Buonaparte might have come last night through this city from Paris ... with a view to flight ... Mr — hastily drops these few lines, to give the British Admiral advice of such intention, that he may instantly take the necessary steps, in order to seize the man ...

24

SURRENDER

Captain Frederick Maitland, HMS Bellerophon[11]
For the information of my Lords Commissioners of the Admiralty, I have to acquaint you, that the Count Las Casses and General Allemand this morning came on board, his Majesty's ship under my command, with a proposal for me to receive on board Napoleon Bonaparte (who had been secreted at Rochefort) for the purpose of throwing himself on the generosity of His Royal Highness the Prince Regent. Conceiving myself authorized, by their Lordships' secret order, I have acceded to the proposal, and he is to embark on board this ship to-morrow morning. That no misunderstanding might arise, I have explicitly and clearly explained to the Count Las Casses, that I have no authority whatever for granting terms of any sort; but that all I can do is to convey him and his suite to England, to be received in such manner as His Royal Highness may deem expedient.

Journal of Lt John Bowerbank, HMS Bellerophon[29]
Early in the morning the *Bellerophon* being then at anchor off Basque Roads, about four miles distant from the French squadron, a brig, under a flag of truce, was discovered working out. At six a.m. the boats of the *Bellerophon* were dispatched to her, and

shortly after, on their quitting her, the crew of the brig cheered, shouting 'Vive l'Empereur.' At seven the barge with Buonaparte and several officers came alongside. Marshal Bertrand first came on board, informing Captain Maitland that the Emperor was in the boat. Napoleon immediately followed. He bowed low and said in French 'Sir, I am come on board, and I claim the protection of your Prince and of your laws.' These words were delivered with a dignified air, then bowing to the officers, he was conducted to the cabin by Captain Maitland. The marines of the ship were drawn up under arms, but did not pay any honours. Buonaparte was dressed in a short green surtout, military boots, and a plain cocked hat. There came with him in the boat, Lieutenants-General Count Bertrand, Grand Marshal of the Palace; Count Montholon-Semonville, and Baron L'Allemand, two of his Aides-de-Camp; Savary, Duke of Rovigo, Minister of Police, the Countesses Bertrand and Montholon-Semonville, with four children. He had scarcely been five minutes on board before he sent his compliments, and requested that the officers of the ship might be introduced to him. This was done by Captain Maitland. He bowed severally to each, and smilingly inquired how each of them ranked. When they were about to leave the cabin he said to them in French 'Well, Gentlemen, you have the honour of belonging to the bravest and most fortunate nation in the world.' Having arranged his dress, he shortly afterwards came upon deck: I had then an opportunity of viewing him more attentively.

Napoleon Buonaparte is about five feet seven inches high, rather corpulent, remarkably well-made. His hair is very black, cut close, whiskers shaved off; large eye-brows, grey eyes, the most piercing I ever saw; rather full face, dark but peculiar complexion, his nose and mouth proportionate, broad shoulders, and apparently strongly built. Upon the whole he is a good-looking man, and when young must have been handsome. He appears about forty-five or forty-six, his real age, greatly resembles the different prints I have seen of him in London. His walk is a march, or (as far as a sailor may be allowed to judge) very like one: and to complete the portrait I must add that in walking he generally carries his hands in the pockets of his pantaloons or folded behind his back. Whilst on the quarter-deck he asked several questions of the officers, took particular notice of the sights on the guns, begged the boatswain might be sent to him, of whom he made many inquiries respecting the ship, and his length of service. This honest fellow, surprised at the unexpectedness of the message, and his sudden introduction to one of whom he had heard so much, to our very great amusement was determined to have the first word: and therefore with cap in hand, a scrape of his foot, and a head almost bowed to the ground in true sailor-like style, saluted him with; 'I hope your honour's well.' ... He speaks French and Italian remarkably well, but does not appear to understand a word of English. About half-past seven he retired for the night. He appeared during the whole of this day very cheerful, frequently playing with the children, etc.

25

TORBAY

John Smart of Brixham, aged fourteen[29]

In common with most English schoolboys of that Waterloo year, we had an extra week's holiday at midsummer ... It was a bright summer's morning when I sallied out after breakfast, with two half-crowns in my pocket, to meet Charlie Puddicombe and his younger brother Dick. We met by appointment on the quay, and at once began to discuss how we should spend the day and my money. Suddenly we spied two ships coming round Berry Head and into the bay, the first a large man-of-war, and the other a three-masted sloop. The ships were coming in quickly with wind and tide, but we heard faintly the sound of the boatswain's whistle, and in a moment the sailors were scrambling up the rigging and out on the yards to take in sail. Then, within half a mile of Brixham Quay, the anchors were let go, and the ships swung round with the flood tide, the large ship being the nearer to the shore. How thankful we were that no school bell would drag us away, but that we might stay to see all the fun! 'Run up to Mrs Hawkins' (the baker's wife), said I to Dick, 'and tell her some King's ships have come in, for she and Michelmore are sure to go off in her boat, and I know she will let us go too. 'And we will shove off the boat meanwhile,' said Charlie. Already several boat-men were unmooring their boats; but just then we saw a boat shove off from the ship, and we all gathered round the steps at the pierhead, for which she was making. As the boat came near we saw it was a large gig, pulled by eight sailors, and in the stern sheets sat three officers.

'Way enough,' said one of them; the oars were tossed, and the coxswain brought the boat as neatly alongside as if he had studied the run of the tide at Brixham all his life. Two of the officers jumped ashore: the one a tall man of about thirty-five, with a cloak on his arm, and the other a younger man, apparently of inferior rank. A portmanteau was handed ashore, and then at once the younger officer gave the order 'Push off!' and as the bow-man, who was ready with his boathook, obeyed, he added to the young midshipman who was sitting in the stern, 'I shall be back in ten minutes; remember orders; no talking.' Then, addressing himself to one of the shore boatmen, who had already shouldered the portmanteau, he asked which was the principal inn where a post-chaise could be obtained. Being directed to 'The London Inn,' the two officers proceeded there, and went in together. Now, it was rather disappointing, and certainly unusual, that the boat did not stop by the quay, for generally Jack is fond enough of putting foot on shore, asking and telling news, besides doing a little shopping. However, the midshipman kept his boat moving a little way off, within easy hail of shore, and seemed to avoid the boats that were putting off to the ships. The officers at the inn proved the attraction for us, and we boys formed part of the group there. It certainly could not have been more than ten minutes before the horses were put in the old yellow postchaise that was as familiar to us as King William's Stone. The two officers came out directly the chaise was ready, the younger one reading from a newspaper to the other, as the latter got into the chaise.

Then, while the postboy mounted, the landlord, who would fain have seen more of them, came out with a bottle and poured out a glass of wine for each. 'Goodbye, Dick,' said the one in the chaise; 'here's to our next meeting!' 'Here's to your safe arrival in London!' said the younger one, 'and good-bye,' he added, as the chaise rolled away up Fore Street. Then, walking back to the pierhead, he held up his hand as a signal to the boat, which speedily came up. 'Now then, men, give way,' he said, as he sat down; and before we could ask what it all meant the oars were in the water and the boat was well on its way to the ship. 'Bean't he in a hurry, then?' said old Michelmore, who, in his floury coat and white hat, had just arrived with his apprentice boy from the shop. 'Come, boys, let's be off to the ship.' We were not long in getting off. Charlie and his brother double-banked one oar, the apprentice pulled another, I sat down in my favourite place right up in the bow, and Michelmore steered. He had a large sack with him containing new loaves, which he was taking as a speculation and as a suggestion for further orders. As we approached the ship, I had the point of vantage as look-out, and I noticed that the shore boats which had preceded us had stopped short of the ship, and were together, while in one of them a man was standing up, who, as we drew nearer, appeared to be in altercation with some one on board. Michelmore steered up to this boat and asked what was the matter. 'They won't let us come alongside, and they say as how they don't want no shore boats at all.' 'But they'll want some shore bread, I reckon,' said Michelmore, letting our boat drift onwards with the tide towards the ship. It was a grand-looking line-of-battle ship, with 74 guns, and with stern galleries and square cabin windows.

The tide took us right under the stern, and there was a sentry with his musket in the poop, and an officer by him leaning over the rail, who said in a loud voice, 'Come sheer off; no boats are allowed here.' 'But,' said Michelmore, as he made a grab at a lower-deck port with his boat-hook, 'I've brought you some bread.' 'If we want bread,' replied the officer, 'we'll come ashore and fetch it, and if you don't let go I'll sink you.' The tide had drifted us right under the gallery, and what was my horror to see the sentry drop his musket and seize a large cannon-ball, which he held exactly over my head. 'Let go, you old fool, or by the Lord I'll sink you!' said the sentry; and to my great relief Michelmore let go, and we were soon out of harm's way. As we pulled away from the ship we noticed that the lower ports were open, and that the decks were crowded with men. But we had not long for inspection, for just then one of the ship's boats, which had been lowered with a crew of at least a dozen men, came up to us, and an officer in her said: 'Now, my man, you had better not get yourself into trouble; we have orders to keep off all shore boats, so you know it's no use trying.' And here we saw that the officer had his sword on and that the men were armed with cutlasses. We rowed back to the other boats to have a conference, Michelmore being most indignant. 'Man and boy,' said he, 'have I sailed on these here waters, and never have I been so treated.' Meanwhile another of the shore boats, which had been to the sloop, came back with the news that there was no better luck there, and then we knew that they must be in earnest, for round each vessel a boat full of armed men was keeping off all comers. One by one the other shore boats departed; but as it was a holiday for us boys, we persuaded Michelmore to stay a little longer. Now, whether it was that we were only youngsters, who, even with the aid of a baker, might be deemed innocent of any sinister intentions, or whether the patrolling boats were content in keeping us outside of their circuit, we were not molested when we again rowed round the ship at a proper distance.

One might well suppose that an English crew, so close to their own shores, would be as eager for communication as we were, and although no word came to us from the ship, we could see the men round the guns peering at us through the portholes. As we rounded the bows of the ship the tide caught us with great force, and at the second time of our doing this, as luck would have it, we were taken a little nearer than we would willingly have ventured. As the current swept us along, I noticed at one of the lower-deck ports a man nodding violently to us, but standing back a little, as if frightened at being seen. His eye caught mine for an instant as he put his fingers to his lips with a warning gesture. We were past him in another moment, but I was greatly excited, and wanted to turn back to see him again. However, Michelmore decided it would be safer to complete our turn; and accordingly we did so, but regulated our pace with the guard boat, so that it was at the ship's stern when we again approached the bows. This time the man was still standing back, and even less visible than before; but his hand was just visible on the port-sill, and as we passed he let something drop from his fingers into the water.

We dared not approach, but we kept it in view as it drifted along. I had my hand dragging as if carelessly in the water, and when we were a good hundred yards clear of the ship, Michelmore steered so as to bring the object into my hand. It proved to be a small black bottle; but as the evident intention of the officers had been to prevent all communication, I was frightened to look at my prize, and could only clutch it in my hand with a fear that some one on board must have seen me. However, our curiosity was too great to brook delay, and we steered towards shore, so that Michelmore's broad body was between me and the ship in case any one was spying at us through a glass. It was a foreign-looking bottle, and as I drew the cork, its oiliness and perfume suggested that it had been used for some liqueur. I kept that bottle for a few years, but even now, without it, I can recall its shape and size and smell. In the bottle was a small piece of paper rolled up, and on the paper was written, 'We have got Bonaparte on board.'

In five minutes after we reached shore, there was not a soul in Brixham, except babies, ignorant of the news ... Every sort of craft that could be pulled by oars or propelled by sail was brought into requisition. The people on board the ship must have suspected from the bustle on the quay that their secret was discovered; but the cries of 'Bonaparte! Bonaparte!' from all the boats, soon told them. Then, finding concealment useless, all the strange visitors showed themselves. We did not know who they all were for some days afterwards, and in fact only got a proper list from the London newspapers when the ships were gone. I can picture at this moment Boney as he appeared in the stern gallery of the *Bellerophon*. My first thought was how little he looked, and that he was rather fat. We were not allowed to come near the ship, but we saw him quite plainly. He wore a green uniform with red facings, gold epaulettes, white waistcoat and breeches, and high military boots. He took off his hat, which had a cockade on it, and bowed to the people, who took off their hats and shouted 'Hooray!' I recall a feeling of triumph mixed with a natural satisfaction at seeing a wonderful sight. Bonaparte seemed to take all the excitement as a tribute to himself. We noticed that the English officers and crew were very respectful, and all took off their hats when they spoke to him. The day was spent by us mostly on the water, and what an afternoon! There never was before or since such an assembly of craft in Torbay as there was the next day ... From Exmouth, Teignmouth, Plymouth, the boats and yachts continued to arrive all day. This was mainly on Tuesday, and on that day all the country seemed to come in. Gentlemen and ladies came on horseback and in carriages; other people in carts and waggons; and to judge by the number of people, all the world inland was flocking to see Bonaparte ... Over the ship's side, the sailors had hung a board on which they had chalked 'He's gone to breakfast.' ... The officer who had gone to London, must have travelled quickly, for on Wednesday morning, as soon after sunrise as the telegraph could work, instructions had been sent to Plymouth, and these had been forwarded to Brixham. The ships weighed anchor at once and sailed for Plymouth, no secret being made of their destination. Boney having gone, the world no longer found anything of interest at Brixham. The visitors left us, and I went back to school.

Francis Horner MP[28]

I was within a very few miles of Exeter, of Buonaparte in Torbay; a number of people went down to get a glimpse of him, and all the worthies of Torquay, and other watering-places, went out in shoals. Nobody was allowed to go on board; but they were happy to row round the ship at a little distance and catch a sight of him as he walked the quarterdeck. How little did we dream of the possibility of such a change when we were at Torquay; he was then in the midst of his plans and preparations for the invasion of Russia ...

Journal of Lt John Bowerbank, HMS Bellerophon[29]

Early this morning we were close in with the land running into Torbay. Between five and six a.m. Buonaparte made his appearance on deck, and continued there until we anchored. He appeared delighted with the prospect, and his approach to England. Looking through his glass he frequently exclaimed in French, 'What a beautiful country!' As we rounded the Berry Head he took notice that the barracks were deserted. At eight a.m. we anchored, and were immediately surrounded with boats. Towards noon several thousand people were collected in hopes of getting a glimpse of our curiosity. He occasionally showed himself through the stern windows, and about three o'clock came upon deck viewing the crowd through his glass. He seemed struck with the beauty of the women, repeatedly crying out: 'What charming girls! What beautiful women!' and bowing to them.

Journal of Lt John Bowerbank, HMS Bellerophon[29]

A few minutes before dinner he came upon deck with no other apparent design than to gratify the surrounding spectators. He looked extremely ill and dejected. I should scarcely have imagined that so great a change could have taken place in so short a period. He was still unshaven and his countenance, naturally sallow, had now assumed a death-like paleness.

Journal of Lt John Bowerbank, HMS Bellerophon[29]

Wednesday, August 2nd. On this day Buonaparte did not once appear on deck, nor did he quit his cabin but to breakfast and dine. His spirits were again at a very low ebb, and Bertrand was frequently with him. Several letters were addressed to Government by Savary and L'Allemand, who were now generally in conversation with each other, and seemed greatly to disrelish the idea of being delivered up to Louis. Napoleon still stoutly avowed his resolution of not being taken from the ship and his generals declared they would themselves be his executioners, rather than he should be forced to St. Helena. While at supper Bertrand waited on Captain Maitland with a request from Buonaparte that the sentinels should be forbidden to call out every half hour as it prevented his rest. I am inclined to think he has latterly slept but little, as he has been heard walking in his cabin much later than usual.

Journal of Lt John Bowerbank, HMS Bellerophon[29]

Friday 4th August. In consequence of orders from the Admiralty we sailed soon after twelve in company with the *Tonnant*, Admiral Lord Keith, and the *Eurotas* frigate; and laid to in the offing for the *Northumberland*. All Napoleon's hopes sank with this movement. He now became very sullen; would not quit his cabin even for meals, but ate alone and rarely saw any person throughout the day. He still refused to name his future companions; declared his resolution never to be removed. We were all now in full expectation of some tragical event. The general conjecture was that he would end himself by poison. It was believed that he had in his possession a large quantity of laudanum. Madame Bertrand even hinted that ere morning we should find him a corpse ... Madame Bertrand told us at supper that his legs were considerably swelled in consequence of his want of exercise during the last three or four days. This observation produced a general remark from his friends that he would not survive a year at St.

Helena. She afterwards declared to one of the ship's officers that 'she really believed the Emperor had now swallowed poison.' The curtain, therefore, must soon drop; but I imagine it will be prudent to leave a door open for escape. Let us then qualify the assertion with a 'perhaps'.

Journal of Lt John Bowerbank, HMS Bellerophon[68]
Monday 8th August. About 10 a.m. the children and nine servants were sent to the *Northumberland*; and about eleven, the Admiral's barge being in waiting, Buonaparte was informed that everything was ready for his removal. We had all assembled on deck to take our last view of him. After a long conversation with Lord Keith, and having taken leave of those officers who were to remain behind, he made his appearance at about twenty minutes before twelve. It was four days since we had last seen him. He was not shaved, and appeared confused. Bowing as he came out, he advanced with a sort of forced smile on his countenance towards the officers of the *Bellerophon*, attended by Captain Maitland ... he bowed to all around, and lastly, turning to the ship's crew, pulled off his hat to them also. He instantly went into the boat ...

Diary of Sir George Bingham[29]
He rather complained of his destination, saying it had been his intention to have lived in a retired manner in England, had he been permitted to have done so ...

Part XII

LOOKING BACK

Such was the significance and sacrifice of Waterloo that for the first time in British Army history every man (including those who fought at Ligny and Quatre Bras) no matter what his rank was entitled to a medal. In addition, every soldier who received a medal had an extra two years added to his military service – the official term being a 'Waterloo Man'.

Many soldiers found themselves surplus to requirements after Waterloo, and faced a desperate struggle to keep body and soul together. Those left with a disability were granted pensions, which varied in size depending on the nature of the injury, but they were not generous; it was common for both the lame and the able-bodied to find themselves destitute and begging in the streets or consigned to the workhouse. The lucky few were accepted into the Royal Military Hospital in Chelsea, but places were limited. Most 'Chelsea Pensioners' were non-residents, and often still resorted to begging to supplement their meagre income.

With Napoleon in exile once more, Marshal Ney became the scapegoat. He was arrested at the beginning of August, and executed three months later.

26

'SUCH HAS BEEN THE BATTLE OF MONT ST JEAN'

Anonymous correspondent[11]
Every tree in the wood of Hougoumont is pierced with balls – in one alone, I counted the holes, where upwards of twenty had lodged: but the strokes which were fatal to human life, have scarcely injured them; though their trunks are filled with balls, and their branches broken and destroyed, their verdure is still the same. Wild flowers are still blooming, and wild raspberries ripening beneath, their shade; while huge black piles of human ashes, dreadfully offensive in smell, are all that now remain of the heroes who fought and fell upon this fatal spot. Beside some graves, at the outskirts of this wood, the little wild flower, 'Forget me not,' 'Myosotis arvensis,' was blooming, and the flaring red poppy had already sprung up around, and even upon them, as if in mockery of the dead. The Chateau itself, upon which the attack was first made by the French, now in ruins, is immediately behind the wood, by the side of the road to Nivelles. It was the beautiful country-seat of a Belgic gentleman, and was accidentally set on fire by shells, during the action, which completed the destruction occasioned by the cannonade. In the garden behind the house, the roses, orange-trees and geraniums were still flowering

240

in beauty, and the fig-tree and the pear-tree bearing their fruits – a melancholy contrast to the ruined house, whose mouldering piles were still smoking, and to the scene of desolation around ...

The poor countryman, who with his wife and infant family inhabited a miserable shed amongst the deserted ruins, pointed out with superstitious reverence, the little chapel belonging to the Chateau, which alone stood uninjured in the midst of these blackened walls and falling beams. There was something inexpressibly striking in the almost miraculous preservation of this simple sanctuary of piety, which the flames of war, and the hand of rapine, had alike spared; and it was affecting to see standing on the spot still reeking with human blood, and heaped with the dreadful and yet undecayed remains of mortality, the sacred altar of that blessed religion, which proclaimed, 'Peace on Earth,' and dispelled the horrors of death by the assurance of immortality. A more mournful scene than this ruined chateau and wood presented, cannot possibly be imagined. Even when the heaps of dead were reduced to ashes, – the broken swords, shattered helmets, torn epaulets, and sabre sashes bathed in blood, told too plainly the deadly strife that had taken place; and the mournful reflexion could not be repressed, that the glory which Britain gained upon this spot, was purchased by the blood of some of her noblest sons.

Anonymous account[11]
During the Battle of Waterloo, some of the horses, as they lay on the ground, having recovered from the first agony of their wounds, fell to eating the grass about them, thus surrounding themselves with a circle of bare ground, the limited extent of which showed their weakness: others of these interesting animals, to whom man so strongly attaches himself, were observed quietly grazing in the middle of the field, between the two hostile lines, their riders having been shot off their backs, and the balls that flew over their heads, and the roaring behind and before, and about them, caused

no respite of the usual instincts of their nature. When a charge of cavalry went past, near to any of the stray horses already mentioned, the trained animals would set off, form themselves in the rear of their mounted companions, and though without riders, gallop strenuously along with the rest, not stopping, or flinching, when the fatal shock with the enemy took place.

Captain Archibald Leach, 95th Rifles[24]

Those amongst us who had witnessed in the Peninsula many well-contested actions, were agreed on one point that we had never before seen such determination displayed by the French as on this day. Fighting under the eye of Napoleon, and feeling what a great and important stake they contested for, will account for their extraordinary perseverance and valour, and for the vast efforts which they made for victory

Charlotte Eaton, travel writer[22]

Many of them [soldiers' wives] rushed forward and carried their wounded husbands off the field at the hazard of their own lives. The wife of a sergeant in the 28th was severely wounded in two places by a shell, which struck her as she was carrying off her wounded husband. This anecdote was related to me by an eye-witness of the circumstance. The woman (respecting whom I inquired since my return to England) has, I understand, been allowed a pension from Chelsea Hospital. I heard of several similar instances of heroic conjugal affection; and I myself saw one poor woman, the wife of a private in the 27th, whose leg was dreadfully fractured by a musket-ball in rescuing her husband. When struck by the ball she fell to the ground with her husband, who was supposed to be mortally wounded, but she still refused to leave him, and they were removed together to the rear, and afterwards sent to Antwerp. The poor man survived the amputation of both his arms, and is still alive. The woman, who was then in a state of pregnancy, has, since her return to this country, given birth to a child, to which the Duke of York stood godfather.

Anonymous account[11]
A private of the 27th, wounded very severely, was carried off the field of battle by his wife, then far advanced in pregnancy, she too was severely wounded by a shell, and both of them lay a long while in one of the Hospitals at Antwerp in a hopeless state. The poor man has lost both his arms, the woman extremely lame, and giving birth to a daughter, to which the Duke of York, it is said, has stood Godfather, by the name of Frederica M'Mullen Waterloo.

Charlotte Eaton, travel writer[22]
An officer, with whom we are well acquainted, went over the field on the morning of the battle, and examined the ghastly heaps of dead in search of the body of a near relative; and after all the corpses were buried or burnt in the same melancholy and fruitless search, many an Englishwoman, whom this day of glory had bereft of husband or son, wandered over this fatal field, wildly calling upon the names of those who were now no more. The very day before we visited it, the widow and the sister of a brave and lamented British officer had been here, harrowing up the souls of the beholders with their wild lamentations, vainly demanding where the remains of him they loved reposed, and accusing Heaven for denying them the consolation of weeping over his grave. I was myself, afterwards, a sorrowful witness of the dreadful effects of the unrestrained indulgence of this passionate and heart-breaking grief. In the instance to which I allude, sorrow had nearly driven reason from her seat, and melancholy verged upon madness.

Sergeant William Lawrence, 40th Foot[8]
Of the general loss on that blood-stained day I am unable to give an exact account, but it must have been enormous on both sides,

for three hundred of my regiment alone were missing; and this was not so great a loss as that of some regiments, for the one on our right lost six hundred, chiefly from the continual fire of shot and shell that the French cannon had kept up between the charges.

'*Extract of a letter from a private of the 42d Regiment*'[11]
It was perhaps the most destructive battle ever fought. The loss fell almost entirely on our division, which, along with the Brunswick troops and some Prussians, was the only one up for the first two hours. The three Scotch regiments are nearly annihilated!! – Ours had only six officers who escaped, and some are so dangerously wounded, as to give little hope of their recovery. We were amply revenged, however; and gave the French a lesson, which they will not soon forget ...

Letter from Prince Bernhard of Saxe Weimar[11]
Dear Father, Thank God, I am still alive and have escaped unhurt from two bloody battles. The first was on the 16th of June, the second was yesterday ... Besides my two battalions of Orange Nassau, I now had under my command three battalions of the Duchy of Nassau; – when my brigade was 4,000 strong: – to-day I have not 1,200 left!

Lady Magdalene, wife of Colonel Sir William Howe De Lancey[3]
It was the prospect of securing this immense benefit to mankind that united all European nations against the ambition of Napoleon, and that afforded the best comfort under the distressing sacrifices made to ensure his overthrow. Perhaps no people benefitted by his fall so much as the French themselves: his triumphs (often great in a military point of view,) left nothing in their hands, whilst they filled every family in France with mourning. The conscription was a more searching tyranny than civilized men had ever before endured; and all this blood flowed in vain. Our Gallic neighbours

have sometimes mistaken the tone of triumph in which we speak of the downfall of Napoleon, and have regarded it as insulting to them: nothing is farther from the mind and heart of the British soldier, who is always ready to acknowledge their military excellence.

Napoleon[9]

Such has been the issue of the battle of Mont St. Jean, glorious for the French armies, and yet so fatal.

27

THE SACRIFICE OF NEY

Marshal Ney in a speech to the Chamber of Peers[9]
Not a man of the Guard will ever rally more. I myself commanded them; I myself witnessed their total extermination, ere I left the field of battle: they are annihilated.

Marshal Ney to the Duke of Otranto[9]
The most false and defamatory reports have been spreading for some days over the public mind, upon the conduct which I have pursued during this short and unfortunate campaign. The journals have reported those odious calumnies, and appear to lend them credit. After having fought for twenty-five years for my country, after having shed my blood for its glory and independence, an attempt is made to accuse me of treason; an attempt is made to mark me out to the people, and the army itself, as the author of the disaster it has just experienced.

Marshal Ney to the Duke of Otranto[9]
Such, M. le Due, is a history of this calamitous campaign ... *Now,* I ask those who have survived this fine and numerous army, how I can be accused of the disasters of which it has been the victim, and

of which your military annals furnish no example. I have, it is said, betrayed my country – I who, to serve it, have shown a zeal which I perhaps have carried to an extravagant height; but this calumny is supported by no fact, by no circumstance. But how can these odious reports, which spread with frightful rapidity, be arrested?

Eyewitness to the execution of Marshal Ney
As he was walking forward to place himself between the Veterans who were to shoot him, and the wall, an officer of the Gendarmerie offered him a white handkerchief to cover his eyes. Ney said, hardly making any stop, 'A soldier like myself does not have his eyes blinded.' When before the Veterans, he said, 'I protest solemnly, before God and man, against the injustice of my sentence. History will be my judge.' Then, walking two paces nearer them, with his left hand he gently took off his hat, and placed his right hand on his heart. 'Veterans,' he said, 'do your duty – *Vive la France! Fire!*' He fell dead instantly … He received a ball very near the heart, two or three in his right shoulder, and one or two at the right corner of his chin. While he lay on the ground, I walked up and put my handkerchief in his blood, which I have by me. This no Frenchman would dared have done.

An officer of the Imperial Guard[9]
Thus was destroyed that fine army, reorganised out of the many brilliant armies already sacrificed by Buonaparte. That monster seems to have issued from his den, enraged that so many thousands of brave men should have escaped his fury, with the purpose of devouring those who were left. Indeed if we might suppose it to have been his intention to render their destruction complete, there would be no difficulty to discover facts on which to found such supposition, in the measures which he adopted during this short and unfortunate campaign. The enormous faults, of which he was guilty, may however rather be imputed to his want of skill,

attended by a temerity without bounds, and to that well known and incorrigible madness, which prompted him on every occasion to push on with blind confidence, without any settled plan of operation, or any calculation of probable occurrences.

28

'MY PAPPER IS DUN'

Lady Magdalene, wife of Colonel Sir William de Lancey[4]
The day I went to Waterloo, Sir William told me the Duke had visited him in the morning. He said he never had seen him so warm in his feelings: he had taken leave of him with little hope of seeing him again, I fancy. The Duke told him he never wished to see another battle; this had been so shocking. It had been too much to see such brave men, so equally matched, cutting each other to pieces as they did. Sir William said there never had been such fighting; that the Duke far surpassed anything he had ever done before. The general opinion seemed to be that it had been a peculiarly shocking battle. Sir William said he never would try it again; he was quite tired of the business. In speaking of his wound he said this might be the most fortunate event that could have happened for us both. I looked at him for an explanation. He said, 'Certainly, even if I recover completely, I should never think of serving again. Nobody could ask such a thing, and we should settle down quietly at home for the rest of our lives.'

Wellington's report to Earl Bathurst, Secretary of State for the War[9]
The artillery and engineer departments were conducted much to

my satisfaction by Colonel Sir G Wood, and Colonel Smyth; and I had every reason to be satisfied with the conduct of the Adjutant-General, Maj.-General Barnes, who was wounded, and of the Quarter-Master-General, Colonel Delancey, who was killed by a cannon shot in the middle of the action. This officer is a serious loss to his Majesty's service, and to me at this moment.

General Miguel Alava, Spanish Commissioner, Wellington's field staff[9]
Of those who were by the Duke of Wellington, only he and myself remained untouched in our persons and horses. The rest were all either killed, wounded, or lost one or more horses. The Duke was unable to refrain from tears on witnessing the death of so many brave and honourable men, and the loss of so many friends and faithful companions, and which can alone be compensated by the importance of the victory.

Wellington's report to Earl Bathurst, Secretary of State for War[9]
It gives me the greatest satisfaction to assure your Lordship, that the army never, upon any occasion, conducted itself better ... The division of Guards, under Lieutenant-General Cooke, who is severely wounded, Major General Maitland and Major Byng, set an example which was followed by all; and there is no officer, nor description of troops, that did not behave well.

Blucher[11]
My dear Wife, You Well remember what I promised you, and I have kept my word. The Enemy's superiority of numbers obliged me to give way on the 17th; but on the 18th, in conjunction with my friend Wellington, I put an end at once to Buonaparte's dancing ... I had two horses killed under me Yesterday. It will soon be all over with Buonaparte. BLUCHER. P. S. (Written by the Prince's son, on the road to Genappe.) Father Blucher embraced Wellington

in such a hearty manner, that every body who were present, said it was the most affecting scene that could be imagined.

P. M. Carpene, miller who had helped the unhorsed Blucher[11]
Prince Blucher, on his return, called at my house with his aide-de-camps; his modesty concealed his illustrious name, and I did not recollect him. He asked me many questions concerning my losses, and my melancholy situation. Alas! it was easy for me to answer that I had saved nothing, either in my house, or on the lands which I farm, and that the war had reduced my family to misery, so that I could not pay my contributions. He asked me the amount of them, I told him 80 francs, which he immediately gave me. He departed, and when he got to Namur, he sent me four pieces of 40 francs each, and one of 20 francs. It was from this messenger, that I learnt the name of this great Prince; his generosity honours him; his modesty ennobles him; and my heart thanks him.

Anonymous account[11]
The Rector of Framlingham, in Suffolk, soon after the battle, wrote to the Duke of Wellington, stating, that in his opinion, the Noncommissioned Officers of the British army had, by their valorous conduct on that day entitled themselves to some distinct marks of their country's approbation, and therefore he felt disposed, for one, to offer his humble tribute to their merit. In order that this might be properly applied, he requested the favour of his Grace to point out to him the non-commissioned officer, whose heroic conduct, from the representations which his Grace had received, appeared the most prominent, to whom he, the Rector, meant to convey, in perpetuity, a freehold farm, value 10l. per annum. The Duke set the enquiry immediately on foot, through all the commanding Officers of the Line, and, in consequence, learnt that a Serjeant of the Coldstream, and a corporal of the 1st regiment of Guards, had so distinguished themselves, that it was felt difficult to point out the

most meritorious; but that there had been displayed by the serjeant an exploit arising out of fraternal affection, which he felt it a duty on this occasion to represent, viz. – That near the close of the dreadful conflict, this distinguished Serjeant impatiently solicited the Officer commanding his company, for permission to retire from the ranks for a few minutes; the latter expressed some surprize at this request, the other said: 'Your honour need not doubt of my immediate return.' Permission being given him, he flew to an adjoining barn, to which the Enemy in their retreat had set fire, and from thence bore on his shoulders his wounded brother, who he knew lay helpless in the midst of the flames. Having deposited him safely for the moment, under a hedge, he returned to his post in time to share in the victorious pursuit of the routed Enemy; we need scarcely add, that the superior merit of this gallant non-commissioned Officer was thus established.

Sergeant Critchley of the 1st or Royal Dragoons[11]
Dear Tom, you hear more news in England than we do here; only what we see is the real thing. The Prussian army plays the devil with the country wherever they go; they made destruction in all the villages on the road from Waterloo to Paris, and beyond. I am not in the least sorry for them, for it just serves them right, and not half bad enough, for the usage they gave the Portuguese and Spaniards; it makes them feel a little of the seat of war as well as the rest of their neighbours.

'Extract of a letter from John Marshall, private, 10th Dragoons'[11]
You may perhaps think, because I have spoke of this, that it shows my vanity; but my motive for having done so, is because I saw in an English newspaper, that the Life Guards were the only cavalry that had been of any service. It therefore did not much please me nor my regiment, that we should not have a little of the credit. The Guards certainly made a very brilliant charge; it ought to be spoken of. You

will, however, see, by what I have here stated, that the regiment did its duty, and that is all we wish to be understood of us.

Lady Magdalene, wife of Colonel Sir William de Lancey[4]
I left Waterloo with feelings so different from those I had on going to it. Then all was anxious terror that I would not be there in time to see one look, or to hear one word. Now there was nothing imaginary – all was real misery. There now remained not even a chance of happiness, but what depended on the retrospect of better days and duties fulfilled ... At eleven o'clock that same day, I set out for England. That day, three months before, I was married.

'Extract of a letter from John Marshall, private, 10th Dragoons'[11]
But how many privates we have lost, I do not know: but not so many as might have been expected; for the French fired so high, that when we was at close quarters with them, half their shot did not tell, or they might have killed every man of us.

Charlotte Eaton, travel writer[22]
On, the morning of Saturday the 15th of July, we set off to visit the field of the ever-memorable and glorious battle of Waterloo ... Upon the doors of many of the cottages we passed, were written, in white chalk, the names of the officers who had used them for temporary quarters on their way to the battle; or who had been carried there for shelter in returning, when wounded and unable to proceed further. Many we knew had died in these miserable abodes.

John Smart of Brixham, aged fourteen[31]
In July the Gazette came down with the lists of killed and wounded at Waterloo. The coach from Exeter brought the first copy, and quite a crowd surrounded the landlord of *The London Inn* who read aloud in his large parlour the names of those regiments that contained Brixham men. I was not old enough to realise the woe

brought by that Gazette, but in later years I have seen the mothers and sisters for whom Waterloo had dismal instead of glorious memories.

Charlotte Eaton, travel writer[22]
Often, as I gazed at the soldier's frequent funeral as it passed along, I could not help thinking that, though no eye here was moistened with a tear, yet in some remote cottage or humble dwelling of my native country, the heart of the wife or the mother would be wrung with despair for the loss of him who was now borne unnoticed to a foreign grave.

'CW, a sergeant of the Guards'[12]
I have, as colour Serjeant, stood by the King's colours from the moment of our march, till borne, in Britain's name, within the gates of Paris. Seven of our colour Serjeants entered the field; and there are only myself and one more that stand.

Colonel Augustus Frazer, Royal Horse Artillery[5]
Are you not tired of battles? Are you not sick of the sanguinary description? Judge then what must have been the reality. The Duke himself said in the evening he had never seen such a battle, and hoped he never should again. To this hope we will all say: Amen.

Private George Farmer, 11th Light Dragoons[25]
I cannot say that the remuneration allotted to me was too great; for my pension, after so many years' service, amounts only to tenpence a-day, and I am far too worn out to add to it greatly by any personal exertion.

'JH', Scottish soldier[27]
Thus ended my campaigning, for I was not likely to do any more good in the army ... the length of my service fell short of the

regulations of the Horse Guards, and I was discharged without a farthing, nor have I received a farthing since.

Solider of the 71st, or Glasgow Regiment, Highland Light Infantry[23]
I left my comrades with regret; but the service with joy. I came down the coast to embark, with light steps and a joyful heart, singing 'When wild war's deadly blast was blawn' [*sic*]. I was poor as poor could be; but I had hope before me, and pleasing dreams of home ... Hope and joy were my companion, until I entered the Firth. I was on deck; the shores of Lothian began to rise out of the mist. 'There is the land of cakes,' said the captain. A sigh escaped me; recollections. I went below to conceal my feelings, and never came up until the vessel was in the harbour ...

Letter by the writer of the journal [above] to his friend, enclosing the last part of the manuscript
Dear John,
These three months, I can find nothing to do. I am a burden on Jeannie [probably his sister] and her husband. I wish I was a soldier again. I cannot even get labouring work ... I would be useful, but can get nothing to do ... I will go to South America. Maria de Parides will put me in a way to do for myself, and be a burden to no one. Or, I shall go to Spain, and live in Boho. I will go to Beunos Ayres. Farewell! John, this is all I have to leave you. It's your's [*sic*]: do with it as you think proper. If I succeed in the South, I will return and lay my bones beside my parents: if not, I will never come back.

Gunner John Edwards, Royal Horse Artillery[1]
I have the onner of waren a blue and red ribbon as a marke of that day ... My account may not be quite so great as you may have it in England – so my papper is dun and I must give over ... so I remain, your loving Brother John Edwards til dath.

KEY TO QUOTATION SOURCES

1. *A Waterloo Letter,* Gunner John Edwards, Royal Horse Artillery in *The Waterloo Archive Volume I: British Sources*, Gareth Glover (ed.). Frontline, 2010

2. 'Diary of Lt Ingilby, R.A. in the Peninsular War and Waterloo Campaign', Lieutenant Ingilby in *Minutes of the Proceedings of the Royal Artillery Institution*, Vol XX, 1893

3. *A Voice from Waterloo*, Sergeant Major Edward Cotton, 7th Hussars. B. L. Green, 1849

4. *A Week at Waterloo*, Lady Magdalene De Lancey, Wife of Colonel Sir William Howe De Lancey, London 1906

5. *The Letters of Sir Augustus Simon Frazer*, Colonel Augustus Frazer, Royal Horse Artillery. Longman, Brown, Green, Longmans and Roberts, London 1850

6. *After Waterloo*, Frye, Major W. E. London 1908

7. *Notes on the Battle of Waterloo*, General Sir James Shaw Kennedy, John Murray, London 1865

8. *The Autobiography of Sergeant William Lawrence*, Sergeant William Lawrence. Sampson Low, Marston, Searle, & Rivington, 1886

9. *Journal of the Three Days of the Battle of Waterloo* by an 'Eye Witness', anonymous French soldier, London 1816

10. *Official Bulletins of the Battle of Waterloo in the Original Languages: With Translations into English*, John Palfrey Burrell (ed.). London, 1849

11. *The Battle of Waterloo*, John Booth, London 1815

12. *Some Particulars of the Battle of Waterloo in a Letter from a Serjeant in the Guards*, London 1816

13. Campaign diary of William Gavin. *Highland Light Infantry Chronicle* 1920–21

14. *Waterloo Letters*, H. T. Siborne. Cassell and Company Ltd, 1891

15. *Douglas's Tales of the Peninsula and Waterloo: 1808–1815*, John Douglas and Stanley Monick (ed.). Pen and Sword, 2014

16. *The Camp & the Sanctuary, a Memoir of Thomas Hasker*, James Everett, London 1859

17. From the diary of Thomas Hasker, 1st King's Dragoon guards. 1st Queen's Dragoons Regimental Museum, CARDG:2075

18. *Adventures in the Rifle Brigade*, by Captain J. Kincaid, London 1847

19. *The Adventures of a Soldier*, Edward Costello, London 1841

20. *Recollections of Military Service*, Sergeant Thomas Morris, London 1845

21. *Eighty Years Ago, or the Recollections of an Old Army Doctor*, William Gibney. Bellairs and Company, London 1896

22. *Waterloo Days: The Narrative of an Englishwoman Resident at Brussels in June, 1815*, Charlotte A. Eaton. George Bell & Sons, London 1888

23. *Journal of a Soldier of the 71st*, Edinburgh 1819

24. *Rough Sketches of the Life of an Old Soldier*, Lt-Colonel J. Leach. London 1831

25. *The Light Dragoon* by G. R. Gleig, London 1853

26. *The Wheatley Diary*, Christopher Hibbert (ed.). Longmans, Green & Co. Ltd, London 1964

27. *Extracts from the Diary of a Living Physician*, ed. 'LFC', London 1851

28. *Memoirs & Correspondence of Francis Horner MP*, Leonard Horner. John Murray, London 1843

29. *Napoleon and his Fellow Travellers*, Clement Shorter, London 1908

30. *Waterloo Roll Call*, Charles Dalton. Eyre & Spottiswoode, London1904

31. *Fifty Years' Biographical Reminiscences*, Lord William Pitt Lennox. Hurst & Blackett, London 1863

32. Letter from Charles Stanley to Lt Colonel Fuller, 1815. National Army Museum, Chelsea, NAM 1973-04-54

33. *With Napoleon at Waterloo*, MacKenzie MacBride (ed.). Francis Griffiths, London 1911

34. *Her Majesty's Army*, Walter Richards. London 1890

35. *Journal of the Waterloo Campaign*, General Cavalié Mercer. Wm Blackwood & Sons, London 1870

36. *Our Fighting Services & How they made the Empire*, Sir Evelyn Wood Cassell 1916

37. *Major General Sir William Ponsonby to his mother Lady Louisa Ponsonby, Borthwick* Institute for Archives, Halifax A1/2/4

38. Letter from Major Anthony Rowley Heyland to his wife, Mary

39. *Words on Wellington*, Sir William Fraser. John C. Nimmo, London 1889

40. *Eyewitness to the Peninsular War & the Battle of Waterloo*, Gareth Glover (ed.). Pen & Sword, Barnsley, S. Yorks 2010

41. *An Historical Sketch of the Campaign of 1815*, Captain Batty. London 1820

42. *The Diary of a Cavalry Officer*, Lt-Colonel Tomkinson. London, 1895

43. Quartermaster-Sergeant's Diary, Royal Scots Dragoon Guards Museum, GB46/G167

44. McDonald Letters, Royal Welch Fusiliers Museum

45. *The Dispatches of Field Marshal the Duke of Wellington*, London 1834

46. *A Surgical Artist at War: The Paintings and Sketches of Sir*

Charles Bell 1809–1815, M. K. H. Starling and P. Starling. Royal College of Surgeons, 2005

47. Letter from Samuel S. Barrington to his mother, in *The Waterloo Archive Volume IV: British Sources*, Gareth Glover (ed.). Frontline Books, 2014

48. *The History of the Second Dragoons 'Royal Scots Greys'*, Edward Almack. London 1908

49. *The Autobiography of Lieutenant-General Sir Harry Smith*, G. C. Moore Smith (ed.). John Murray, London 1901

50. *The London Medical Repository and Review*, George Man Burrows and Anthony Todd Thomson. London 1816

51. *Liverpool Mercury, 22 December 1815*.

APPENDIX: BIOGRAPHICAL NOTES ON PEOPLE MENTIONED IN THE TEXT

Adair, Captain Robert (1st Regiment of Foot Guards). Mentioned in *The Battle of Waterloo* (Booth); born around 1787; aged around twenty-eight at Waterloo; wounded Quatre Bras; died from wounds in Brussels on the 23 June.

Adam, Maj-General Frederick (3rd (Light) Brigade). Mentioned in *Adventures in the Rifle Brigade*; born in Scotland, 1781; aged thirty-four at Waterloo; joined army at fourteen; left arm broken and hand shattered in Peninsula, 1813; *The rout of the Old Guard at Waterloo by General Adam's Brigade was the turning-point of the battle, and ensured victory* (Waterloo Roll); seriously wounded at Waterloo; died in 1853 aged seventy-two.

Alava, Lt-General Miguel. Mentioned in *Journal of the Three Days of the Battle of Waterloo;* born in Vittoria, 1770; aged forty-five at Waterloo; reputedly the only man at Trafalgar and Waterloo (was a captain in the navy and transferred to the army); was seconded to British army to act as aide-de-camp to Wellington and was Spanish Commissioner at Waterloo in rank of Lt-General; died in Bareges in 1843 aged seventy-three.

Alten, Lt-General Sir Charles. Born in Hanover, 1781; aged thirty-four at Waterloo; fought in the Peninsular campaign; severely wounded at Waterloo; died in 1840 aged fifty-nine.

Askew, Lt-Colonel Henry (1st Regiment of Foot). Mentioned in *The Battle of Waterloo* (Booth); born in 1775; aged forty at Waterloo; wounded at Quatre Bras; died in 1847.

Barclay, Lt-Colonel Delancey (1st Foot Guards). Mentioned in *A Week at Waterloo*; served in Flanders; died in 1826.

Barnes, Maj-General Sir Edward. Mentioned in *Journal of the Three Days of the Battle of Waterloo*; born in 1776; aged thirty-nine at Waterloo; known at Waterloo as 'our fire eating adjutant-general' (*Waterloo Roll Call*); wounded; died in 1838 aged sixty-two.

Barrington, Ensign the Hon. Samuel S. (1st Regiment of Foot Guards). Born in 1796; aged nineteen at Waterloo; killed at Quatre Bras.

Baynes, Lt George M (Royal Horse Artillery). Mentioned in *The Letters of Sir Augustus Simon Frazer*; served in Peninsula campaign; died in 1874.

Belson, Lt-Colonel Sir Charles Philip (28th Foot). Mentioned in *The Battle of Waterloo* (Booth); born in around 1774; aged forty-one at Waterloo; served in Peninsula campaign; died in 1830 aged fifty-six.

Bernhard, Saxe Weimar, Prince of. Mentioned in *The Battle of Waterloo* (Booth); born in 1792; aged twenty-three at Waterloo; *Son of Duke Bernard of Nassau, who sent a contingent of Nassau troops to fight at Waterloo. In the Wellington Despatches is a letter from Wellington to Duke Bernard, in July, 1815, in which* *he speaks highly of the bravery of the young Prince* (*Waterloo Roll Call*); died in 1862 aged seventy.

Von Blucher, Gebhard Leberecht, (Prussian field marshal). Mentioned in *Journal of the Three Days of the Battle of Waterloo*; born in Rostock, 1742; aged seventy-two at Waterloo; died in 1819 aged seventy-seven.

Bolton, Captain Samuel (Royal Artillery). Mentioned in *Waterloo Days: The Narrative of an Englishwoman Resident at Brussels in June 1815*; born in Suffolk, 1783; aged thirty-two at Waterloo; *This officer was killed towards the close of the battle, when directing the fire of his battery against the Imperial Guards ...* (*Waterloo Roll Call*).

Bonaparte, Napoleon. Mentioned in *Journal of the Three Days of the Battle of Waterloo;* born in 1769; aged forty-six at Waterloo; returned to Paris after the defeat, but unpopularity and hostility caused him to abdicate; he fled Paris hoping to escape to the USA, but, finding Rochefort and other ports blockaded, surrendered to HMS *Bellerophon;* died at St Helena, 1821, aged fifty-two.

Brown, Captain Thomas (1st Regiment of Foot Guards). Mentioned in *The Battle of Waterloo* (Booth); killed at Quatre Bras.

Bull, Captain Robert (Royal Horse Artillery). Mentioned in *The Letters of Sir Augustus Simon Frazer*; born in Stafford, 1778; aged thirty-seven at Waterloo; served in West Indies and Peninsula; died in Bath in 1835, aged fifty-seven.

Cameron, Sergeant Alexander, Pipe Major (92nd Reg of Foot). Mentioned in *With Napoleon at Waterloo*; served in Peninsula campaign; *It is recorded of this gallant Scot, on the 18th June,*

1815, that not content with piping at the head of his regt. he marched forward with a party of skirmishers, and placing himself on a height, in full view of the enemy, continued to animate by playing favourite national airs (*Waterloo Roll Call* quoting *Scots' Magazine*); died in Belfast, 1817.

Cameron, Lt-Colonel John (92nd Regiment of Foot (Gordon Highlanders). Mentioned in *Battle of Waterloo* (Booth); born in 1771; aged forty-four at Waterloo; *He met his death at Quatre Bras whilst leading the 92nd against a large body of French troops. Never was a commanding officer more universally lamented. He was buried on the 17th June during the height of the storm which raged that day. His grave was dug in a quiet lane by his devoted foster-brother, Ewen McMillan, a private in the 92nd, who had accompanied his master through all his campaigns. By desire of his family, Cameron's body was aftds. disinterred and removed to Scotland, where it was re-interred in Kilmallie churchyard, where a tall obelisk, with an inscription by Sir Walter Scott, marks his grave.* (*Waterloo Roll Call*)

Clarke-Kennedy, Captain Alexander Kennedy [*sic*] (1st Dragoons). Born in Knockgray, Scotland, 1782; aged thirty-three at Waterloo; served in Peninsula campaign; *captured the French eagle of the 105th Regt ... after a desperate fight, in which he was severely wounded* (*Waterloo Roll Call*); died in 1864 aged eighty-two.

Cooke, Maj-General George. Mentioned in *The Battle of Waterloo* (Booth); born in 1768; aged forty-seven at Waterloo; lost right arm; died in 1837 aged sixty-nine.

Cooke, Colonel Richard Harvey (1st Foot Guards). Mentioned in *The Battle of Waterloo* (Booth); fought in Peninsular campaign; died in 1856.

Costello, Sergeant Edward (Rifle Brigade). Mentioned in *Adventures of a Soldier*; born in Ireland, 1788; aged twenty-seven at Waterloo; wounded at Quatre Bras (which seems to have caused him to miss the battle on the 18 June); made Yeoman Warder of Tower of London; died in 1869 aged eighty-four.

Cotton, Sergeant Major Edward (7th Hussars). Author of *A Voice from Waterloo*; born on the Isle of Wight, 1793; aged around twenty-two at Waterloo; made Mont St Jean his home and became a battlefield tour guide; died in 1849 aged fifty-six; buried in gardens of Hougoumont; later disinterred and reburied in Brussels.

Croft, Ensign Thomas Emsley (1st Regiment of Foot Guards). Mentioned in *Battle of Waterloo* (Booth); born in 1798; aged seventeen at Waterloo; survived wounds at Quatre Bras; died in 1835.

Dalrymple, Lt-Colonel Leighton Cathcart (15th Light Dragoons). Mentioned in *Wellington's Doctors*; born in Ayrshire, 1785; aged thirty at Waterloo; fought in Peninsula campaign; lost left leg Waterloo; died in Herefordshire, 1820.

De Lancey, Lady Magdalene. Author of *A Week at Waterloo*; born in 1793; aged twenty-two at Waterloo; she followed in her new husband's footsteps to Brussels a few weeks after his departure, and her account of the events that followed were originally written to keep her brother informed of events and not published till 1906; originally told her husband was dead, she hurried to nurse him on learning of his whereabouts; after his death she remarried and died in 1822, aged twenty-nine, giving birth.

De Lancey, Colonel Sir William Howe (Deputy Quartermaster-General). Born in New York, 1778; aged thirty-seven at Waterloo;

mentioned in despatches several times during the Peninsular campaign; *Waterloo Roll Call* says *the wind of a cannon ball knocked him off his horse. This, it was afterwards found, had separated the ribs from the back-bone, and caused a fatal injury.* [Although seemingly far-fetched, reports of death or injury from the 'wind' of a high velocity cannon ball is not uncommon in eye-witness accounts from this period, but other accounts say the ball hit him in the back.] *Wellington caused De Lancey to be removed to a hut in a blanket*; Wellington's own version of the incident runs: *De Lancey was with me, and speaking to me when he was struck. We were on a point of land that overlooked the plain. I had just been warned off by some soldiers (but as I saw well from it, and two divisions were engaging below, I said 'Never mind'), when a ball came bounding along en ricochet, as it is called, and, striking him on the back, sent him many yards over the head of his horse. He fell on his face, and bounded upwards and fell again. All the staff dismounted and ran to him, and when I came up he said, 'Pray tell them to leave me and let me die in peace.' I had him conveyed to the rear, and two days after, on my return from Brussels, I saw him in a barn, and he spoke with such strength that I said (for I had reported him killed), 'Why! De Lancey, you will have the advantage of Sir Condy in 'Castle Rackrent' – you will know what your friends said of you after you were dead.' 'I hope I shall,' he replied. Poor fellow! We knew each other ever since we were boys. But I had no time to be sorry. I went on with the army, and never saw him again.*

Dick, Major Robert Henry (42nd Royal Highlanders – the Black Watch). Mentioned in *The Battle of Waterloo* (Booth); born in 1787; aged twenty-eight at Waterloo; served in Peninsula campaign; succeeded to the command after Macara's death; wounded at Quatre Bras; killed leading a charge during Sikh War, 1846.

Dorville, Major Philip (1st, or Royal, Regiment of Dragoons). Mentioned in *The Battle of Waterloo*, Booth; born in Fulham, 1774; aged forty-one at Waterloo; fought in Peninsular campaign; *At Waterloo Col Dorville commanded the two squadrons of the 1st Dgns. 'which rushed into the second column of the enemy, consisting of about 4,000 men, and after a desperate fight returned with a French eagle.' In this gallant charge Col Dorville had the scabbard of his sword shot away, and a bullet passed through the breast of his coat. Had three horses shot under him* (*Waterloo Roll Call*); died in Malvern in 1847.

Douglas, Sergeant John (3rd Battalion, The Royal Scots). Author of *Douglas's Tales of the Peninsular & Waterloo*; born in Lurgan, Ireland, around 1789; aged around twenty-six at Waterloo; fought at Walcheren and in the Peninsular campaign; died in 1866.

Dumaresq, Captain H (aide-de-camp to Bing). Mentioned in *The Letters of Sir Augustus Simon Frazer*; born around 1792; aged around twenty-three at Waterloo; *Fought in 13 battles during the Peninsula campaign ... Was shot through the lungs at Hougoumont, but, being at the time in charge of a message to Wellington, he went on to the Duke and delivered it. Ball never extracted* (*Waterloo Roll Call*); died in 1838.

Dyneley, Captain Thomas (Royal Horse Artillery). Mentioned in *Waterloo Diary*; *served at the battle of Maida, and in the Peninsula. Was taken prisoner at Majalahonda, when engaged with the rearguard of the French army, 11th Aug., 1812, but escaped from the enemy* (*Waterloo Roll Call*); died in 1860.

Eaton (*née* Waldie) Charlotte Ann, traveller and travel writer. Mentioned in *Waterloo Days: The Narrative of an Englishwoman Resident at Brussels in June, 1815*; born in 1788; aged twenty-seven at Waterloo; also wrote *Continental Adventures* and *At Home and Abroad*; died in 1859 aged seventy-one.

Edwards, Gunner John (A Troop, Royal Horse Artillery). Mentioned in *A Waterloo Letter*, written to his brother in Wales; tentatively identified (by editor/transcriber of letter) from among at least three others of same name as being born in Flintshire, Wales, in 1775; aged forty at Waterloo; 5' 7 ¾, brown hair and eyes, fair complexion, could read and write; fought through whole Peninsula campaign.

Erskine, Captain the Hon. Esme Stuart (Deputy-Assistant Adjutants-General, 60th Foot). Mentioned in *The Battle of Waterloo*, Booth; born in 1789; aged twenty-six at Waterloo; taken prisoner after being wounded; died in 1817.

Evans, General Sir George De Lacy (aide-de-camp to Ponsonby). Mentioned in *With Napoleon at Waterloo*; born in Ireland, 1787; aged twenty-eight at Waterloo; had two horses shot from under him; died in 1870.

Ewart, Sergeant Charles (Scots Greys). Mentioned in *The Battle of Waterloo* (Booth); born near Kilmarnock in 1769; aged forty-six at Waterloo; experienced soldier and fencing master; said to be 6' 4" tall and of 'Herculean strength'; capture of French eagle made him a national celebrity; in 1816 he was invited to a Waterloo dinner at Leith near Edinburgh, where Sir Walter Scott proposed his health and invited him to speak. 'Ewart begged that he might be excused, saying that *he would rather fight the battle of Waterloo over again, than face so large an assemblage*'; died in Salford 1846 aged seventy-seven.

Farmer, Private George (11th Light Dragoons). Mentioned in *The Light Dragoon*; taken prisoner during Peninsula campaign; served in India after Waterloo; discharged in 1836 after twenty-eight years' service.

Fitzgerald, Captain (brevet Lt-Col.) Richard (2nd Life Guards). Mentioned in *The Battle of Waterloo* (Booth); born around 1774; aged forty-one at Waterloo; fought in Peninsular campaign; killed by cannon shot leading a charge.

Fludyer, Ensign George (1st Regiment of Foot Guards). Mentioned in *Battle of Waterloo* (Booth); survived wounds at Quatre Bras; still living in 1876.

Frazer, Lt-Colonel Augustus Simon (Royal Regiment of Artillery). Author of *The Letters of Sir Augustus Simon Frazer*; born in Dunkirk in 1776; aged thirty-eight at Waterloo; severely wounded at Battle of Bayonne year before Waterloo; died in Woolwich in 1835.

Frederick, Duke of Brunswick. Born in 1771; aged forty-four at Waterloo; formed his volunteer corps, the Black Brunswickers, after his Duchy was taken by Napoleon; killed by musket ball at Quatre Bras.

Frye, Major William Edward. Author of *After Waterloo*; born in 1784; aged thirty at Waterloo; in Brussels at time of battle but not on active service and took no part; died in 1858.

Gardiner, Lt-Colonel Sir Robert (Royal Horse Artillery). Mentioned in *Waterloo Diary*; born in 1781; aged thirty-four at Waterloo; *His troop was most severely pressed in covering the left of the army on the retreat from Quatre Bras on the 17th* (*Waterloo Roll Call*); died in 1864.

Gavin, Quartermaster-Sergeant William (71st Highland Light Infantry). Author of *Waterloo Diary*; born in around 1775; aged around forty at Waterloo; veteran of numerous campaigns; died in 1834.

Gibney, Assistant Surgeon William MD (15th King's Hussars). Account from *Wellington's Doctors*; born in Ireland; on half-pay in 1818.

von Gneisenau, August (Prussian Field Marshal). Mentioned in *The Battle of Waterloo* (Booth); born in 1760; aged fifty-five at Waterloo; died in 1831.

Halkett, Maj-General Sir Colin. Mentioned in *Recollections of Military Service*; born in 1774; aged forty-one at Waterloo; wounded four times and had four horses shot from under him; died in 1856.

Hamilton, Lt-Colonel James Inglis (Scots Greys). Mentioned in *With Napoleon at Waterloo*; born in New York in 1777; aged thirty-eight at Waterloo; *While leading a charge on horseback, he lost his left arm. He put the reins in his mouth and continued the charge, even after his right arm was severed by a French lancer. Moments later he was shot and killed. He was found with a bullet wound through his heart, as well as other injuries; Hamilton's scabbard and silken sash were sent to his brother. (Who Was Who at Waterloo, Summerville)*

Hankin, Major Thomas Pate (Scots Greys). Mentioned in *With Napoleon at Waterloo*; born in 1766; aged forty-nine at Waterloo; survived wound and died in 1825.

Hasker, Private Thomas (1st King's Dragoon Guards). Mentioned in *The Camp and Sanctuary*; born in Birmingham in 1789; aged twenty-six at Waterloo; died in 1858 aged seventy.

Hay, Lt-Colonel James (16th Light Dragoons). Mentioned in *The Diary of a Cavalry Officer*; right arm broken in Peninsular campaign; *was so seriously wounded at Waterloo that he could not be moved from the field for eight days* (*Waterloo Roll Call*); died in 1854.

Hay, Ensign James, Lord (1st Regiment of Foot Guards). Mentioned in *The Battle of Waterloo* (Booth); born around 1797; aged around eighteen at Waterloo; fought and wounded in the Peninsula campaign; killed at Quatre Bras; *Was acting as adjutant to Lord Saltoun. His horse, a fine thoroughbred, refused a fence, and tried to wheel round. As Lord Saltoun was passing down a path close by, a body fell across his horse's neck and rolled off. It was poor Hay, who had been picked off by a French cavalry skirmisher, who was, in his turn, shot dead by a Grenadier.* (*Waterloo Roll Call*)

Hervey, Colonel Felton Elwell (Wellington's Staff). Mentioned in *The Battle of Waterloo* (Booth); born in 1782; aged thirty-three at Waterloo; lost right arm in Peninsular campaign; *always mounted himself and his orderly upon English hunters, so as to make his escape should he at any time be unexpectedly surrounded. Upon one occasion, when reconnoitring, Hervey rode up, by mistake, to a small detachment of French cavalry. Fortunately for him, the men were dismounted, and busily employed in cooking their rations; but no sooner was the colonel discovered, and his rank recognized, than the order to mount was given. Hervey and his orderly, finding the odds greatly against them, immediately started off at a tremendous pace to reach our lines. The French dragoons were quickly in their saddles, for the prize was worth gaining, and amidst wild shouts and loud halloes, gave chase to their tiring foes. The noise attracted the attention of some of the enemy's lancers, who, being posted nearer the English forces, were enabled to cut off* *the retreat of the fugitives. The clattering of the horses' hoofs, who had thus joined in the pursuit, sounded like a death-knell to the two gallant soldiers. 'Your only chance, colonel,' said the faithful orderly, 'is to make for that ravine.' Hervey followed the suggestion; the ravine was narrow, with only room for one horse to enter. No sooner had he gained it than, on looking round, a terrible sight presented itself. The devoted soldier, knowing that the life of his commanding officer could alone be saved by the sacrifice of his own, had placed himself across the narrow opening, and was literally pierced and cut to pieces. The delay thus occasioned enabled Hervey to pursue his flight. Gaining the open, he charged a stiff fence, and was soon out of sight of his pursuers* (Waterloo Roll Call); died in 1819.

Heyland, Major Arthur Rowley (40th Regiment). Account from british-cemetery-elvas.org; born in Belfast in 1781; aged thirty-four at Waterloo; wounded at least twice in campaigns before Waterloo; killed by ball to neck during attack on farm of Mont St Jean late in the battle.

Hussey, Maj-General Sir Vivian. Mentioned in *Waterloo Diary*; born in Cornwall in 1775; aged forty at Waterloo; died in 1842.

Ingilby, Lt William Bates (Royal Horse Artillery). Mentioned in *Waterloo Diary*; born in 1791; aged twenty-four at Waterloo; *was present at the sieges of Ciudad Rodrigo, forts of Salamanca (wounded) and Burgos. Also at the battles of Busaco, Fuentes d'Onor, and Salamanca* (Waterloo Roll Call); retired General Sir W. Bates Ingilby, KCB; died in 1879 aged eighty-nine.

Irby, Captain Henry Edward (2nd Life Guards). Mentioned in *The Battle of Waterloo* (Booth); born in 1783; aged thirty-two at Waterloo; died in 1821.

Jeffs, Sergeant Major Thomas (18th Hussars). Mentioned in *Our Fighting Services & How they Made the Empire*; promoted for gallantry; still living in 1830 (Waterloo Roll Call).

Kelly, Captain Richard (28th Foot). Mentioned in *The Battle of Waterloo* (Booth); born in Leicestershire in 1786; aged twenty-four at Waterloo; *A bullet passed right through his cheeks carrying away the roof of his mouth* (*Waterloo Roll Call*); survived wound and died in 1851.

Kempt, Maj-General Sir James. Mentioned in *The Battle of Waterloo* (Booth); born in Edinburgh in 1764; aged fifty-one at Waterloo; took over 5th Division when Picton was killed; wounded; died in 1854.

Kennedy, General Sir James Shaw (43rd Foot). Mentioned in *Notes on the Battle of Waterloo*; born 'James Shaw' in 1788 in Scotland, assumed wife's name upon marriage in 1820; aged twenty-seven at Waterloo; wounded in the Peninsula campaign and suffered from fever 'from which I never fully recovered'; *On 18th June, 1815, he was allowed, in presence of Wellington, to form the 3rd Division (to which he was attached), in a new and unusual order of battle, to meet the formidable masses of cavalry seen forming in its front, and in this formation the division resisted, successfully, repeated attacks of Napoleon's cavalry.* (*Waterloo Roll Call*); died in 1865.

Kerrison, Lt-Colonel Sir Edward (7th Hussars). Mentioned in *A Voice from Waterloo*; born in 1774; aged forty-one at Waterloo; fought in Peninsula campaign; died in 1853.

Kincaid, Lt John (95th Rifle Brigade). Author of *Adventures in the Rifle Brigade*; born in 1787 in Scotland; aged twenty-eight at Waterloo; wounded several times in the Peninsula campaign;

severely wounded and had horse shot from under him at Waterloo; knighted in 1844; died in Hastings in 1862 aged seventy-four.

Kinchant, Cornet Francis Charlton (Scots Greys). Mentioned in *With Napoleon at Waterloo*; born in Hereford in 1790; aged twenty-five at Waterloo; killed in battle.

Lambert, Maj-General Sir John. Mentioned in *The Battle of Waterloo* (Booth); born in 1772; aged forty-three at Waterloo; *Succeeded to the command of the British troops before New Orleans, in Jan 1815, on the deaths of Generals Pakenham and Gibbs* (*Waterloo Roll Call*); died in 1847.

Lawrence, Sergeant William (40th Foot). Author of *The Autobiography of Sergeant William Lawrence*; born in Dorset in 1791; aged twenty-four at Waterloo; wounded in Peninsular campaign; died in Dorset in 1867.

Leach, Captain Jonathan (95th Rifles). Account from *Rough Sketches of the Life of an Old Soldier*; *the command of the battalion devolved upon Leach when his two senior officers were wounded* (*Waterloo Roll Call*); wounded himself; died in Worthing, aged seventy.

Lloyd, Captain William (Royal Artillery). Mentioned in *The Letters of Sir Augustus Simon Frazer*; born in 1778; aged thirty-seven at Waterloo; died from wounds on 29 July.

Lockwood, Lieutenant Purefoy (30th Foot). Mentioned in *Her Majesty's Army*; *Lockwood of ours had gone home with a silver plate in his skull, on which was engraved 'bomb proof'* (*Waterloo Roll Call*); still living in 1846.

Lygon, Lt-Colonel Hon. Edward Pyndar (Life Guards). Mentioned in *The Battle of Waterloo* (Booth); born in 1786; aged twenty-nine at Waterloo; died in 1860.

McMullen, Private Peter (27th Foot). Mentioned in *The Battle of Waterloo* (Booth); severely wounded in the knee; his wife suffered a fractured leg from a musket-ball while trying to carry him from the field; his wife later gave birth to a girl who was christened Frederica McMullen Waterloo. His Royal Highness Frederick Augustus, Duke of York and Albany, commander in chief in the British Army, stood godfather to the infant.

Macara, Lt-Colonel Sir Robert (42nd Royal Highlanders – the Black Watch). Mentioned in *The Battle of Waterloo* (Booth); *He was wounded about the middle of the engagement* [Quatre Bras], *and was in the act of being carried off the field by four of his men, when a party of French unexpectedly surrounded and made them prisoners. Perceiving by the colonel's decorations that he was an officer of rank, they immediately cut him down with his attendants* (Waterloo Roll Call).

Macdonald, Captain Alexander (Royal Horse Artillery). Mentioned in *The Letters of Sir Augustus Simon Frazer*; *served at the capture of the Cape of Good Hope in 1806, and was taken prisoner at Buenos Ayres in 1807 ... Served in the Peninsula campaign* (*Waterloo Roll Call*); severely wounded; died in 1856.

Macdonald, Captain Robert (1st Regiment of Foot – Royal Scots). Mentioned in *Douglas's Tales of the Peninsular & Waterloo*; severely wounded in the Peninsular campaign; died in 1860.

Macready, Ensign Edward Nevil (30th Foot). Mentioned in *Her Majesty's Army*; born around 1798; aged around seventeen at Waterloo; died in Clevedon, Somerset, in 1848.

Maitland, Captain Frederick, RN. Mentioned in *The Battle of Waterloo* (Booth); born in Fife in 1777; involved in numerous sea battles; reached rank of Rear Admiral and was knighted; died at sea in 1839.

Maitland, Maj-General Peregrine. Mentioned in *Journal of the Three Days of the Battle of Waterloo;* born in Hampshire in 1777; aged thirty-eight at Waterloo; fought in the Peninsula campaign; *The example he set, both at Quatre Bras and Waterloo, had much to do with the victory then obtained over the French. When Napoleon's 'Old Guard' made that gigantic and final effort, on the evening of June 18th, to retrieve the fortunes of the day, it was Maitland's brigade which checked their advance and drove them headlong down the bloody slope. 'Now, Maitland, now's your time!' said Wellington, as the leading column of the French Guards approached. (Waterloo Roll Call)*; died in 1854.

Menzies, Captain Archibald (42nd Highlanders). Mentioned in *The Battle of Waterloo* (Booth); acted as major after Sir R. Macara's death until wounded himself; promoted to major on the day of the Battle of Waterloo; died in 1854.

Mercer, Captain Alexander Cavalie (Royal Horse Artillery). Author of *Journal of the Waterloo Campaign*; born in Hull in 1783; aged thirty-two at Waterloo; rose to rank of general; died in 1868.

Miller, Lt-Colonel William (1st Regiment of Foot Guards). Account from *Waterloo Roll Call*; born in Edinburgh in 1785; aged thirty-one at Waterloo; *'I feel I am mortally wounded ... I should like to see the colours of the regiment before I quit them forever ... ' They were brought to him and wrapped around his wounded body. His countenance brightened and he smiled, declared himself well satisfied, and was carried from the field*; died in Brussels on 19 June.

Ney, Marshal Michel. Mentioned in *Journal of the Three Days of the Battle of Waterloo*; born in 1769; aged forty-six at Waterloo; called 'The bravest of the brave' by Napoleon; arrested and tried for treason (he had campaigned for Napoleon and against the king before Waterloo); executed on 7 December 1815.

von Ompteda, Colonel Christian Friedrich Wilhelm (King's German Legion). Mentioned in *Notes on the Battle of Waterloo*; born in 1765; aged fifty at Waterloo; killed in attempt to retake La Haye Sainte.

Pack, Sir Denis (Scots Greys). Mentioned in *With Napoleon at Waterloo*; born in Ireland in 1772; aged forty-three at Waterloo; experienced officer, known for his bad temper, but brave and wounded eight times in Peninsula alone; wounded at Quatre Bras; died in 1823.

Pardoe, Ensign Edward [Purdo in text] (1st Regiment of Foot Guards). Mentioned in *Some Particulars of the Battle of Waterloo* ...; born in 1796; aged nineteen at Waterloo; severely wounded at the siege of Bergan-Op-Zoom in 1814; killed at Waterloo.

Picton, Lt-General Sir Thomas. Mentioned in various accounts. Born in Wales in 1758; aged fifty-seven at Waterloo; vastly experienced officer; wounded in the Peninsular campaign; *Received a probably mortal wound at Quatre Bras, but concealed the fact from everyone, excepting an old servant, in order that he might be present at what he foresaw was to be a tremendous struggle. Fell whilst gloriously leading a charge of infantry to repel 'one of the most serious attacks made by the enemy on our position.' It is said that on the morning of the 18th June, one of the first questions asked by Napoleon of his Staff was: 'Ou est la division de Picton?' A few hours later, the broken ranks* *and decimated companies of many French regts. answered the question* (*Waterloo Roll Call*).

Ponsonby, Lt-Colonel Sir Frederick. Cousin of Sir William Ponsonby. Wounded in the lung and both arms, lay on the field all night and was plundered. Not expected to survive, he was nursed back to health by his sister Caroline (*Oxford Dictionary of National Biography*).

Ponsonby, Maj-General Sir William. Mentioned in various accounts; born in Ireland in 1772; aged forty-three; *Lost his life at Waterloo from being badly mounted. Whilst leading a cavalry charge against the Polish Lancers his horse stuck in a heavy ploughed field and was unable to extricate itself. He took a picture and watch out of his pocket and was just delivering them to his A.D.C. to give his wife when the lancers were on him. Both Ponsonby and his companion were immediately killed by the Polish cavalry* (*Waterloo Roll Call*).

Purdo, Ensign Edward – see 'Pardoe'

Ramsay, Captain William Norman (Royal Horse Artillery). Mentioned in *The Letters of Sir Augustus Simon Frazer*; born in 1782; died at Waterloo, aged thirty-three; his body was later moved to Edinburgh and buried beside that of his wife, according to his own wishes (his brother Lt William Ramsay, RA, was killed at Battle of New Orleans in January of same year as Waterloo).

Robe, Lt William Livingstone (Royal Horse Artillery). Mentioned in *The Letters of Sir Augustus Simon Frazer*; born in 1791; aged twenty-four at Waterloo; fought in Peninsula campaign and decorated for bravery; *My Dear Sir William, I should have written to you long ere this had not a wound, which deprived me of the use of my arm, prevented me. As to the fall of your son, and my* *esteemed friend, I can only say that few young men have left this life more sincerely regretted, and his exertions on the 18th will ever endear his memory to all who witnessed his noble conduct on that day. Major Ramsay's last words to me were as follows: 'Did you ever witness such noble conduct as that of Brereton and Robe?' In short, it is a most painful task to relate the history of a man whose fall I sincerely lament, and I cannot without tears of sorrow think of your son, and my esteemed friend Major Ramsay. About five o'clock on the 18th your son received a mortal wound, and about the same time the following day he died at the village of Waterloo, after twice having taken leave of me in the most friendly and affectionate manner. I was too ill to ask him any questions; indeed, I was so distressed when I saw him at his last moments, that I could only shake him by the hand, and in the course of a few minutes he expired. His remains were interred in a beautiful spot of ground in the village of Waterloo, where I intend to raise a monument to his memory. Yours most truly, A. Mcdonald* (Letter to Robe's father, from *Waterloo Roll Call*).

Smith, Major H. G. W. (95th Foot). Author of *The Autobiography of Lt-General Sir Harry Smith*; born in 1787; aged twenty-eight at Waterloo; widely experienced officer, including New Orleans and the Peninsula, and campaigns after Waterloo; *He married ... in 1816, a young Spanish lady, Juana Maria de los Dolores de Leon, who had appealed to him for protection on the day after the assault on Badajoz in Apr. 1812* (*Waterloo Roll Call*); died in London in 1860.

Stanhope, Lt-Colonel the Hon. James (1st Foot Guards). Mentioned in *Eyewitness to the Peninsular War & the Battle of Waterloo*; born in 1778; aged thirty-six at Waterloo; died in 1825.

Stanley, Private Charles (1st King's Dragoon Guards). Born in Nottinghamshire in 1792; aged twenty-three at Waterloo; listed as missing for several months; finally confirmed as killed at Waterloo.

Strangways, Lt Thomas Fox (Royal Horse Artillery). Mentioned in *The Letters of Sir Augustus Simon Frazer*; born in 1790; aged twenty-five at Waterloo; served in numerous campaigns and decorated for bravery; *Dangerously wounded at Waterloo, and his recovery was miraculous* (*Waterloo Roll Call*); continued his army career and was killed in action in 1854 in Crimea.

Streatfield, Captain Thomas (1st Regiment of Foot Guards). Mentioned in *Battle of Waterloo* (Booth); survived wound at Quatre Bras; died in 1864.

Stuart, Major the Hon. William (1st Regiment of Foot Guards). Mentioned in *Battle of Waterloo* (Booth); born in 1778; aged thirty-seven at Waterloo; served in the Peninsula campaign; died in 1837.

Tomkinson, Lt-Colonel William (16th Light Dragoons). Author of *Diary of a Cavalry Officer*; born in Nantwich, Cheshire, in 1790; aged twenty-five at Waterloo; severely wounded in the Peninsular campaign; died in 1872.

Townshend, Col the Hon. Horatio (1st Regiment of Foot Guards). Mentioned in *Battle of Waterloo* (Booth); born in 1780; aged thirty-five at Waterloo; served in Peninsula; severely wounded at Quatre Bras; died in 1843.

Uxbridge, Lt-General, Earl of. Mentioned in various accounts; born in 1768; aged forty-seven at Waterloo; would have assumed overall command if Wellington had been killed; *this brilliant cavalry leader served with distinction in the early part of the war in the Peninsula ... wounded in the right knee during the last charge;*

his right leg was amputated after the battle and buried under a tree. A board was afterwards affixed to this tree with this verse: 'Here lies the Marquis of Anglesey's leg/Pray for the rest of his body, I beg' (Waterloo Roll Call); died in 1854.

Varender [variously spelt Verender/Verrinder], Private Benjamin (32nd Regiment). Born in Somerset in around 1790; enlisted aged 16; *In consequence of Amputated Right Arm is rendered unfit for further service and is hereby discharged ... He is about twenty-six years of age, five feet eight inches in height, brown hair, grey eyes, fresh complexion, by trade a Cooper* [Army discharge papers from Royal Chelsea Hospital].

Wellington, Arthur, Duke of. Account from *Journal of the Three Days of the Battle of Waterloo*; born in 1769; aged forty-six at Waterloo; entered politics and became prime minister in 1828; fought a duel in 1829 while in office; given a state funeral on his death aged eighty-three in 1852; buried in Westminster Abbey next to Nelson.

Wheatley, Ensign Edmund (King's German Legion). Author of *The Wheatley Diary*. Born in around 1793; aged twenty-two at Waterloo; emigrated to France after marrying; died in Trèves in 1841.

Whinyates, Captain Edward C. (Royal Horse Artillery). Account from *The Letters of Sir Augustus Simon Frazer*; born in 1782; aged thirty-three at Waterloo; fought in numerous campaigns; *at Waterloo he had three horses shot under him, was struck by a round shot on the leg, and severely wounded in the left arm towards the close of the day* (Waterloo Roll Call); died in 1865.

William, Prince of Orange. Account from *Official Bulletins of the Battle of Waterloo*; born in 1792; aged twenty-three at Waterloo;

educated at Oxford and joined British army as aide-de-camp to Wellington; fought in Peninsula campaign; wounded at Waterloo; became King William II of the Netherlands in 1840; died in 1849.

Wood, Colonel Sir George Adam (Royal Regiment of Artillery). Account from *Journal of the Waterloo Campaign*; born in 1767; aged forty-eight at Waterloo; died in 1831.

BIBLIOGRAPHY

Published Books

Black, Jeremy, *The Battle of Waterloo: A New History*. Icon Books, London 2012

Bowen, H. V., *War & British Society 1688–1815*, Cambridge University Press 1998

David, Saul, *All the King's Men: The British Soldier from the Restoration to Waterloo*. Viking Penguin, London 2012

Eaton, Charlotte, *Waterloo Days: The Narrative of an Englishwoman Resident at Brussels in June, 1815*. George Bell & Sons, London 1888

Fletcher, Ian, *Galloping at Everything: The British Cavalry in the Peninsular Way & at Waterloo, 1808–15*. Spellmount Ltd, Staplehurst, Kent 1999

Glover, Gareth, *Eyewitness to the Peninsular War & the Battle of Waterloo: The Letters & Journals of Lt-Col James the Hon. Stanhope*. Pen & Sword, Barnsley, S. Yorks. 2010

Hamilton-Williams, David, *Waterloo New Perspectives*. Brockhampton Press, London 1999

Hibbert, Christopher (Ed.), *The Wheatley Diary*. Longmans, Green & Co. Ltd, London 1964

Holmes, Richard, *Wellington – The Iron Duke*. HarperCollins, London 2002

Howard, Dr Martin, *Wellington's Doctors: The British Army*

Medical Services in the Napoleonic Wars. Spellmount, Staplehurst, Kent 2002

Knollys, Major, *Shaw, the Life Guardsman.* Dean & Son, London, 1885

Miller, David, *Lady de Lancey at Waterloo.* Spellmount, Stroud, Glocs., 2008

Monick, Stanley (Ed.), *Douglas's Tales of the Peninsular and Waterloo.* Leo Cooper, Barnsley, S. Yorks. 1997

Price, Sian, *If You're Reading This ... .* Frontline Books, London 2011

Snow, Peter, *To War with Wellington.* John Murray, London 2010

Summerville, Christopher, *Who Was Who at Waterloo.* Pearson 2007

Tomkinson, Lieutenant Colonel William, *The Diary of a Cavalry Officer 1809–15.* Spellmount, Staplehurst, Kent 1999

Weller, Jack, *Wellington at Waterloo.* Greenhill, London 1967

Wootten, Geoffrey, *Waterloo 1815: The Birth of Modern Europe.* Osprey, Oxford 1992

Miscellaneous

A Waterloo Letter. Edited by Lt-Col M. E. S. Laws, O. B. B., M. C., R. A. (Retd.), F. R. Hist. S.

Principal Websites

Google Books – books.google.com
Internet Archive – www.archive.org
Project Gutenberg – www.gutenberg.org
Waterloo Diary – www.waterloodiary.net
Friends of the British Cemetery – british-cemetery-elvas.org
The Discriminating General – www.militaryheritage.com

Also available from Amberley Publishing

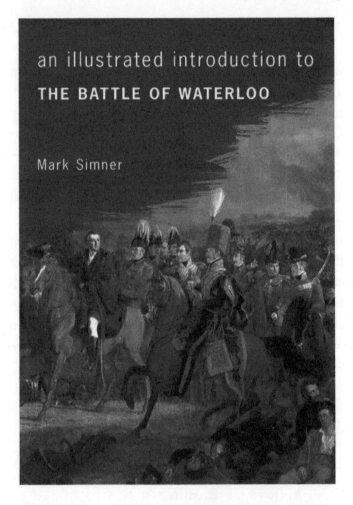

an illustrated introduction to
THE BATTLE OF WATERLOO

Mark Simner

Fascinated by history? Wish you knew more? The Illustrated Introductions are here to help. In this lavishly illustrated, accessible guide, find out everything you need to know about the Battle of Waterloo.

£9.99 Paperback
96 pages
978-1-4456-4666-4

Available from all good bookshops or to order direct
Please call **01453-847-800**
www.amberleybooks.com

Also available from Amberley Publishing

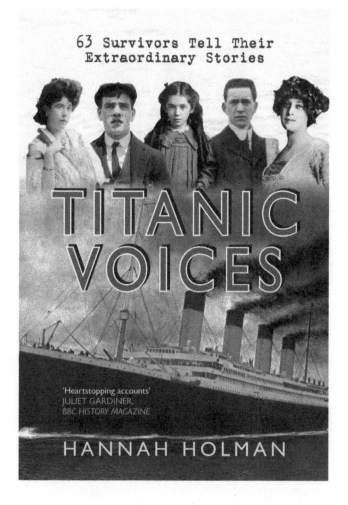

There were over 700 survivors of the *Titanic* disaster and their horrific experience has captivated readers and moviegoers for over 100 years. But what was it actually like for a woman to say goodbye to her husband? For a mother to leave her teenage sons? For the unlucky many who found themselves in the freezing Atlantic waters?

Titanic Voices is the most comprehensive collection of *Titanic* survivors' stories ever published and includes many unpublished and long-forgotten accounts, unabridged, together with an authoritative editorial commentary. It is also the first book to include substantial accounts from female passengers and those travelling third class.

£14.99 Paperback
448 pages
978-1-4456-1443-4

Available from all good bookshops or to order direct
Please call **01453-847-800**
www.amberleybooks.com

Also available from Amberley Publishing

EYEWITNESS ACCOUNTS

BATTLES OF THE CRIMEAN WAR

WILLIAM H. RUSSELL

The allied expeditionary force landed on the beaches of Calamita Bay, on the south-west coast of the Crimean Peninsula, in September 1854. The campaign that followed would create such iconic figures as the nurses Florence Nightingale and Mary Seacole, and iconic images such as the Thin Red Line of the 93rd Highlanders at the Battle of Balaclava and the Charge of the Light Brigade. Reporting it all was William Howard Russell, special correspondent of *The Times*. Russell's articles, transmitted back to Britain by electric telegraph, shocked the public and made him world famous. This book reprints Russell's vivid accounts of the battlefields of the Alma, Sevastopol, Balaclava and Inkerman.

£8.99 Paperback
224 pages
978-1-4456-3789-1

Available from all good bookshops or to order direct
Please call **01453-847-800**
www.amberleybooks.com

Also available from Amberley Publishing

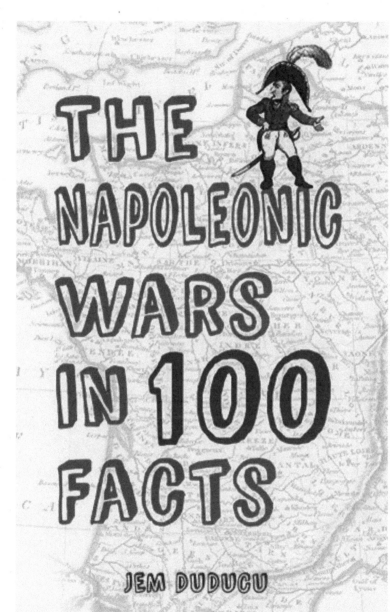

THE NAPOLEONIC WARS IN 100 FACTS

JEM DUDUCU

Available from all good bookshops or to order direct
Please call **01453-847-800**
www.amberleybooks.com